IN A DIFFERENT TIME

PETER HARRIS

IN A DIFFERENT TIME

The inside story of the Delmas four

UMUZI

for my mother

Published by Umuzi 2008
P.O. Box 6810, Roggebaai 8012, South Africa,
an imprint of Random House Struik (Pty) Ltd
Company Reg No 1966/003153/07
80 McKenzie Street, Cape Town 8001, South Africa
P.O. Box 1144, Cape Town 8000, South Africa
umuzi@randomstruik.co.za
www.umuzi-randomhouse.co.za

First edition, first printing 2008
Second printing 2008
Third printing 2009
Fourth printing 2009

3 5 7 9 8 6

ISBN 978-1-4152-0049-0

Cover image by Sean Wilson
Text design and layout by William Dicey
Set in Aldus

Printed and bound by Pinetown Printers,
Pinetown, KwaZulu-Natal

AUTHOR'S NOTE

This is a story that has never left me. It has visited and haunted me from the very days on which the events took place. My challenge was to write it, a task that took me, intermittently, about ten years. It is now finished and I have many to thank for their support and assistance. Ivan Vladislavic for his faith in the book and for his advice and assistance over the last five years. Stephen Johnson, the MD of Random House, for taking the time to read my manuscript in November 2007, and for liking it. To Annari van der Merwe and Frederik de Jager of Umuzi for bearing with their first-time author.

My thanks particularly to Mike Nicol who sacrificed his entire December 2007 and early January to undertake an outstanding edit of the manuscript in an utterly professional manner. I must acknowledge Jacques Pauw's books *In The Heart of the Whore* and *Dances with Devils*, which were a valuable source of information.

My gratitude goes to Helen Seady for her input on the text, and Norman Manoim for advice on some of the long-forgotten legal issues.

Finally, to Caroline who has been a constant source of support and provided invaluable advice in relation to all of the many drafts of the book over the last ten years, drafts which she painstakingly read and on which she provided meticulous comment. She has been central to the writing of this book and, with my beloved children Simon, Isabella, Dominic and Luke is, of course, central to me.

PH
April 2008

I should have been a pair of ragged claws
Scuttling across the floors of silent seas

– from 'The Love Song of J. Alfred Prufrock' by T S Eliot

THE BOMB

The man leaning over the bench is focused on his work – a study in concentration, as you should be when constructing a bomb. His name is Japie F Kok and he works for the mechanical department of the technical division of the security branch of the South African Police.

The division's workshop is located at Rebecca Street in Pretoria West. Security around the workshop is tight, for this is the place where the 'unofficial' devices are made: the special phone taps, the booby traps, silencers, timing devices, detonators, grenades without the time delay. Here too containers are specially constructed to carry carefully designed weapons of assassination: poisons made of various toxins and poison dispensers, and, of course, bombs. Parcel bombs, letter bombs, letter-box bombs, pen bombs, jump bombs, landmine bombs, car bombs, suitcase bombs, limpet-mine bombs, fire bombs, bombs powerful enough to blow up buildings and bombs designed merely to blow off your hand. Bombs in all shapes, forms, intensity and guises.

1

It is April 1987. I'm on the Pretoria highway in the fast lane, ears pinned back, being pulled along in the slipstream of a seventy-seater school bus going like hell, the children clustered up against the large back window, pulling faces at me, smiling and waving. I am not enjoying myself.

This morning the phone rang at five o'clock. Not a good time for me.

I come up from a heavy sleep, grope clumsily for the instrument on the bedside table. Alongside me my wife Caroline turns away from the noise and pulls at the duvet. She's a journalist. I'm a lawyer. Because of our jobs the phone rings at all hours of the day and night. It's something we never get used to.

My voice is a croak when I answer.

'Is that Peter Harris?' says someone I don't recognise.

'I'm afraid so,' I reply.

'This call is from Lusaka. Please visit Jabu Masina, Ting Ting Masango, Neo Potsane and Joseph Makhura in Pretoria Central Maximum Security, they need to see you urgently. Please see what you can do to assist them.'

I have notepaper and a pen beside the phone. I scribble down the names. 'No problem,' I say, but the caller has cut the connection.

'What is it?' mumbles Caroline.

'That's what I've got to find out,' I say, heading for the bathroom.

Maximum Security means 'political', nothing else. Serial killers, sadistic rapists, wild psychotics, mass murderers never make it close to Maximum Security. Maximum Security is for the 'politicals', my clients.

I've got the easy job. They get charged, I represent them, and then they go to jail, usually for lengthy periods. Then I visit them. In places like Pretoria Central or the 'snakepit' in Kroonstad, on Robben Island or at Diepkloof prison, otherwise known as 'Sun City' after the fantasy pleasure dome built by Sol Kerzner in Bop. Bophuthatswana to the apartheid architects.

'Are they guilty?'

Well, yes, they are … mostly. At least the ones who end up in those kinds of places are, if guilty is the right word. Sadly, I suppose, I don't have that many innocent clients. Not many lawyers do. Worse still, my clients are generally accused of the big things like treason, murder, conspiracy, trying to overthrow the State, sabotage, crimes which carry the death sentence. This is why these people are hard to defend, particularly if they are, in fact, guilty.

Even worse, my clients often don't want to deny the charges against them; they're not interested in their own innocence. This is in stark contrast to most people charged with criminal offences. Most people protest their innocence, even in the face of overwhelming evidence. Murderers holding a smoking gun proclaim their innocence. Try it for yourself: walk – or run – through your average prison on any day of the week and ask the prisoners convicted of criminal offences which of them are innocent and were wrongly convicted. Every hand will go up.

What distinguishes my clients is that they are politicals. Ask them if they intended to overthrow the State and you will get a strong yes. Unfortunately, though, even if they are separated from the criminals, they still end up in the same place, prison. This is depressing for a lawyer, demoralising.

Since this morning's phone call I have made some enquiries about Jabu Masina and the Three Others, as we refer to our clients in legal parlance. I've found out that they were part of an African National Congress special operations unit that had been on a mission in the country for about ten months before they were caught. This in itself is interesting as a lot of Umkhonto we Sizwe (MK) operatives are caught a lot sooner. Askaris (captured and turned MK guerrillas), now in the employ of the security police, are deployed at all railway stations, taxi ranks, border posts and potential entry points looking for their ex-colleagues who, once identified, are quickly arrested. The border patrols and perimeter farm commandos take care of those who jump the fence.

The arrest of a unit like this will have been kept a secret so that the police could run their 'investigation' without the irritation of lawyers wanting to see their clients. That would have interfered with the careful construction of the State's case. Depending on the circumstances of their arrest, their families tend to learn of their detention only much later.

There is a pattern in the way the State handles arrested MK soldiers. Generally, once arrested, they refuse to talk. There are threats of torture and then some talk, which, frankly, is precisely what I would do in that position. I would sing an aria if it helped. Others will not talk. So they are tortured according to the creativity and inclination of the security policeman involved. They talk and give a 'confession'. Most talk in the end. For the brave it's a matter of how long you can last and how complete your confession is.

Once there's a confession, they are taken before a magistrate who, in all seriousness, asks the battered and exhausted accused if they have been tortured or if they have given the confession 'freely and voluntarily'. The accused, avoiding the eye of the security policeman who has tortured them, reply that the confession was freely and voluntarily given. The magistrate attests to this and, hey presto, the primary building block of the State's case slots into place. 'Investigative technique?' you ask. 'Tip-offs and torture.' Not too subtle, but effective. Betrayed by their bodies, the accused are dragged back to their separate cells in a mist of pain, shock and regret.

Now accomplices are arrested, the interrogation process is repeated and the investigation completed. Only when the case is virtually ready for trial are the accused brought to court for their first appearance. Of course, if there are decent channels of communication with other MK units or with headquarters in Lusaka, then word would have got out about their misfortune, particularly if a reporting date was missed. In Lusaka's books, if a unit goes quiet for too long they are assumed arrested and the appropriate steps are taken to protect other groups. In most cases, however, MK guerrillas operate in small, discrete groups with little or no contact between them, particularly on special missions. Generally, the first court appearance is the first time that the outside world knows of their arrest.

Often, this appearance coincides with a front-page exposé in the Sunday papers. The story will have been leaked by the police to the newspaper's friendly crime reporter who has no problem firing the opening salvo for the security police in the impending battle.

By 1987, the government's use of 'unofficial' methods has become accepted practice and the use of torture in interrogation is not the worst of it. We're ten months into the second state of emergency and the townships are literally under military occupation, many cordoned off by barbed wire and patrolled by soldiers and dogs.

South Africa, I believe, is not in a good place. In fact, black people contend that it has been in a shocking place for some three hundred and thirty-five years.

The figures of the mass detentions vary. Depending on whom you talk to they are as high as thirty thousand and as low as ten thousand. If ten thousand is low! Each day resistance by the United Democratic Front (UDF) and the Congress of South African Trade Unions (Cosatu) gathers force in every corner of society, from the workplace to the schools. Increasingly, anti-apartheid activists are assassinated, disappear, or are booby-trapped and bombed. This is not official policy, but we know it's happening. We just can't prove it. And a lot of people don't want to know for fear of what they might hear and the personal consequences of that truth.

This is all below the surface. Above it, there is a legal and judicial order that provides, within the narrow confines of the security laws, for the representation of political organisations and political prisoners. The government, caught between its urge to deal violently with all opposition and its strange, desperate pursuit of international credibility and legitimacy, has left the legal door ajar. It's a door into a small room. But people use the opportunity. As you do when you have nothing else.

It is in this context that political trials have become public contests between the government and the resistance organisations. A courtroom battle for the moral high ground, legitimacy and credibility. This is 'hearts and minds' stuff, and exposure is key.

I am one of those defence lawyers who get called in, purveyors of the meagre legal meals. I have been doing this for some years now, and, at the age of thirty-three, I alternate between spikes of energetic commitment to my clients, anger, exhaustion and a laconic cynicism that I try to disguise. Alarmingly, I sometimes experience a number of these states simultaneously. I see my clients at their weakest and most vulnerable. They speak to me of their fears and frailties, their relationships, childhoods, prejudices and insecurities.

Try visiting detainees who are in solitary confinement once every two weeks for years and you end up discussing very little law – not much point when they are detained under draconian security legislation that allows little room for legal movement. We spend the time talking about politics, family, how they feel, their conditions. I give them some idea of what's happening outside and verbal information gets relayed. I understand it from their point of view. I know how I would behave: with double their vulnerabilities and half their courage.

When they are finally released, there is often a sense of embarrassment when we meet 'outside'. Is it me or my client who becomes distant? Or do we both withdraw to our secret places, neither of us digging too deep, the revelations never mentioned? Perhaps it interferes with their reconstruction. You never want your therapist at your party.

Uncomfortable thoughts as I hunch over the steering wheel at high speed driving to Pretoria Central to meet four new clients, worrying that I might not have the energy to stay the course.

2

It was close to midnight when Jabu Masina jolted awake, the glare of headlights filling the room. The car slowed and stopped in front of the school classroom where Jabu hid. He checked his handgun, a Tete pistol, and stuck it back in his belt. His shirt was wet with sweat. Surprise was his only ally against a man like Orphan 'Hlubi' Chapi.

This was the second time he had come back to get Chapi. He'd tried a month ago but Chapi was too well protected and always alert. He'd followed him for two weeks and never got close enough, eventually returning to base in Swaziland shortly before his Swazi passport expired. A passport supplied by his commander, Solly Simelane.

After completing basic military training in the Funda camp close to Luanda, Jabu had been taken to a safe house in that city. There he was told he would be posted to Swaziland to join a unit that would specialise in assassinations – the 'Icing Unit', as it came to be known.

Before Jabu left for Swaziland, Oliver Tambo, the president of the ANC, visited him at a safe house in Luanda. The two men met alone in a sparsely furnished room. Jabu felt honoured to be sitting with a man he revered so much. The president asked about his training and where he'd grown up. Jabu spoke of his home in Rockville and life in South Africa before he left. The meeting ended with Oliver Tambo shaking his hand and wishing him luck.

On 11 June 1978, Jabu was given two hundred rand and a passport, with a visa valid for fourteen days, by his commander Solly Simelane. He was instructed to enter South Africa and 'sanction' Chapi, a policeman notorious in Soweto for atrocities against his own people. Jabu knew of Chapi. The man was a legend in Soweto and boasted that he had killed a number of students. Always armed, he rode seemingly invincible through the township in the company of his fellow policemen. Bullet proof.

There had been previous attempts on Chapi's life. All had failed. People were terrified of him. Quick to use his gun, he had the reputation of being an outstanding marksman.

Crossing through the Oshoek border post, Jabu arrived in Soweto at seven the same evening. Again, he spent his days and nights tracing Chapi, but with little success. Although he knew where Chapi lived, he did not want to be seen too close to the house. On those occasions he ran a stakeout, the man was nowhere to be seen.

The days passed. Jabu became desperate. On the morning of the fourteenth day, while waiting at a traffic circle near the Anglican church close to Chapi's Rockville home, the policeman's brown Ford Grenada pulled up close to him. Two women got out. Jabu walked quickly towards the vehicle, reaching for the pistol tucked into the front of his pants and covered by his loose blue shirt. Suddenly a police van turned the corner and stopped next to Chapi's car. Jabu paused. This was too dangerous. Moroka police station too nearby. He walked away slowly. From a distance he watched the Ford Grenada drive off. The hit would have to be that night. He would need cover of some sort.

In the late afternoon, Jabu returned and checked the area around Chapi's house once again. The houses were bigger here, not the small matchboxes that dotted Soweto. The property was larger too, and Chapi's house had a drive-in garage. Comparing it to his own house fuelled Jabu's resentment, justified his intention. This man was enjoying the fruits of collaboration, and everything had a price. Jabu made his plans.

The Ndondo school opposite Chapi's house would provide good cover while Jabu waited. Once night fell he entered the school and took up a position in a classroom facing the street. Previously he'd avoided this option, thinking it too obvious. But this was his last chance. Because of the tension, the waiting was long and tiring. Eventually Jabu sat down, propped himself against a wall, and drifted into sleep. He would jerk awake, chide himself, but a heaviness behind his eyes sent him back to sleep.

Then the headlights flooded the classroom. It was Chapi's Ford Grenada.

Now he had to make his move. The car stopped opposite Chapi's house and a man got out, walked towards the yard gate and opened it. In the dull orange light cast over the township by the 'Apollos' on their tall masts, Jabu realised that the man was Chapi. Quickly, he left the classroom, keeping to the shadows. Chapi's house was on his left, the Grenada on his right. Chapi was opening his garage door. Jabu hurried towards him. Hearing footsteps, Chapi spun round, his gun in his hand. So fast, Jabu knew he wouldn't make it. He staggered drunkenly and lurched across the road towards the policeman. He was close now, level with the car. Chapi lowered his gun, asked if he was okay. Jabu slurred a reply. Simultaneously, he drew his pistol and shot Chapi high in the body on the right. Chapi fell to a crouch and lifted his gun. Jabu squeezed the trigger again. It jammed. Chapi levelled his weapon. Jabu cursed, dived over the Ford's bonnet, trying to fix the gun. Chapi was firing now, six shots or more. At each explosion Jabu expected the shock of metal tearing into his flesh. He scrambled to the front of the car as the wounded Chapi moved to the rear: the hunter suddenly become the hunted. It was true what they said about Chapi: he couldn't be killed. The shots were deafeningly close. This is it, thought Jabu, the end. And then silence. He raced wildly down the street. Alive. Once round the corner, he walked slowly up the street behind Chapi's house and, jumping a fence, hid in a garden.

He pushed the gun into his pants. To think that such a small weapon could take the life of a man, although the indestructible Chapi would surely survive only one bullet. And then the police would hunt him down. Yet Jabu couldn't move. The night was filled with sirens as police vans accelerated from Moroka police station. Anyone on the streets would be stopped and questioned. He wouldn't stand a chance. He knew that no one would leave their houses. The brave might peep out a window, but no one would go further than that. This was Soweto and what you didn't know couldn't hurt you. An hour passed. Another. Until early in the morning, cold and scared, he was finally able to creep away.

The next day Jabu made preparations to get out of the country. His passport had expired. He would have to jump the border. This presented dangers of its own. Another possibility of arrest. To add to his anxiety he still knew nothing of Chapi, of whether his mission had been successful.

Jabu decided to cross the border into Botswana as he had been instructed to do if something went wrong. Mozambique was out of the question as it would be an embarrassment to the Mozambicans if he were caught.

At Johannesburg's Park Station that afternoon, the *Sowetan*'s billboards proclaimed the death of Chapi. Jabu bought a copy. He read that the residents of Soweto had 'danced in the streets'.

That night he slipped through the fence into Botswana and made his way to a refugee centre. Refusing to speak to anyone at the camp, he demanded to see a senior ANC official. Two days later he received a visit from Joe Modise, to whom he told his story.

Afterwards, exhausted, aware of the finality of his act, he wondered why he felt no regret, why he was infused with a sense of victory.

His first mission was over. He had committed murder.

3

Getting to Pretoria Central Maximum Security Prison takes you through the massive military complex of Voortrekkerhoogte, the headquarters of the South African Defence Force. Army camps lie on the right and left, uniform brown barracks matching the dry, brown veld. The largest military complex in Africa. This is an ugly place. Behind the grey walls of the camps lies an alien terrain of numbing rules and soldiers, sad people who find comfort in the camaraderie of procedure and the invigoration that the distant prospect of death brings. I know, I have been there. Very often, I see the air force's C130s taking off: dark olive green birds with bulging stomachs of bile, heading for Angola, Mozambique, Namibia (still called South West Africa at the time) to fuel dubious and unpublicised wars. These conflicts in the north, on which we quickly turn the page, are never real until someone we know does not come back. And most of us know someone.

I have to admit that I am prejudiced against Pretoria. I have never been able to distinguish the pretty purple of the jacaranda trees that line every avenue from the suffering that is planned and implemented from this city. I have been involved in too many trials and made far too many visits to a prison that smothers all within it for me to appreciate the jacarandas in blossom. There is little beauty in Pretoria. The city streets are always filled with bureaucrats, police or soldiers scurrying between great concrete blocks – the massive government departments that administer the country – the heat rising from the tarred roads in the city centre visible and choking.

Another reason I dislike Pretoria is because bombs go off there. The ANC's military struggle, focused originally on 'hard targets' like military and security installations, has intensified over the past few years. Greater numbers of units come into the country and the line between 'hard' and 'soft' targets has blurred. I suspect that Pretoria is regarded as a hard target and the ANC doesn't know or care if I am visiting. The thought of leaving this world in pieces along with people I dislike is not only sickening, it scares me. A lot.

Even restaurants are targeted. I don't particularly like Wimpy Bars, but now they're being blown up, and hamburger-eating civilians are dying. This bizarre choice of target makes me wonder about the mind of the bomber and fills me with unease and fear, for both the burger and the bomb. The lines are hazy out there. Being in the wrong place at the wrong time can get you killed.

The prison is squat and square, the interior courtyards surrounded by high yellow walls and steel walkways. Successive, impenetrable steel doors lead through the sections into the depths. The outer section facing the street houses the common criminals. One of the busiest roads in the country goes right past the white windows of the biggest prison in the country. Passing by, you see hands waving imploringly at you. It's uncomfortable. Disconcerting. Not the best entrance to our capital city, but then Pretoria is a city without manners. From the monolith of the Voortrekker Monument, visible from twenty kilometres away, to the rifle design of the University of South Africa that looms above the road into the city, and the clammy embrace of the massive prison, you get the message, and the message is a crude one: power.

I drive down Potgieter Street, turn onto the bridge and suddenly I'm in the 'secure' complex. To my left, the officers' club and other headquarter buildings. Left, and left again, and I'm facing the neat and ordered houses of the prison warders. No shortage of gardeners for their green lawns and clipped hedges. Serious criminals serving out their last days at Pretoria Central manicure these pathways. They know that cutting blades of grass, even one at a time, in the sun with soil beneath your feet, cannot compare to the concrete vacuum of the prison.

I feel the trim lawns and pathways of the houses, made more clinical by the scarcity of flowers, mirror the minds of the occupants. Their stoeps gleam, red, polished. Children play and laugh on the grass, while sprinklers lazily loop a glittering silver spray over the austerity. The lace curtains at the windows hang in the stillness. These houses are all the same, the difference lies in the gardens, the cars and the cut of the hedges, but all is dwarfed by the great yellow-brick prison towering above them. In that shadow, the complex seems invulnerable.

On the hill above the prison squats Death Row, a separate prison for those sentenced to death. It is where the hangings occur, a frequent occurrence in these times. I have never been there.

The cheap facebrick of the prison, almost white in the sun, contrasts with the bottle-green bullet-proof glass of the protruding observation posts. I see movement behind the glass as I squint up at the tower: the boy at the gates of the castle waiting to be let in. Two cameras swivel in an arc and I know that the warders are watching me. The game begins.

I don't get angry, because there are rules to this game. They set them and I obey them, but they also know that they can't go too far. Even if we both misbehave, we respect the boundaries and act within them. If they go too far, I will report them and someone senior may act on my complaints. It's the least you can do when you hold all the cards. So they are rude and I am, I hope, contemptuously professional.

I press the intercom button. No answer. If someone were to respond immediately, I would be surprised. I wait for two minutes and press again. Wait some more and press again. Third time lucky. I know we are close to the limit now. A response from the box: 'Ja.'

I give my name. Say I am an attorney on a legal visit to Jabu Masina, Ting Ting Masango, Neo Potsane and Joseph Makhura.

Silence.

'Hello?'

Silence.

I swear, unable to contain myself. I know they are listening. I can hear sniggering through the crackly intercom.

I turn around. There must be other ways of doing this. What the hell am I doing here anyway? How can this childishness amuse them? They are bored and I am angry, not a good cocktail. In the glare of midday, the dry heat bounces off the tar, and cooks my brain as my anger rises.

A voice says, 'You didn't make an appointment.'

'Yes, I did.'

Silence. I had once tried to break the impasse by being nice, asked how they were, were they having a good day? They stayed mute, stared at me, as I probably would if I worked in Pretoria Central and someone asked me the same question. Ever since, I've understood that mutual enmity is the natural order. Suits me. Sometimes I like being disliked, which concerns me. But today it is all too much. A friend, Karel Tipp, with whom I worked some years ago once told me, when he was in the middle of a huge and complex case, that all he really wanted to do was to work on one of those old tugboats that never leave Durban harbour, look out to sea and polish the brass. At times like these, I slowly polish the brass, the rolling sea clear and pure.

Suddenly with a whoosh of hydraulics, the great black steel door in front of me opens. Warder van Rensburg beckons me in.

THE BOMB

The commander of the technical division of the Security Branch is Colonel WAL du Toit, known as Waal to his friends. Colonel du Toit is highly regarded within the police and respected for an uncanny creativity when it comes to the construction of killing instruments. As one of his former colleagues once put it, 'Waal made the most beautiful little devices.'

Colonel Waal du Toit has given his blessing for the bomb to be made in the mechanical department. Influential people in the police have asked that a bomb be specifically constructed for a critical target. As Japie Kok is one of Colonel du Toit's most innovative technicians, he has been assigned the job.

Japie has been briefed on the concept of the bomb. Consequently, he has spent a considerable amount of time thinking about the specifics of its design and construction. This bomb has to last a long time and survive much wear and tear. The target of the bomb is an individual.

4

Jabu and Ting Ting moved from house to house in Mamelodi. Jabu, from Soweto and less likely to be recognised in Mamelodi, occasionally went out during the day to meet their contacts. Ting Ting stayed indoors, only venturing out at night. The two men hadn't been in the country long and were nervous of being identified.

First they stayed at the home of Dr Fabian Ribeiro. Dr Ribeiro was their initial contact and he spent time briefing them on the situation in the country and in Mamelodi. While still in Botswana preparing for their mission, they had decided that they would carry out their first action in Mamelodi. They had chosen Mamelodi for a reason. Six months earlier, in November 1985, police had fired on a crowd in the township, killing thirteen people and wounding nearly eighty. As trained soldiers, they felt acutely the unfairness of police firing on an unarmed crowd in the very place where Ting Ting had grown up and which was now under army occupation. Driven by a hot rage, they decided that this would change. Whatever the cost, their first attack would be on the security forces occupying Mamelodi.

The township was crawling with police and soldiers, as Mamelodi was regarded as a flashpoint. It had become an occupied zone. There were roadblocks daily. Once a week, a section of the township was cordoned off and every house searched. The police and soldiers showed little regard for the occupants, smashing doors and windows and breaking crockery and ornaments. Young girls and women were pulled out of bed in the middle of the night in their nightdresses and made to stand with the men and shivering children in the small sitting rooms of the matchbox houses under the scrutiny of soldiers with R4 combat rifles, while the rest of the search and seizure team moved from room to room tipping out drawers.

Jabu and Ting Ting knew that they couldn't stay long in the area. They also had a strong chance of being caught in their first few weeks and were determined to carry out an 'action' before that happened. They could not wait for the other members of the unit to arrive; it was time for the mission to start.

The two men buried most of their weapons beneath a pile of rubble and stones close to a dumping ground, not far from the house of an ANC contact, Harold Sefula. They each kept a 9 mm Makarov pistol and a Russian F-1 defensive hand grenade. These were easy to conceal and provided an element of reassurance should they run into trouble.

Jabu and Ting Ting made contact with an activist called Moss Morudi who supplied information about a military observation post on a hill overlooking the township and the regularity of patrols. He also told of a dirt road leading to the hill station. The two MK soldiers decided to mine this road.

On the night of 15 February 1986, Jabu and Ting Ting retrieved a TM-57 landmine (designed to trigger beneath heavy vehicles) and its detonator from their cache. This they carried back to Morudi's house in a sports bag which in turn they hid in a bedroom cupboard. The two comrades had dinner with Moss and his family.

The next afternoon, wearing overalls similar to those worn by municipal road workers, they set out with the bag and a spade. They were both armed with a pistol and a grenade. The operation was risky. There was a strong possibility of being apprehended. But they were both convinced they needed to make a move.

At the designated spot, Jabu stood watch while Ting Ting dug. The ground was hard and compacted and the spade bounced off the surface. Fortunately, at that time of the afternoon, the army's movements were infrequent. Ting Ting laboured quickly, a hole opening up. When it was deep enough, Jabu laid the mine and Ting Ting inserted and tightened the small MVZ-57 detonator cap. The mine was armed. Jabu covered the device with gravel and they both sprinkled white surface dirt over the area they'd disturbed. The tip of the detonator was invisible among the stones.

The two men walked slowly away, the spade slung casually over Ting Ting's shoulder.

Back among the houses, they wiped the spade clean of prints and left it standing up against a house wall, knowing it would not be there for long. The whole operation had taken ten minutes.

Jabu and Ting Ting moved from Morudi's home to another safe house in the township.

At six thirty the mine was detonated by a Casspir. By then it was dark. Moss Morudi heard the explosion and left his house to visit the site. Soon the area was swarming with soldiers taking up defensive positions. The shouts of the men were interrupted by the sound of a helicopter coming in low overhead. In the darkness, he saw the great swirls of dust, murky in the white searchlight of the chopper as it briefly landed within the cordon of soldiers before clattering off over the township. Later that night Morudi saw a heavy-duty army truck towing a long trailer. On the trailer was a large vehicle covered by a brown tarpaulin. The convoy of vehicles slowly left Mamelodi.

In the weeks that followed, the landmine attack was the main topic of conversation in the Pretoria townships. Surely an MK unit was operating in the area?

As far as Jabu and Ting Ting were concerned, their message to the authorities was clear: 'We are here.'

5

You really have to admire these guys for their attention to detail. They occupy the lowest level of the security apparatus and they wear a mud-brown uniform. But the buttons shine, the boots gleam and the belt buckle is a beacon. There are, incongruously, three straight lines ironed across the middle of the back of their shirts. Having done my military service in 1974, conscripted at the tender age of seventeen and ending up a platoon commander with the rank of lieutenant, I know that these lines, so painstakingly ironed into the back of the shirt, serve no purpose whatsoever other than to indicate that some cretin, wishing to impress his superiors, has spent a precious extra two hours ironing them in. Welcome to the logic of South African military life.

To me, these men with their chests puffed out and their brown shirt-sleeves rolled the regulation three fingers above the elbow, when the arm is extended, are familiar animals. Warder van Rensburg is in good shape. Tall, broad shouldered and fit, he regards me as dirt. I am used to this. He nods and ushers me to a yellow line one metre inside the room. I move quickly and stand on the line, knowing that if you don't step smartly, you run the risk of being crushed to death by the massive steel door as it silently swings closed. What a mess. Sometimes, they close the door while you're entering and when you curse they fake irritation with their colleague who is operating the system but they never apologise. This is all part of the game.

As the door shuts behind me, the barred steel door in front of me opens. Cameras mounted high on the wall watch as my briefcase goes into the metal detector. I follow Warder van Rensburg through the doorway, pick up the case, wait for yet another barred door to open and enter a brick-lined passage with steel mesh walkways above it. Warders patrol the walkways. At roof height are triangular windows of bottle-green glass behind which sit more warders. It always makes me think of those advertisements for luxury resorts, which claim to offer great service by virtue of having five staff members for every guest.

I have been to this prison many times and should be inured to its charms. But I'm not. The cold hostility of the building and the warders depresses me. This place is not about rehabilitation, this is confinement, a fortress in a war with no foreseeable end. And that is a lonely thought.

Warder van Rensburg carries that most essential item of equipment, a large bunch of keys, attached to his belt by a length of olive-green nylon cord. He uses the keys to unlock a succession of steel-barred doors as we go deeper into the prison and finally reach the consulting room. In fact, it is not a proper legal facility: it's the prison doctor's consulting room and surgery. I go in and the door slams shut behind me. Warder van Rensburg and I have not exchanged a single word.

I am alone, except for the small square window in the door at which the head of my host, like Banquo's ghost, appears periodically. He stares at me intently.

This is what is called an 'in-sight but out-of-sound' consultation. It will be some time before they bring my clients. These warders are in no rush, and why should they hurry? Prisons are about spending time.

It may seem strange that a prison should have no consulting room, but I suppose when it was built no one could imagine prisoners affording legal advice, or that such advice would be allowed even if they could. Not this type of prisoner anyway. But here I am and I have to be accommodated, and so the surgery suffices.

On another occasion, I consulted in the garage into which the top security prisoners were driven in escorted armoured vehicles. Once, seated at a table in the middle of the cold and echoing space, I was talking with clients who faced charges of sabotage and high treason when the garage door rumbled slowly open. We faced the street, stunned. Jaws dropped. Freedom beckoned, but where to run? Was it a trap? Would they be waiting outside and open fire as my clients ran into the road? Was it just a mistake, a trick, a game? Then wild shouts and swearing sounded above and the door slowly closed. No one said a word except me. 'Shit!' I said.

Consulting in a doctor's surgery inside a prison may bother some attorneys, but I rather like it. It makes a pleasant change from the dull tranquillity of a lawyer's office. Maybe it's because I admire doctors greatly. I feel that if I were a doctor, I would do something useful. I suppose that because I am constantly afflicted by a variety of illnesses which require serious and immediate medical attention, I have real respect for doctors. I admire someone so learned that he can listen calmly to my complex and disturbing symptoms then nod sagely and prescribe Streptomycin twice a day for the bacteria, Clarityn at night with dinner, an Imovane sleeping tablet to assist my slumber, and then an assortment of Myprodol and Stopayne at breakfast for the pain and generally to see me through my day until I can get to some refreshment in the evening. Now that's service. In my book, people who are on first-name terms with the rare illnesses I suffer from, not to mention the remedies for these afflictions, warrant real respect.

No sign of my clients.

Bored, I weigh myself. Seventy-four kilograms. Take a look around. This place is not one your average patient would feel at home in. No windows, no air, mean-looking pieces of surgical apparatus lying about, huge needles and steel implements, rubbish bins filled with used band-ages and other items too sordid to describe. I so fear these things that I take a white towel from the back of a chair and cover the bin, as if to prevent some dreadful disease from leaping out. I imagine prisoners, warders and a lawyer desperately crawling down the passages of the sealed prison that is to be our common tomb. I need to see my clients before I deteriorate further.

A metal rattle at the door and Warder van Rensburg's face at the small window. Then my clients walk in. All four of them. I give them the familiar handshake. Surprisingly, they look in good shape, strong and fit. I am greeted by the one who walked in first. Tall, dark, well built, a handsome man with strong features and a smile curling his lips up at the edges.

'My name is Jabu Masina, we are glad that you have come. It has been a long time. We thought you would come earlier.'

He is followed by a man who introduces himself as Ting Ting Masango.

24

He is shorter, broader, smiling as he takes a seat at the table. His left eye squints. I have to avoid focusing on it. Lighter in complexion, he wears a spotless white T-shirt, beneath which I can see he is carrying a bit of weight. He has that kind of build.

Neo Potsane is shorter than Jabu and Ting Ting. Small featured with a pockmarked face, wiry and alert. He's nervous, constantly glancing around, unlike the first two who seem at ease.

The last is Joseph Makhura, the smallest and the youngest of the four, seemingly out of place among these older and tougher men. I wonder how he got here.

I am nervous. The first time you meet clients is always difficult. If they don't like you from the start, they generally fire you quickly. I've never been dumped by a client, and I don't want that to happen now. At the beginning, we merely need to like each other; the trust can come later.

I smile and say, 'I have just weighed myself, but I must tell you, I think they have loaded some extra kilos on this scale just to discriminate against me, these swinish warders.'

Jabu smiles sardonically, gets up and weighs himself. Just on eighty-three kilos. Satisfied, he sits down.

With Ting Ting the scales dip and clang and he has to slide the weight along. Exclaiming, he turns to me. 'I agree with you, this machine has been sabotaged.'

We burst out laughing in relief.

'I am sorry that I didn't get here sooner,' I say, 'but I only got the call this morning.'

Jabu raises his eyebrows but makes no comment.

We exchange pleasantries as if we are meeting for the first time in the lobby of a hotel.

'How was your trip here?' Jabu asks.

'Not bad, but you know they're redoing the highway and at times it can be frustrating. Are you okay here? How is your health?'

'Here it is much better, at least there are rules, although the weather is very hot.'

'Are you getting any exercise?'

'There's an exercise yard, but it's very small.'

'You look in good shape,' I comment.

'Not bad, not bad,' says Ting Ting politely.

25

Ending it, I say, 'I think it's important before we start for you to know who I am and where I come from, so that you can make a decision about whether we should go forward together.'

I know that many prisoners in their position are only too overjoyed to have someone come and visit them, never mind represent them. But these guys are different. At ease with their situation, they will make their own decisions, and anyway, I want them to know that they have a choice.

I tell them I'm from the law firm Cheadle, Thompson and Haysom. That it's a human-rights firm that started a few years back. Most of us came from the big established law firms. In the early 1980s, we felt there was a need to build a practice that would represent resistance organisations and individuals needing representation in their battle against the apartheid government. At that stage, there'd been only two or three firms, small ones, prepared to do political work. In fact, this kind of work was tough, poorly paid and made you unpopular in certain circles. All good reasons why most lawyers avoided it.

I tell them about Halton Cheadle who specialises in representing the black trade union movement. Banned and under house arrest in the 1970s, a brilliant lawyer. Fink Haysom, a former Nusas president frequently detained and held in solitary confinement. Also Azhar Cachalia, one of the leaders of the United Democratic Front, detained more times than I can remember. All fine lawyers. I talk about the cases the firm has handled, including the big treason trials like the Maritzburg Treason Trial and the Alexandra Treason Trial, both run by Norman Manoim, one of the partners.

I mention a few of the cases I've handled, trying to pick on those that show my experience and expertise in these areas. They listen intently, occasionally putting questions. It turns out they know some of the accused we've represented, many having been trained in the same MK military camps in Angola.

We're using valuable time but the links need to be made. As in most new relationships, the sniffing out is important, how you relate to the client, the way you speak, avoiding legalese and jargon, not being flashy with your knowledge but showing enough, revealing political sense but not taking your clothes off or dropping too many names. Just saying enough to show you have some connection.

I have to see it from their point of view. They've probably been inside for some time, been tortured and maybe face serious charges. Then in walks this white boy in a suit (although, unlike some colleagues, I've never been a snappy dresser) who says he's been told to assist them. Hell, I could even be in the pay of the security police. In their shoes, I would be cautious if not suspicious. Although simply being asked to represent them is an indication of some degree of credibility. But who knows?

For me, it's important that I like my clients. They may irritate me, which some of them do, but it isn't enough to have a working relationship. I need something stronger. I need to be motivated, otherwise it becomes a chore and I get bored. This isn't just a job.

Out of the blue, Ting Ting, who has been quiet, asks me what car I drive. I'm taken aback. I know that a lot of clients like their lawyers to drive large, fancy cars. I reply sheepishly that I drive a Honda Ballade. Ting Ting's silence is telling. After a moment, perking up, he says, 'We were driving the latest Audi when we were caught.'

'Sies man,' I exclaim. 'That's the car of choice of the security police.'

'I know,' says Ting Ting, 'that's why we drove it. But it didn't help.'

We laugh and move into other areas. Family stuff. I need the details of parents and contact addresses, phone numbers, financial obligations. Girlfriends? They laugh and look at each other.

'Do we have time for that?' Neo asks.

I leave it there for the moment. I need to find out what we're facing. 'Do you have a copy of the charge sheet?'

'No,' says Jabu.

Typical, they have been given nothing.

'Okay,' I say, 'then tell me some of the details so I can get a sense of it.'

They exchange glances and Jabu says, 'They say we have done everything.'

I lean forward. 'Help me to understand. "Everything" is a big word.'

'Everything means undergoing training, possession of weapons, sabotage, assassination and murder, planting landmines and a bomb.'

Shit, I think, they are right, there is nothing else. I clear my throat, which has gone tight. 'The assassinations,' I say quietly, 'give me an example.'

Masina looks me in the eye. 'Have you heard of Brigadier Molope?'

I go cold. 'Yes, I've heard of him.'

We are in trouble.

6

Driving back to Johannesburg thinking of the policeman Brigadier Molope, I am in another place, a prisoner of memory. I remember the Winterveld massacre, as it became known.

Winterveld is an arid and dusty area of mud houses outside Pretoria, part of the Bophuthatswana Bantustan. In Winterveld there is one hundred per cent unemployment, no running water or electricity. It is an empty dust bowl of hunger.

On Wednesday 26 March 1986, the people of Winterveld protested against the detention and torture of their children by the Bop police. There was speculation that the chief of police would come to the soccer field to speak about the detainees. Some residents said they had heard the police announcing the meeting the day before on loudhailers.

The people, mostly women and children, gathered slowly on the gravel soccer field in the middle of the settlement. There were a few men, but most had gone to Pretoria looking for work. A tattered barbed-wire fence surrounded the field. It was a windy day and dust swirled across the field and the surrounding houses. In some of the tiny gardens people had sparse vegetable patches but the soil was too hard and dry to produce much greenery.

By nine o'clock, the crowd numbered more than five thousand, their ranks swelled by curious schoolchildren. Also people from adjacent settlements and some of the youth had come from the nearby township of Garankuwa. Trucks arrived and police and soldiers dismounted. More police arrived in armoured vehicles. They wore full riot gear and were armed with R4 combat rifles. The mothers and elders realised that the situation was explosive and tried to calm the crowd. Opposite them, the police formed a defensive line.

The area police commander arrived and conferred with his subordinate. The police were now facing the crowd, rifles at the ready but pointed down. The commander admonished the gathering through a loudhailer and a rumble of annoyance went through the people. The commander shouted louder that he 'would leave them lying all over the field like ants' and bulldoze their houses. The crowd's voice rose in anger. The police raised their rifles. Some of the protesters sensed danger and tried to get away but those at the back were pushing forward. A stone sailed out and landed close to the police. They watched. There was more shouting as mothers and fathers appealed to the police for information about their children. More stones. Suddenly the police opened fire. The harsh bang bang bang of semi-automatic rifle fire. The shots, sporadic at first, escalated to a crescendo, the bullets smashing into soft flesh. No more stones now, just the police target shooting.

Chaos. A wild rushing panic as people ran for safety, snagging in the barbed wire. Screaming. Dust in the faces of the fleeing crowd, blinding them, blurring the scene in a red-brown haze. The shooting died out. The people had disappeared, leaving only the wounded and dead on the ground and hanging on the fence. A silence, then the bawling of children and the groans of the wounded.

Eleven people, mostly women and children, died that day. Two hundred were injured and more than a thousand people arrested, loaded with kicks and swinging rifle butts onto the police armoured vehicles and driven to neighbouring police stations.

By the time we lawyers got there, called in by the Catholic Church, all that was left were mounds of clothing dotted across the field and scraps of material flapping on the barbs of the fence. Dark patches of blood swarmed with blue flies. And scattered in the dust were shoes, lots of them.

We based ourselves in the church of Father Smangaliso Mkhatshwa in Soshanguve, a Catholic haven with outbuildings that could serve as a makeshift medical station and from which we could work to take statements. Through the rest of that day and night and all of the next day, teams of doctors and nurses treated the wounded brought to the mission. Had these people gone to any hospital, they would have been arrested and interrogated. Social workers spoke with the families of the dead, while foreign camera crews filmed the scene.

Gathering evidence of the atrocity and trying to trace the missing became a desperate time of hoping against hope that they had been detained, and were not lying dead in the police or hospital morgues. It would take many visits to the sparse concrete cold rooms of the mortuaries to identify all those who had died on that day.

The massacre was followed by mass arrests in the area, and the random torture continued. The Winterveld massacre, as it became known, became an infamous incident, not least because Bénédicte Chanut, a white French doctor from Médecins du Monde, was also arrested and viciously sjambokked. Chanut had been working at a clinic run by the Catholic Church and Médecins du Monde near Winterveld and, on hearing the shooting, had grabbed her medical case and driven to see if she was needed. She ran straight into the Bop police, who concluded that if black people were causing trouble, there had to be a white person behind it. Not knowing that she was a French national or that she was a doctor, she was arrested and brutally flogged. The French government intervened and she was released.

The Winterveld massacre received considerable media exposure. The Bophuthatswana government called a commission of inquiry and Norman Manoim and I ended up representing the Winterveld community with the brilliant pair, Wim Trengove and Bob Nugent, as our counsel. The commission went nowhere. During May 1986, while the commission was still under way, the two senior police officers commanding the police responsible for the massacre were promoted. It was a clear signal to the people of Winterveld. The commission had become a farce.

The policeman whose promotion got the most publicity was the officer in charge of the entire area, Brigadier Molope. He had been in command on the day of the Winterveld massacre and had given the order to fire. He was known to be leading the offensive against the youth and many of those who survived the torture and thrashings talked of how he would use a wire whip on their backs.

Brigadier Molope was a giant of a man who wore black reflective sunglasses and drove a black bullet-proof Mercedes Benz with tinted windows. Gliding through the bleak townships of Garankuwa, Soshanguve and Mabopane, Brigadier Molope became the source of an almost mythical horror.

THE BOMB

Bombs, like most things in life, are best kept simple. The explosive must be durable, malleable, depending on the vehicle, not volatile and unobtrusive. The vehicle or casing is critical, particularly when the bomb has to travel. Bombs that will be on the move and have to deceive the recipient take careful consideration. The key in this case is that the intended target must not know that he is about to flick the switch on his own life. This is where the bomb manufacturer's real cunning comes in. Japie Kok is an expert in this field.

7

The few months after the Winterveld massacre were good to Colonel Molope. With his promotion to Brigadier in May 1986 had come more responsibility in terms of his command. In charge of all police and security operations in the massive ODI area of Bophuthatswana, his reputation instilled total fear. The fear was based on a brutality that was unpredictable and often irrational, although not without calculation of consequence. As far as the citizens of Winterveld were concerned, for Molope there was no way back, no redemption. Not after the massacre. Merely to maintain the status quo in the area and protect his own policemen, Molope had to increase the use of force and violence.

When Molope's large Mercedes Benz drove through the streets, people looked away, afraid that he might stop if they stared. Everyone speculated about his eyes, always invisible behind the sunglasses. No one had seen his eyes. It was rumoured that even when beating suspects in the cells he wore his sunglasses.

Molope always travelled with bodyguards and at least one police escort car. Any bystander who attracted attention stood a good chance of being taken to police headquarters in that escort car for interrogation and sport. Such misfortune was a matter of fate.

It was luck that Selina, a friend of Ting Ting's from Winterveld, introduced him to the woman who was Brigadier Molope's mistress. A sheer coincidence to which Ting Ting feigned indifference. Selina didn't know Ting Ting's real identity. In effect, she was unwittingly part of his cover. Molope's mistress lived in the 'Beirut' section of Mabopane. The section had been named 'Beirut' and the area adjacent to it 'Lebanon' after extreme fighting there some years earlier between police and residents.

Over the next few weeks, Ting Ting and Selina met the woman from Beirut several times. Molope had bought his mistress a house and often on a Friday or Saturday night his black car would be seen parked beneath a shade-cloth lean-to.

Slowly Ting Ting pieced together details about Molope's daily life. On one occasion the mistress wanted to invite Selina and Ting Ting to her house but was worried that Molope would discover that she was entertaining guests. She could lose the house for such an indiscretion, she told them.

The house in Mabopane where Molope lived with his wife and family had extensive security, as did another house he owned in Mafikeng. Yet he visited his mistress alone, without his bodyguards. Ting Ting duly briefed the unit.

The following Friday night, Ting Ting waited near the mistress's house. He parked the unit's green Audi 500 (bought from a second-hand car dealer on Bloed Street, Pretoria) some blocks away and walked back. The black Merc wasn't parked under the shade cloth awning, and although he waited some hours Molope didn't arrive. Eventually, concerned that the woman might spot him loitering in the street, Ting Ting decided to leave.

He was back the next night. Lights were on in the house but no sign of Molope's car. Again he waited. Again it was wasted effort. He realised this was going to take time.

The following Friday, 20 June 1986 at six o' clock, Ting Ting again drove past the house. This time the car was parked beneath the shade cloth. The chances were that Molope was there for the weekend.

The next morning the unit met up and Jabu listened to Ting Ting's information. After a brief discussion, they decided to assassinate Brigadier Molope that night. The task went to Ting Ting, Joseph and the fifth man in the unit, Justice Mbizana. The men parted, the three heading off to retrieve weapons and ammunition from a secret cache.

On the way to Molope's house, the three were stopped at a police roadblock. To turn round would be dangerous. There was no alternative but to sit it out. Yet surely the car would be searched. A policeman in full combat gear holding an R4 rifle approached them. Ting Ting rolled down the window and politely greeted the officer. The policeman glanced into the car, hesitated, then waved them through.

Despite a kick of adrenaline at this close encounter, the three reconnoitered the mistress's house: Molope's car was in the yard. Ting Ting stopped the Audi in a nearby street. It was night but the township was bathed in the orange glow of the tall arc lights, the Apollos. The men went over the operation. Ting Ting would wait in the car. Justice was to take the lead, Joseph to cover him. They were to saunter to the house. The woman should not be hurt. Afterwards they should walk calmly back to the car. No running or they would attract attention.

Joseph and Justice went off. Ting Ting placed his Makarov pistol between his legs. He felt the reassuring shape of the hand grenade in his pocket and wondered if he would have to use it.

He watched Joseph and Justice round the corner and head towards Molope's house. They were both wearing overcoats over dark tracksuits bought specially for night missions. Each was carrying an AK-47 beneath his overcoat, as well as a hand grenade.

They went through the garden gate and onto the stoep to the left of the front door. Joseph remained in the shadows at the corner of the stoep while Justice, his AK-47 at the ready, knocked loudly. They heard footsteps. The door opened. It was the woman. She saw Justice and the AK-47 levelled at her and screamed. She tried to slam the door but Justice kicked it open. He saw the massive frame of Molope coming up fast behind the woman, protected by her. Justice froze, not wanting to shoot the woman but knowing that if he didn't open fire first, they were in big trouble.

Suddenly the woman, still screaming, threw herself behind the door. Molope was close now, grabbing at his gun in its holster. Justice pressed the trigger of the AK-47, the recoil pushing him backwards. The volley caught Molope full in the chest, but still the policeman advanced. Now he was in Joseph's line of sight and he too fired a short burst into the giant man. Molope went down, his body falling forwards, face first. He lay jerking, thick blood spreading beneath him. The woman was silent. Joseph walked up to Molope and fired short automatic bursts into him, one two, one two, as he had been trained, holding his accuracy, wanting to make sure the hated brigadier was dead.

Then the two men walked away holding their AK-47s in the air, Justice telling the gathering onlookers, 'Ngenane ezindlini, singabe MK.' Go into your houses, we are MK.

The next day the unit heard radio reports of Molope's killing. There was spontaneous celebrating in the streets of Winterveld.

8

Liaising with the office of the attorney-general in Pretoria on the case of Jabu Masina and the Three Others is only a marginally better experience than dealing with the prison warders at Maximum Security. No legal collegiality here, just the same obstructive treatment. Cold enmity behind a

34

veneer of legal professionalism. But when I finally get the charge sheet, I start to regret the rush. There are forty-nine charges and I realise that, if anything, the accused have been somewhat modest about their activities, and with good reason.

The charge sheet, dated 15 May 1987 and signed by the deputy attorney-general of the Transvaal, MT van der Merwe, senior counsel, states that from 1977 to 1986 all four of the accused received intensive and specialised military training in a number of countries, including Mozambique, Zambia, Angola, Tanzania and the German Democratic Republic.

The main charge says it all: 'And whereas the accused during the period 1977 to September 1986 and in the Republic and elsewhere and with hostile intent against the state to overthrow the government of the state and through force to endanger it (a) conspired with the ANC and its members ... to promote the aims of the ANC and to commit the acts set out in the annexure hereto ... therefore the accused are guilty of the crime of high treason.' It is downhill from there.

There are three charges of contravening the Terrorism Act of 1967, involving the commission of what the Act describes as 'a range of terrorist activities'. Six charges that relate to contravening the provisions of the Internal Security Act, 74 of 1982. Four charges of murder. Three charges of attempted murder. Twelve charges of malicious damage to property. And the cherry on the top, the main charge of high treason. As usual in these cases, there are a number of alternative charges. It reminds me of that song about a man loading sixteen tons of coal, one fist of iron and one of steel, '... and if the left don't get you, then the right one will ... dum dum dum.'

If I have been left in any doubt as to how serious these charges are, there are also charges of contravening the Arms and Ammunition Act, 75 of 1969, by unlawful possession of the following assortment of weapons: two Makarov pistols and their fully loaded magazines, five AK-47 combat rifles and twenty-three fully loaded magazines, two Russian SPM-2 limpet mines and related components, four 158 mini limpet mines with igniters and time fuses, two Russian defensive F-1 hand grenades, eleven RGD offensive hand grenades and a variety of igniters, six military-type mechanical detonators, one TM-57 landmine and its detonator, numerous rounds of ammunition and, just in case things got out of hand, one RPG anti-tank rocket launcher.

I know that if the accused are found guilty on any one of the charges of murder there is a strong likelihood of the death sentence. There are four such charges here, as well as the main count of high treason, which also carries the death penalty. There's something else: I know that the State justice system is an efficient one and that they would never put up charges of murder in a high-profile political trial unless they had a rock-solid case. Treason is possibly arguable. But a murder trial probably based on confessions, with the type of judges allocated to political trials, makes conviction highly likely. If no extenuating circumstances can be found, it is obligatory for the judge to pass the ultimate sentence. Death by hanging.

9

Jabu Masina had never been in such a big lorry. Climbing over the stacked furniture, he shouted to his brothers and sisters, looking forward to the move to a new house in a different area. The flurry and fuss of the white men added to the excitement although the men were loud and frightening. On the truck his mother cried softly. But to a nine-year-old, the prospect of the big move was thrilling.

The day had started early with the police and the council workers coming in their vans and massive trucks. The night before, his stepfather had told them they'd have to move from the small house in Western Native Township where they'd lived for as long as he could remember. The two-bedroomed house with a kitchen and dining room and an outside toilet was home to the family of thirteen. Jabu's grandmother and his mother's younger sister, an uncle and two cousins also shared the house. Jabu slept in the kitchen with his five brothers, head to toe.

Jabu Masina, born on 26 December 1950, was the second-eldest child. The eldest, his brother Nodo, had died, stabbed at the age of fifteen in a fight trying to shield a friend. Jabu had never known his father and his mother never mentioned the man. The boy didn't know if he was dead or had abandoned them. Nor did he ever raise the topic as it angered his mother. His stepfather, Jumbo, was a good man, and looked after them as his own children.

Jumbo was a domestic worker, a servant for a white family in the

Johannesburg suburb of Highlands North. From time to time, Jabu went with his mother to visit the house where his stepfather worked. He never went inside. He waited at the back near the staff quarters, occasionally seeing the white occupants, distant but not unfriendly. A different world. Jumbo gave them leftovers, bread and sometimes vegetables and meat. It was delicious and a change from the pap and wild spinach that was their staple diet.

Once a week, usually a Saturday, his mother cooked meat on a coal stove. It was a great treat. There was no electricity in the house. Jabu helped with the washing up, taking the plates and pots out to the only tap on the property a few metres from the house.

He was close to his mother. A large and enveloping woman, she was strong and always in control. Yet she never seemed to sleep. His grandmother made *umqombothi*, selling the traditional beer from the front room of the house.

Jabu did not have much contact with white people. He grew up afraid of whites, although he'd never met any whites or talked with them. He thought they hated him. Surely that was why they made black people stay in distant places. He heard stories of black people being arrested and beaten for being in white areas or for being 'cheeky'. The white police, cruising the township in their vans, dogs snarling in the back, were trouble. They terrified Jabu and he ran whenever he saw them. To Jabu, whites had big houses and cars; all the black people he knew served them or worked for them.

His first encounter with whites occurred when he was about eleven years old while visiting Jumbo at the Highlands North house. Jumbo had given him a packet of leftovers and on the way to the bus stop Jabu ate from the packet. He hadn't gone far when he noticed a white boy with an Alsatian on a leash, the kind of dog that barked in the back of police vans. The white boy, about his age, looked at him expressionlessly as he passed. Keeping his eyes down, Jabu quickened his pace, but the white boy's stare made him uneasy. He didn't want to be thought 'cheeky' but he couldn't resist a backward glance. As he turned, he saw the white boy let go of the leash, just letting it drop from his hand. The dog sprang forward.

Jabu ran, clutching the packet of leftovers. The dog was gaining. He looked back to see the boy standing still, curious but detached, and the dog racing at him. Jabu dropped the packet of food, even as he did so worrying that his mother would be cross with him. On his left was the open gate of a house, it was his only escape. He rushed through and shut the gate. In the street the dog snapped and snarled, bearing its teeth. Jabu stood petrified.

He didn't hear the white man approaching. The first he knew of him was when a large hand gripped his shoulder. He screamed. Terrified of the dog and the man, he cowered speechless.

'Are you trying to break into my house?' the man asked loudly in Afrikaans.

'No, baas, the dog wanted to bite me,' said Jabu but the man wasn't listening, was dragging him to the house, hitting him, kicking him.

The man phoned the police. 'I caught a small kaffir breaking into my house,' he told them. Soon two white policemen arrived and Jabu was thrown into the back of their van. The boy and the dog were nowhere to be seen. In the van, the fear gone, Jabu got angry. At the police station he was uncooperative and a black police constable threatened to lock him up for the night if he didn't make a statement. Jabu spent his first night in prison.

Meanwhile Jabu's mother was frantically searching for him. Like Jumbo she too was a domestic worker. The next day she explained the situation to her white employer and asked for time off. The woman kindly offered to help her and, after phoning a number of police stations, tracked down Jabu and had him released. On the way home, the boy told his mother what had happened. She said nothing. It was the way of things.

Throughout his school years, Jabu got good marks and sometimes first-class passes. He was among the smartest in the class, although no match for a stocky boy called Cyril Ramaphosa. They became friends. But at the age of sixteen Jabu was taken out of school and the friendship dwindled. Times were hard for the Masinas; they needed Jabu to start earning.

For the next eight years he worked in factories and warehouses until he felt doomed to a life of manual labour and wages that were a pittance.

At the age of twenty-four, Jabu went back to high school where he had to repeat Standard Seven. He passed and went into Standard Eight, determined that he would get his matric. But there were no exams in June that year due to student protests and boycotts. It was 1976. Jabu was not involved in the student movement or in politics, determined to keep his promise to his headmaster who had said that he would only take him back if he stayed away from the girls and did nothing wrong. It wasn't easy. The events of June drew him in. The primary cause of the protests was the use of Afrikaans as the language of instruction. Jabu had no problem with Afrikaans, having grown up in Western Native Township where the majority of the residents were 'coloured' and spoke Afrikaans. But he sympathised with the other students. He also knew that this was not purely about Afrikaans, but also about the youth who would not accept their fate, like their parents and, perhaps, as he did. So he went with the crowd, but he did not lead it.

He joined the rampaging students. Police firing teargas were everywhere. In the chaos of burning buildings, he saw the bodies of those who'd been shot, heard mothers screaming as they searched for their children in the black smoke. Saw dogs scavenging among the bodies and the debris. Watched as police vehicles appeared out of the smoke and gunfire rang out as the students dispersed, only to regroup and converge on another target. The night brought some relief to the noise and the gunfire.

The uprising continued for the rest of 1976 and schooling was disrupted. Jabu saw his dream of getting an education fading. Through the first half of 1977 he worked hard. In June, the unrest erupted again in commemoration of those who'd died the previous year. Again schooling ceased. Again there were no exams.

Jabu was becoming frustrated and despondent. He was now twenty-six years old. He heard of students leaving the country, of ANC recruiters offering passage to Mozambique and Swaziland. There was talk of joining the ANC in exile to fight the Nationalist government. At first Jabu thought the talk mere bravado. He returned to school, but a police presence on the grounds meant frequent disruptions. Studying was impossible.

Jabu's thoughts turned to the ANC. He heard from a friend called Caesar that if you joined the organisation in exile you would be looked after and get a good education. He decided to leave the country and made the necessary contacts. Some nights later, with Caesar and a woman, Popone Dube, he climbed through the border fence into Swaziland.

They were met by an ANC representative and taken to a house in Manzini, called the 'White House'. Here they ate and spent the night. Jabu was exhausted and scared, but convinced an education was worth the hardship.

The following day, the three were visited by a man who introduced himself as John Nkadimeng. He'd arranged their passage into Mozambique and that night they were driven across the border in a Land Rover. The well-built man at the wheel said, 'Welcome to the ranks of the ANC. I am Jacob Zuma.' He was at ease, friendly, cracking jokes, interested in them. Eventually they reached Maputo and a large house that Jabu learnt was a 'transit' house called Matola, after the suburb.

The next morning, Jabu met Solly Simelane, the ANC area commander. Did he want to finish his education or go for military training? Jabu opted to finish his schooling. That day he and a host of young people sat about in the house and its orchard, talking, already missing home. Jabu contributed little. He wondered if he'd done the right thing. If he'd ever see his family again. He was comforted by the fatherly figure of Jacob Zuma, moving in and out of the house, smiling, bringing documents for them to sign, making them feel at home in a foreign place.

That night Jabu woke drenched in sweat. It was hot and stifling in the room and he needed air. Outside in the orchard he was confronted by a guard carrying an AK-47. It was the first time he had been so close to a gun. The legendary status of the weapon tantalised him. He wanted to touch it. Gradually he and the guard fell into easy conversation. They talked about the gun and military training, and the camps in Angola that sounded heroic and exotic. Soldiers training with AK-47s and hand grenades, the camaraderie, an MK army united in reclaiming the country. Wondering how he could go to school when others were fighting, Jabu decided to change his option.

The next morning he nervously told Simelane that he'd changed his mind. The man was irritated but agreed to reassign him.

A week later, Jabu flew with seven other MK recruits in a civilian aircraft from Maputo to Luanda, Angola. He was anxious and excited during the first flight of his life. On arrival, the recruits were escorted by an ANC official through passport control and out into the sharp sunlight. For a country at war, it looked so normal and peaceful. After a night at a safe house, Jabu was driven into the bush outside the city. An hour later he arrived at Funda, an ANC basic training camp. There was no turning back.

10

I like the parents immediately. I arrange that they come to our offices in Johannesburg and we meet in the boardroom. They know what the matter's about, as I'd told them on the telephone and, in any event, the word is already out on the street.

I always make a point of taking detailed statements from the parents. I find that, taken together with the statements of the accused, it gives a more rounded picture. And this is a picture that will need a lot of rounding. Generally, by the time the accused get to the awaiting trial stage – and there are exceptions – they project themselves as warriors, martyrs for the struggle and believers in the oft chanted slogan 'liberation or death, victory is certain'. I suppose it is necessary 'to hold the line', as people in the struggle are fond of saying. Fearing that if it should slip, it will be gone forever, leading to weakness and perhaps betrayal. Personally, I don't really buy the 'charge of the Light Brigade' stuff. But I don't go as far as some cynics who have changed the slogan to 'liberation or victory, death is certain'.

While many ANC members that I have defended held true to the image of strength and commitment, there is another side that is also important and which is often neglected. This is the humanity and vulnerability of the accused. What circumstances and events drove them to this point? What were the determining influences that made these individuals different from the broad mass of people who remained spectators?

To me, the four accused seem typical at first with their jokes and their apparent strength and confidence. But these accused are different: they are more considered than some of the other people I've defended. I wonder if this is because they've run their course, and been caught. For them, it is not just the end of liberty. It is final, the end of life.

But they are the sons, and these are the mothers and fathers.

Mr Simon Potsane is an old man of average height, erect in his bearing, with distinguished grey hair. Bushy grey eyebrows frame eyes no longer a clear brown but milky, marked and creased by age and a fierce sun. His suit is worn, pressed and clean, and his shoes are polished to perfection. His calloused hand rasps against mine as he introduces himself and the others: Mrs Joyce Masina, and Mrs NaSindane Masango, and the aunt of Joseph Makhura, Mrs Maria Sithole. Mrs Masina is big and broad, a generous, beautiful face now blurring with maturity, the skin dark and shiny smooth, wearing a headdress over her hair in the tradition of African women.

I don't want to take statements now. As with the accused, we need to deal with the preliminaries and establish trust. I am also concerned that if they see all the charges they'll panic and not be able to address the issues calmly. I've been involved in cases where the accused didn't want their parents to know exactly what they had done. That they had killed people. Even though my clients knew that their mothers would be sitting in court and would listen to every detail, in the beginning they did not want them to see the charge sheet. Mostly this is because what is typed on white paper in thick black ink is starkly upsetting. Murder and attempted murder, even when seen in context, remain profoundly shocking acts.

Many of the parents of the accused that I've defended were deeply religious people. Christians who would find it hard to condone the taking of a life, would have difficulty reconciling themselves to the fact that their child had killed another human being. In the end they learnt to live with, if not accept, their child's actions, but this was a process that could never be rushed. In other instances, where the family was not religious, there was still a shock as the parents came to terms with the circumstances and the knowledge that their child faced a lengthy jail sentence or even execution. For accused from 'political' families it was easier, as their loved ones immediately understood and were supportive of their situation and motivation. The difficulty at the beginning of each case was that you didn't know where you and the families stood on these sensitive issues.

In this instance, I realise that I cannot delay the truth. I tell them that the charges are serious.

'What do you mean?' asks Mrs Masango.

'I mean that the State is alleging that they killed people, policemen. That they were part of an MK assassination unit that was highly trained. They were instructed by the ANC to carry out certain high-profile assassinations and they did this. But now they have been caught.'

There is silence as my words sink in. I don't tell them that the State will be asking for the death penalty. I don't have to. Everyone knows that for murder you hang. It is unspoken, but there.

I fill the gap taking down their personal details.

'You must help us,' says Mrs Masina quietly.

I choke as I see the desperation in her eyes. Not wanting to raise expectations, I say, 'I will, but you must know that this is a very difficult case. It will be a long battle but we will not stop fighting.'

They look at me expectantly and I think, Who am I to tell them about difficult battles? Who am I to tell them anything? I know the law is almost useless in such cases and soon I will get into my nice car and go home to my nice house.

My thoughts are interrupted by Mrs Masina who says, 'About the money for the case, we will give you what we have but we do not think that it will be enough. We will speak to our families to see what can be done.'

Relieved that at least I can address this, I reply, 'You mustn't worry about the money for the case. The ANC has made arrangements for the money for their defence. This money will come from overseas and you will not have to pay anything. They will also pay you a small subsistence allowance to help you cope with the expenses that you will incur in attending the trial and coming to the consultations. So the money is the one thing that you don't have to worry about.'

The provision of finance for political trials and detainees was an important component of the ANC's resistance struggle. It was critical for ANC members and guerrillas to know that they would always get access to a good legal defence and that their families would be supported. Such financial support was the one certainty that those who were captured could rely on.

The money came via the law firm of Carruthers & Company in London who, in order to disguise the source of the money, took their instructions from another London law firm by the name of Birckbeck Montagu's, an upper-crust, well-established firm that represented the International Defence and Aid Fund (IDAF). The partner at Birckbecks responsible for disbursing the money and paying our accounts was a man called Bill Frankel, a well-spoken and clever solicitor of great integrity. Bill would be the last person anyone would associate with the provision of funding for the legal defence of the guerrillas of a liberation movement. In fact, the money was raised from a variety of sympathetic sources and countries. The Scandinavians, particularly the Swedes, were generous donors, with

Bengt Save Soderberg, the Undersecretary of State in the Foreign Office, playing a leading role.

The key person responsible for raising the funds was the chief executive of IDAF, Horst Kleinschmidt, a South African exile and ANC member. Horst, a backroom person by nature, played a critical role in coordinating donor funding to IDAF. Quiet and enormously professional, he moved through Europe establishing contacts and setting up the conduits to get money into the country to fund most of the political trials and support political prisoners and their families after sentencing. If you had seen Bill Frankel and Horst Kleinschmidt having coffee in Covent Garden, you might have assumed that they were investment analysts discussing commodity prices.

The other key funder of political trials was Gay McDougall's Washington-based organisation, the American Lawyers' Committee for Civil Rights Under the Law. Gay was a hugely impressive and well-connected lawyer who ran her organisation with efficiency and integrity and who could always be relied on to help out when things were dire.

Despite the sometimes splintered nature of the international anti-apartheid movement, there were a large number of groupings and individuals who did fine work. Bill Frankel and Horst Kleinschmidt were two such people. They delivered the goods yet never claimed public credit.

Without this legal funding from outside, it would have been impossible to run the trials. Nationally, there were simply not enough anti-apartheid organisations with access to resources to pay for these cases. The few attorneys prepared to do political work generally charged fees that were about a third of the going rate. Likewise, sympathetic counsel charged a fraction of what they could charge commercially. However, these costs combined with the expenses of running a trial that could last as long as three or four years, amounted to large figures. The big commercial law firms that could sustain the costs simply refused to do it. And so, it fell to Carruthers and the American Lawyers' Committee to provide the funds.

However, the financing of the trial was not uppermost in the minds of the parents. They wanted to know if the group had committed these deeds.

'I don't know,' I respond to Mrs Masina, who has taken the lead. 'I have only just got this information and will have to discuss it with them at our next consultation.' The families are confused, and I feel powerless to comfort them. I cannot say that justice will take its course or that their sons are innocent and will be set free. These are not detainees in a state of emergency where you know that eventually they will be released. This is different. These men have accomplished their objectives. And now the State is going to make them pay.

The difference between the families and me is that they still think something just or fair will happen, that the actions of their sons will be understood in the broader context and that they will not go to prison or worse. I know differently. I know the kind of people who will be prosecuting this case, the type of investigating officers, the judge, and I know that their job is to ensure that these men receive the maximum sentence.

11

HOJE YA HENDA CAMP, MALANJE PROVINCE, ANGOLA

It had been a Cuban camp and was well fortified with three anti-aircraft batteries. During the 1980s it became one of MK's major training camps. It was here that Joseph Makhura received his training.

Joseph Makhura: 'There was a big fight between MK and Unita in eastern Malanje Province near a town called Cacuso. I was sent there along with a friend called Jeff, who had been with me in the Swapo camp. He was a nice guy from Rockville in Soweto. When we got to Cacuso, Jeff stayed there and I moved to a village called Musafa, about fifty kilometres away. There was nothing but jungle between the two villages which were connected by a gravel road. Musafa was deserted. The war had driven out the locals a long time ago.

'We were about fifty or sixty MK at Musafa, an outpost really. Our mission was to stop Unita from taking the area. We lived in some destroyed houses and I was the medic there. It was a strange place. The villages around us had been destroyed by Unita and were deserted, but the people had to live and to eat and so they returned during the day and tended their land. At night they disappeared. They would tell us if Unita was in the area and we would hunt them down. There were frequent firefights.

'To get supplies, we had to go to Cacuso. The MK commander there was a man by the name of Bra T – T for Timothy, I think. He had a reputation for bravery. I admired him because whenever there was trouble he would be there, which you couldn't say for some other commanders. Chris Hani and Bra T were always there for us.

'Unfortunately, Cacuso was a mess. The people robbed the stores, stole supplies to buy liquor, there was no discipline. The worst thing was the journey to and from Cacuso. Often on our way back to Musafa, we would find that the road had been mined by Unita. Once a tractor driven by a farmer was blown up and locals were also sometimes shot by Unita. We tried to help them, but usually it was no use, their injuries were too severe.

'There was a lot of complaining on that eastern front. We wanted to fight at home, not in Angola. In late 1983, Chris Hani and Bra T came to listen to our complaints. There was a lot of talk about the guys in London and in the diplomatic missions in Europe while we were in the camps fighting a war against Unita in Angola. Personally, I was not happy, but I knew I had volunteered. It was my decision to join and so I had to take what was given.

'But it was very bad. Once, when we were travelling back to our camp, we came across bodies on the road, poor villagers who had surprised Unita laying a landmine. Unita shot them, just like that. When we got there people were crying and removing the bodies from the road. It was terrible. And then I knew that I must get out of this place. This wasn't why I'd left South Africa. This wasn't my war.

'Driving on from there to Musafa was one of the worst drives of my life, not knowing whether Unita had chosen another place to plant their mines. Every bump we went over, every jolt of the truck, which was filled with supplies, could have set off a landmine. I was tense. The sweat poured off us in the heat. The road itself was bumpy and potholed, some of them easily big enough to put a few mines in. We drove slowly looking for signs of freshly dug earth, not even checking the bush next to the road for an ambush.

'I'll take my chances in an ambush, I was thinking. But with a landmine there was no second chance.

'Eventually we got to Musafa. My uniform was wet right through. I pulled up in a clearing in the village and my MK comrades came out firing their AK-47s in the air in celebration that the truck had arrived with supplies. I went to my medical room and waited there until it was quiet.

I didn't want to be shot by mistake by my own men. That place was wild, anything could happen.

'On the day after Christmas, 26 December 1983, we got word that Unita had ambushed and killed a large MK unit near the Kwanza River in the south. We took a platoon from Musafa and teamed up with another two platoons from Cacuso. We moved to the ambush point in six large Russian trucks, called Urals. It took us about two hours to get to the river and by then it was already dark. We found a lot of MK bodies and also soldiers from the Angolan army. The Angolan army in the area was not well trained, we called them People's Militia or "Odepe".

'The Odepe were undisciplined, always complaining. We had to rely on them because they knew the terrain but in a skirmish they just shot randomly and wildly. When you asked them why they were firing like that, they said they were scaring the enemy. Hell, they scared us and we were their allies! Shame, we used to treat them badly and tell them to carry our heavy stuff, like the RPG with the rockets in the backpack. But we stopped this practice because in the first few contacts they would shoot those RPG rockets off like fireworks, hitting trees and rocks, very dangerous, crazy I tell you. We even stopped telling them to carry our ammo as they would shoot it off on any excuse, just so they wouldn't have to carry it. Actually, maybe they weren't so stupid after all, although when you got into a real firefight and needed it, the ammo was all used up.

'The good Angolan soldiers were fighting the South Africans on the Namibian border. Besides the Urals, we had with us an even larger truck, a huge thing, which we filled with the bodies of our comrades. It was terrible. They had been surprised and slaughtered. We worked right through the night and into the next day. The flies and the stench from the bodies made us sick. It was swampy ground and thick bush with mosquitoes that ate us alive.

'While searching for the wounded in the bush, I found my friend Jeff. He had crawled under a small bush but was in a very bad way, shot in the stomach and his right leg was broken. I tried to help him, but it was no use. He could barely speak. He said he could hear us moving in the night but did not have the strength to cry out. He died half an hour later. I was holding him in my arms as he died. I picked him up and carried him to the truck, gently laid him down on the great pile of bodies.

Other bodies soon covered him. We climbed on the trucks and left that killing ground.

'It just went on and on, from camp to camp. February 1984 I was back in Viana Camp near Luanda. While I was there, Bra T approached me and asked if I wanted to fight in South Africa. I said yes. Later, in September 1984, I went to Pango Camp in the north of Angola for specialised training in explosives and assassination. I enjoyed the training, but my instructor almost killed me there.

'We were being trained in how to use and throw the F-1 hand grenade. You would pull the pin, the lever arm popped off in your hand and you had to wait until the instructor told you to throw the grenade. It was nerve-racking. The instructor was close to you but protected by a thick shield, so he was okay. On this one occasion I pulled the pin, the arm popped off and my instructor waited ... and waited ... and waited ... until in a panic I threw the grenade, which exploded very close to us. I yelled at the instructor that he had nearly killed me. I think he forgot what was happening. Maybe he was thinking of something else, dreaming.

'I was at Pango Camp for a full year, training and training, thinking that I would never go home. In September 1985, I got called to Lusaka where I met Jabu, Neo, Rufus and Justice. I was finally going home, almost six years after I had left.'

THE BOMB

Building a bomb for a fixed object, such as a building or an installation, has its own peculiarities but is an easier device to put together. The challenge in such instances is about what sort of bomb is most appropriate and how the bomb will be attached to the target so that it will cause the most damage.

The bombs that exploded on 27 May 1987 in the headquarters of the Congress of South African Trade Unions in downtown Johannesburg did precisely that. Experts specifically constructed the bombs to the required strength and trained saboteurs cut through the bars on the back wall of the building, gained entrance to the parking basement, and placed the explosive charges around the main supporting pillars of the building and the lift shaft. They did it in the middle of the night when no one was around, so it didn't matter what the bombs looked like. They weren't designed to deceive, merely to destroy, which they did, rendering an entire eleven-story building permanently unusable. Very effective.

In the case of a living target, an individual, it is more difficult. One scenario is to place the bomb at a place frequented by the target. Hence at a home, a car, a place of work, a restaurant or a street. In circumstances where the individual has no known allegiance to a place or an object, the bomb must travel to the individual or they must travel to meet each other. A meeting of coincidence, so to speak.

12

Last night was a bit of a scene at Sam's Cafe with my partners after our monthly partners' meeting. Always a torrid and difficult meeting with the colliding egos and stresses of running a political practice on very little money. Drinking too much at the dinner, swapping stories of State stupidity as we talk ourselves up to heights of brilliance and legal cunning.

On the highway to Pretoria, the sun knifing in through the window combines with my dehydration to launch me into a bout of mild depression, induced by a vitamin B deficiency. Generally, I never smoke during the day as it makes me feel tired, but I light a cigarette. It's a habit, when I feel bad, to do things that make me feel worse. Pitiful really.

I'm thinking of my approach to the accused and what they will say in relation to the charges. Deciding on the nature of the defence is a difficult phase in any trial preparation. It has to be handled carefully. The accused have to be guided by the correct considerations, both legal and political, in order to construct a responsible defence. I know that conventional lawyers would decry taking political issues into account and would only consider the legal questions. But in a case where both sides are driven by power, punishment and political advantage, such concerns can never be ruled out. This is a political trial. So these matters have to be considered and the accused must come to a decision about their defence by themselves.

If I suggest they adopt the defence that would result in the lightest sentence, I would be naive and they would be outraged. I would be dismissed as their defence attorney. Similarly, I would be doing them a disservice if I advised a purely political stance towards the court and its proceedings. In all likelihood, this would result in an excessively stiff sentence. The ideal defence in a political trial has to encompass complex and sensitive considerations in order to meet both the legal and political needs of the accused. The wishes of their families must also be considered.

In some political trials, the accused have jettisoned their cause in favour of the lightest possible sentence. They admit culpability and state that they were brainwashed by the ANC. There are numerous variations on this theme of distancing the accused from the ANC. Usually, this tactic ends up a mess. Branding your erstwhile comrades sick manipulators places you forever on the political perimeter.

This is not an easy game to play, particularly for novices, and most accused are first timers. The security police are experienced and often exhibit masterful insights into the character of the accused, exploiting divisions within groups as well as personal weaknesses and insecurities. In the end, hungry, hurt and scared, most people will do anything to please their captors. If they don't like what you've written, they'll tell you to write it again. And again and again until it fits the bill, their bill. And then, back in your cell, the guilt seeps through you. You're humiliated, sore and alone, trying to justify what you've done. Hoping that your comrades will understand, which, of course, they won't. And that's how it starts.

This is serious stuff. The one component common to most political trials is the challenging of the accused's confession. In legal jargon, this is known as 'the trial within a trial'. In many MK trials, most of the evidence comes from the confession of the accused, usually extracted under torture and duress. The admissibility of the confession then becomes contentious. And so battle is joined.

I approach the prison, feel the eyes of the warders looking at me through the thick glass. I bark my name into the intercom, the sun on my head shooting pain across my thin skull. The immaculate Warder van Rensburg, reassuringly exhibiting the same distance and contempt towards me, ushers me in. The clanging of the massive hydraulic doors jars my delicate senses, makes me wish that I had shown more restraint the previous night.

We go in through one door after the other until the door of the doctor's surgery closes. I stretch out gratefully on the bed. As I lie there I wonder why the beds in doctors' surgeries are always uncomfortable. Maybe they don't want the patients settling in. The frowning eyes of the warder appear at the peephole in the door and I can see that he is irritated by this lazy lawyer stretching out on the starched white sheets of the prison doctor's bed. It's just too much! Although it's good to know that I am irritating him, I realise sadly that a few hours alone on this bed in this prison would be something that I would welcome, perhaps even pay for. Two hours of sleep would see me right. I close my eyes.

Unfortunately, this time my clients are brought in promptly. I greet them and we weigh ourselves. It is becoming a ritual and prison is about rituals. We go through the niceties as if we were meeting for coffee in a café, discussing the surroundings, their daily routine, the gym. I pass on good wishes from the families. There is no passing or keeping of written messages. A friend of mine was barred by the Law Society from visiting clients in prison after he was caught smuggling out a message on a piece of paper. Such a mistake would be pounced on and give Warder van Rensburg more pleasure than his Sunday braai.

To business. 'This is serious now and I want you to listen closely.'

They pull their chairs closer and go silent, totally absorbed. I give them some options about the type of defence that can be mounted.

'Each option has serious consequences and needs to be thought through carefully. Don't make a decision now. Take your time, discuss it among yourselves and in a few days we can discuss it further and I can answer any questions you may have. I also want to take detailed statements from each of you and analyse them at length before advising you of what I think your best defence should be. I'm going to detail all of the options so that you get a precise picture of your legal position. I appreciate that some of them may not be acceptable to you, but you still need to know about them.'

I work through the particulars of each charge and relay the types of sentences that each offence would attract on conviction. They are silent.

I tackle the big issue. 'What do you say about the murder charges? Have you confessed to them?'

Jabu is slow in replying. 'Yes, we have confessed to the murders and the other charges. It was part of our mission.'

'Yussus,' I respond, having got much more than I expected. 'Look, we will need to explore the facts and circumstances of each charge. But I must tell you, you can't get more serious charges. If convicted, you face the death sentence.'

There, I have said it. The death sentence. I needed to do that, to get it onto the table, make them realise the utter gravity of their situation. I tell them that the death sentence is mandatory unless extenuating circumstances are found, explaining that those are factors associated with the case which diminish the moral, if not legal guilt of the accused. I give examples. They look at me steadily. They are not talking, waiting for me to finish, watching me. This is my test. What is this lawyer going to advise?

There is a long silence and then Ting Ting speaks. 'We know what the penalties are for what we have done. We knew that before we even came back into the country. These are things that must be faced. How we handle it is very important to us. There can be no going back, we are soldiers.'

Strong stuff.

'That's fine,' I say.

As we work through the different types of defence, I realise that they are not being charged with what they did in Bophuthatswana, with the murder of Brigadier Molope. Who would have thought that the 'independent' country would be helpful in such circumstances? Anyway, the security police don't need the Bop charges, the South African ones are enough. Besides, too many accomplishments would turn these men into heroes.

13

The woman, tall and blonde, came out of the large house towards Ting Ting. He saw that she was carrying a book and wondered what it was. She wore an orange floral dress and even though her hair was tied back, there was no escaping her youth. From inside the house, he could hear the radio commentary of a rugby game. Saturday afternoon in the suburb of Gezina in Pretoria. The woman was close now. Lifting his head to look at her, Ting Ting saw that tears rolled down her cheeks. The book she carried was a Bible. Ting Ting knew that he had not done a good job in the garden. He had lost this job. The racing pigeons were really to blame. There were fourteen of them in a mesh cage and every time he passed the cage, he stopped to watch them. He spent long moments gazing and talking softly to them and did not complete the tasks that the woman's husband had set for him. This family paid well at five rand for a day's work. The normal rate was two rand. The husband had told him that the family was moving and they would no longer need his services, but he knew this was a lie. The man felt he had not done his work properly and wanted to get rid of him.

The woman had always been kind to him, had given him food and old clothes that he took back to his family. It was a great saving. Desperately wanting to ask for another chance yet too proud to plead, he wished that they would reconsider but he knew that the man had made up his mind.

It was over. Looking at her as she stood before him, he too started to cry, overcome with strange emotions. The woman looked him in the eyes, opened the Bible and read out a verse about how Jesus would come and wipe off the tears of all those who were crying. He looked down, embarrassed by his own tears, and tried not to notice hers. She gave him some clothes and money and told him that her husband had said that he could take six of the racing pigeons. It was kind of them. He left taking the pigeons with him in a small wire cage that she gave him.

Ting Ting was the seventh of ten children and he knew that this 'weekend' money would be much missed in the household. His mother, NaSindane, worked as a domestic worker at a house in Meyer's park opposite the suburb of Silverton. Ting Ting went to visit her at the house and was struck by its size. On these visits, he rang the bell at the front gate and waited for his mother to come and let him in. She would give him bread and tea and he'd sit in the sun on the stairs of an outside storeroom to eat. But he had to eat quickly so that he was gone by the time the owners returned.

On one visit, he saw the daughter of the owner, a young white girl who his mother called 'Nonnatjie' – little madam. He noticed that his mother, who was always in command at their home and very strict with her own family, behaved differently here. It bothered him that this little girl did not respect his mother and called her by her first name. At home, he would never call an older person by their first name, always by their title, like aunt or uncle.

His own home was one of the tiny matchbox houses in Mamelodi. His father John Thulare Masango, a large, but mild mannered man, rose every morning at half past four to report for work at six. His job at a construction company in Silverton was to open and close the entrance gates. John Masango worked an eleven-hour day and returned exhausted in the evening. Even when his father was very sick, he never missed a day's work.

His mother ran the household. She was always talking and giving orders, making sure that the little food in the house was meticulously shared. Even an orange was shared out piece by piece.

Ting Ting's three sisters shared a small room while the seven brothers slept on the floor in the dining room and kitchen. Ting Ting made sure that he slept on the kitchen floor which was warm from the fire.

The house attracted people: friends, relatives and neighbours were constantly popping in. A visitor who made Ting Ting uneasy was Mrs Msezane, the headmistress of his school. Whenever he misbehaved, she stopped at his house to tell his mother of his transgressions. Ting Ting would make himself scarce, knowing that when he returned home, he was in for a tough time. Despite this he passed in the top five in his class of fifty pupils every year.

Mrs Msezane seemed ever present as, even on weekends, he sat close to her at the Baptist church that he attended with his family. A highlight of going to church was riding through the streets on the handlebars of his father's bicycle. Flying down the dusty roads, Ting Ting would feel like a champion, his father's strong arms around him while he waved and shouted to friends.

Ting Ting's school days were far from carefree. During one year he developed pneumonia and had to be admitted to hospital. The illness had been caught late and his condition deteriorated quickly and he lapsed into a coma. The hospital contacted his mother and told her that he had died. She rushed to the hospital beside herself with anguish.

In the depths of his coma, Ting Ting found himself in a room filled with a radiant light. He felt his sister Sesi pulling at him, away from the comfort of the room. After a while he woke up to see his mother at his bedside.

Once he'd recovered, Ting Ting was enrolled at another primary school in Mamelodi. One of his teachers, a Mr Babsie Mkhize, habitually beat the children. The disruptive Ting Ting with his squint became a special focus for Mkhize. He mocked Ting Ting's squint so cruelly that Ting Ting thought of running away. But he didn't want to disappoint his family. His mother particularly.

The one thing that Ting Ting wanted most was a bicycle. He nagged his father, unable to understand why his father wasn't obliging. One day his father snapped at him, 'And what will the family eat if I buy you a bicycle?' It was a rare outburst from this calm man who never raised his voice and Ting Ting never asked for a bicycle again. One day, he decided, he'd earn money by working as a gardener and support his entire family.

He looked for work on weekends in the white suburb of Silverton. He got his first Saturday job with an Afrikaans family. The work was not difficult and they paid him two rand.

It was his first sustained contact with whites, and although the family was not unpleasant to him, he noticed his tea was served in a jam tin and his plate of food was put on the ground, the way you would feed a dog. Ting Ting was impressed by the furniture in the house and asked his mother how whites could afford these things and why black people had nothing. His mother retorted, 'If you ask questions like that, you will end up on Robben Island, like Mandela. Just be thankful that you have a job and are not in jail.'

At school Ting Ting's good academic record continued. His ambition was to become a dentist – surely education would open opportunities for a better way of life? Then in June 1976, the world changed. After the uprising in Soweto, Ting Ting was elected onto the Student Representative Council at his school. The SRC met regularly and picked up on the issue of Afrikaans being forced on the students as the language of instruction. As it happened, Ting Ting was completely fluent and at ease in Afrikaans but that was not the issue. It was not the language of his choosing. In July 1976, the students of Mamelodi were boycotting classes and targeting liquor outlets as they believed the government used alcohol to turn blacks into ineffectual drunkards. Bottle stores were set alight. So were municipal buses.

Ting Ting was at the forefront. He enjoyed the excitement and the action. It was a wild power he had never known before and everything seemed possible. Schooling was disrupted to such an extent that it ceased. The headmaster threatened Ting Ting with expulsion if he didn't stop stoking unrest. In response Ting Ting organised demonstrations against the headmaster who sought police protection. Ting Ting was expelled.

In early 1977, Ting Ting found employment at a salary of R90 a month. The money was welcome as his mother no longer had her job as a domestic worker. She now sold vegetables on the roadside and did not make much money, returning home at night to cook the evening meal, mute from exhaustion. Despite his job, Ting Ting continued his activities as a student organiser and became active in community affairs.

One day while visiting his father at the construction company in Silverton, Ting Ting witnessed the behaviour of a young white man towards his father. The man drove up to the entrance gate and shouted, 'John, open the gate,' blustering and gesticulating rudely.

Much offended, Ting Ting told the driver not to speak to his father in that way. An argument started that was only stopped when Ting Ting's father intervened. Enough, he said to his son. Or he would lose his job. The young white man drove off. Beside himself with anger, Ting Ting's father instructed his son never to visit him at work again. Powerless, Ting Ting promised to stay away.

In 1978 Ting Ting was arrested during a protest march in Soweto and detained in a police station. The sheer power of the police, their weaponry, armoured vehicles and equipment, the radios constantly crackling with reports, the helicopters disgorging police and troops, made him question what chance he and his comrades had with their petrol bombs and stones.

That year, an MK member, Solomon Mahlangu, was convicted of murder and charges under the Terrorism Act and sentenced to death. He was a man from Mamelodi; in fact, his family lived not far from Ting Ting's home. The campaign to keep Mahlangu from the gallows captured the popular imagination and became a focus of political mobilisation, culminating in an all-night vigil. Ting Ting convened the meeting and in the early hours of the morning made a passionate speech. 'If he is hanged,' he told the gathering, 'I am going to take his place and I urge all those who are able to do the same.' His plea was met first with silence then with applause. Ting Ting realised he had crossed a line: he would now be a marked man as there were bound to have been security police in the crowd. Early the next morning the radio carried news that Solomon Mahlangu had been hanged at Death Row in Pretoria Central Prison.

The customary place for the State to bury those it hanged was the Mamelodi Cemetery. Ting Ting and Mahlangu's mother rushed to the cemetery to retrieve the body before it was buried by the authorities, without prayers and ceremony. The cemetery was deserted. Instead, Mahlangu had been buried at the Atteridgeville Cemetery.

By the time they got there, some fifty activists had gathered and others were arriving. Armed police in riot gear faced the crowd. An officer with a loudhailer intoned monotonously: 'This is an unlawful gathering, you have three minutes to disperse or force will be used against you.' The crowd moved forward. The police fired teargas canisters and then charged, wielding batons and sjamboks. In the chaos Ting Ting escaped. Solomon Mahlangu was buried in the cemetery in a plot marked only by the number of the grave.

During the next few days Ting Ting moved between the houses of his friends. He had word from his mother that the security police were looking for him and he should not come home. He decided that he would leave the country and go into exile. He would become a soldier.

Without being able to say goodbye to his family, Ting Ting made his way to Mozambique and joined the ANC. He was warmly welcomed by a thickset man who appeared to be in charge of the new arrivals. Later Ting Ting learnt the man's name was Jacob Zuma.

Like Jabu, Ting Ting ended up in the Matola transit house with its orchard of mango trees. Before being sent to Angola for military training he was asked to choose a nom de guerre. He chose 'Qondile', meaning 'Bells', which, he thought, chimed nicely with his name.

14

In the surgery in Pretoria Maximum Security there is little small talk after the ritual weigh-in.

Ting Ting leads the discussion. 'I know that there is still a lot of work to be done but we want you to be aware of our thinking. We want to ask a question. What is the consequence of us not giving evidence? We ask this because we have a problem, and that is we are not prepared to take the stand and deny that we have done the things that we have done. I say this because the acts described in the charge sheet were committed by us as soldiers of Umkhonto we Sizwe, and we will not distance ourselves from what we have done.'

Jabu adds, 'In any event, we have confessed in writing to all of these acts, so how can we now deny them?'

I look from one man to the next. They gaze back, earnest, solemn. 'Well, let me deal with your first question about the implications of your not going into the witness box to give evidence. In a criminal trial, if the accused plead not guilty and then are not prepared to give evidence in their own defence, which means going into the box and denying their actions and being subjected to cross-examination, the court will draw what is known as an "adverse inference". At the end of the trial when the judge is weighing up all the evidence, this factor will count against the accused.'

They nod understandingly.

'You see,' says Jabu, softening the tough stand taken by Ting Ting, 'it is not just that they have all the evidence against us from the confessions and when we pointed out the places where the acts took place and described them, it is also that we will not deny these things from a political point of view.'

We look at one other, the implications and the consequences writ large.

Ting Ting continues, 'We have had long and hard discussions about all the options you presented to us. We have taken each one, worked it through and in each case we have rejected the possibility of using that type of defence. We cannot plead not guilty. Firstly, because we will not allow them to place us on trial according to their rules for fighting to liberate this country. They have no right to do that. Secondly, we did the acts alleged, mostly on the instructions of the ANC and we will not back away from that.

'At the same time, we cannot plead guilty. Although we are, in fact, guilty, our acts cannot be seen in purely criminal terms, just as those who killed the enemy in the fight against fascism in the Second World War were not tried for murder. The acts we committed were carried out against an enemy that has made us victims in our own country and taken any rights that we had away from us. Our rights to land, to move freely, to work in a fair manner, to be educated, and a range of others. This government is murdering our youth and has our leadership in prison. The people we killed were at the forefront of the apartheid regime's attack on black people and they deserved what happened to them. While we have killed and each of us has to deal with that inside ourselves, we are not murderers. We are not normal criminals.'

We all smile at the 'normal criminals' bit.

'Do you follow me, that this is a war in which they hold most of the cards and we cannot simply play their game when we have had no part in forming the rules?' asks Ting Ting.

'I follow you very well,' I say, 'and I appreciate your position.' I know where this is going, but it cannot come from me.

'Look, let's also be honest here,' says Ting Ting, 'we know that we probably cannot avoid the death sentence. We have to face that fact, so we need to conduct our trial and go our way in a manner which does not compromise our beliefs and the reputation of the ANC. That is why we like the last option that you presented to us. It may be radical and not the norm in ANC trials, but it is the one we would like to follow. By doing this, we get to the same conclusion as the other defence options, but in a way of our choosing and which will also highlight what we are doing and the nature of the conflict we are involved in.'

They are talking of the prisoner-of-war option. This was the last option I had presented to them. I had done this knowing it was an extreme course of action, but that at least it deserved consideration, given their desperate situation.

In this option, they are acting as soldiers under orders from the ANC and are involved in a 'just war' against an illegal and illegitimate minority government. This government, by implementing the system of apartheid, declared an international crime against humanity, and has oppressed and caused the deaths of many of its citizens. The court represents this illegal government and therefore has no authority to try the accused. On this basis, they do not recognise the jurisdiction of the court and refuse to participate in the proceedings. They insist on being accorded prisoner-of-war status in terms of the Geneva Convention.

Heavy stuff. Quite so, but I knew the system and I knew that the accused would, in all likelihood, have difficulty denying the charges against them. There would be a 'trial within a trial' but afterwards the proceedings would follow a predictable path. The judge would admit the confession and the State would be home and dry. But I also knew that choosing this 'soldier option' would send them down an avenue from which there was no return.

By rejecting the jurisdiction of the court, the four would not be able to participate in their own trial and mount a defence. In the light of this refusal, the judge would be compelled to enter a plea of 'not guilty' on their behalf. The trial would then proceed as if they had entered the not-guilty plea. However, the evidence of the State, in the form of documents or witnesses, would be unchallenged and admissible. There would be no cross-examination of witnesses and no challenging of the confessions. Barring a miracle, not a frequent occurrence in our courts, they would be found guilty on all counts.

I explain to my clients that after being found guilty of murder, an accused is entitled to mount an extenuation case. The sentence for murder is death. Only if the court finds extenuating circumstances, can a lesser sentence be passed.

My clients listen intently.

'A wife who murders her drunken husband in self-defence when he's coming at her with a knife after she's proved that he has violently abused her and her children for ten years, will have an excellent extenuation case,' I explain. 'The problem for you is that if you do not participate, you will not be able to mount an extenuation case and therefore the death sentence is a certainty.'

Their guard drops. There is silence. We look at each other and I see confusion and loneliness in their eyes. Vulnerability. Caught in the head-lights and blinded, they nevertheless choose not to run.

'But, Peter, are we not finished anyway?' says Neo Potsane. 'Whatever we do, we are dead men.'

The words 'dead men' ring in my ears. And this is what goes through my mind: if they choose the prisoner-of-war option, it will be a grand and brave gesture. But when they are dead and buried, their mothers will look at me and believe I failed them, that I should have saved their sons. That I should have stopped them making heroic but fatal stands and kept them alive at whatever cost. I also know that once the death sentence has been passed, the accused will be quickly hanged if there is no appeal.

The State will do this to avoid the lengthy and very public campaign that would almost certainly be mounted for their reprieve and release. It is a fact that if they do not participate in the trial, they could be hanged within three months of sentence.

'Look,' I say, 'the State has a strong case against you and you have a major problem if you don't plead. If you enter a not-guilty plea we may be able to spin out the trial for a long time. With postponements and appeals, we could even stretch it for a few years. At the same time, we can get an international campaign started that may place sufficient pressure on the government to ensure that you are given a reprieve even if you do get the death sentence.'

They are silent, watching me.

'Things can happen in the trial that may assist us. We may get lucky and be able to prove torture and get your confessions thrown out. The judge may make a mistake or behave so badly and show so much bias that we could take him on review. Hell, the judge may even die and we would then have to start the trial all over again and that would take a few more years and who knows what might happen then.

'Some of the judges they allocate to these trials are so old that it's difficult knowing if they're alive in the first place.'

They smile.

'What I'm saying is there are things we can do to keep you alive and I have an obligation to do that. But if you do not participate, these doors are all closed to you. The trial will proceed very quickly and you stand every chance of going down. Maybe I am wrong. I'm a firm believer that something will turn up. I am an optimist.' Thinking to myself that you bloody well have to be an optimist to do this work.

But I still need to make my point.

'Seriously, we need to understand that even though your chances on trial may be bleak, there are hidden possibilities that may delay or change things. If you take this political stand, these possibilities will no longer be open to you. The option of standing on principle comes at a terrible price, and you must be aware of that. This is also a strategy that is untested. It is not as if you are putting up a defence or an argument in extenuation, and even if you were, no ANC cadre has ever been granted POW status or anything even approaching it.

'But you will not even get that far. Your stand on non-participation will prevent you from doing anything other than making a statement, and I am not even sure if the judge will allow that as he may think that you are making a mockery of his court and his authority. However, you must also know that if you choose this route, I will give you total support and do everything I can to keep you alive for as long as possible.'

Businesslike, Jabu replies, 'We know you are doing your job by saying these things. We appreciate that. It shows us that you have our interests at heart. But it was you who sketched out the POW option to us in detail and we have discussed it and come to the conclusion that it is the one we want to follow. We would like you to consult Chris Hani, our commander in Lusaka, as well as Govan Mbeki. We would have liked to consult with the leadership on Robben Island but we know that that is obviously not an option. We will try to get word to them and see what they have to say. In the meantime, we will continue with our own discussions.'

15

In 1978, front page photographs of ANC men in a shootout with police convinced Joseph Makhura that he was wasting his time as a gardener at the Berea Park Sports Club in Pretoria. He was tending bowling greens while others were dying for his freedom. Joseph decided to travel to Swaziland and join the ANC.

Joseph Makhura: 'My family had always stayed in Lady Selborne near Pretoria where we had a decent house and land that we could farm. My mother told me that when I was two years old, my family was forcibly removed from the land and taken to a small house in Mamelodi. All the people from Lady Selborne were split up and resettled in Mamelodi and the townships of Garankuwa and Atteridgeville. My mother and my uncles often talked about Lady Selborne for hours. My mother would bring out her pictures of our house. Mamelodi was different, it was a tough place.

'My mother was not happy about her children growing up in Mamelodi, with all the drinking and crime and violence, so she sent me to live with my grandmother Sina and my grandfather Joseph, who worked on a farm at Hartebeespoort Dam. I was three years old. I remember crying at being separated from my mother, desperately wanting to stay with her, but I also think that she was battling to cope in many ways. She was a single mother. I never saw my father and she never mentioned his name. I also think that the move from Lady Selborne really affected her and made her very depressed.

'The farm my grandfather worked on was owned by a white man called Koos Viljoen. My grandfather looked after the cattle. My grandmother was a domestic worker and gardener for a white family who had a house in the suburb of Cosmos near the dam. They were absentee owners and would use the house on the occasional weekend. My grandfather was a kind and gentle man who never hit us, even though we were quite naughty.

'Initially the house my grandfather lived in was a single room. He built on a kitchen and bedroom and we were joined by my sisters and some cousins whose parents were also living in Mamelodi. They worked during the day and worried about leaving the children alone from five in the morning until eight at night.

'The farm had its own troubles. Koos, "Baas Koos" as we called him, was a man with a terrible temper. From time to time, he would arrive and count the cows, and if there was anything wrong he would scream and shout, calling us "kaffirs" and my grandmother a "kaffermeid". We were frightened of Baas Koos when he behaved like this and would run into the house and peek through the curtains, praying that he would not hit my grandfather. On these occasions, my grandfather would explain to Baas Koos, but he wouldn't listen. I remember him shouting at my grandfather to be quiet: "Shut up, kaffir!" Then my grandfather would stand there, head bowed, looking at the ground. One day I asked what "kaffir" meant. He replied, "Kaffirs are white people." It was a strange answer. I didn't understand it then, and I'm not sure I do now.

'I remember another day Koos came with a sjambok and thrashed my grandfather, shouting at him that he was stupid and needed to be taught a lesson. My grandfather sank to his knees in the dust in front of Baas Koos, covering his head with his hands while he was whipped. Watching through the window, I started to cry, wanting to go out there and do something although I was too afraid. I heard Baas Koos shouting and swearing at him, the sjambok cutting through the air, and then I heard my grandfather start to beg for mercy in Afrikaans. I couldn't really understand the language then, but it was obvious that he was crying and pleading with Baas Koos to stop, which he did after a while, panting from the effort. Shoulders heaving, he turned, threw the sjambok into the back of his truck and drove off fast, leaving my grandfather lying on the ground. I rushed out and helped him into the house. He never said a word as I laid him on his bed, bleeding, eyes closed in pain. He turned to face the wall so I could not see his face. I climbed onto the bed with him and put my arms around him, hugging him tight. He didn't move. When I asked if I could help, he waved me away. I did not know then but I know now that he was ashamed. He did not want me to come too close to his humiliation.

'I don't know if Baas Koos was in trouble or drunk or what, but he began to beat my grandfather more often. Each time it was the same thing. He would never listen to my grandfather, just whip him until he lay cowering on the ground. It got to the stage where my grandfather, when he heard the truck coming, would stay in the house, too terrified to go out. Baas Koos, sjambok in hand, would stand in the yard, shouting at him to come out. My grandfather would go out and sometimes he would be beaten and sometimes not.

'I was very close to my grandfather. He was the father I never had and he treated me like a son. I asked him once why he didn't fight back. He said, "If I fight back, my son, we will have to move from this place – and there is nowhere to go." I understood that this was the way things were. I accepted it and also became afraid. Then something else happened.

'To make extra money, my cousins and I and some other local boys would sell earthworms to the white fishermen at the dam. On one occasion a white boy came up to me. He was smaller and younger than me. He asked me something in Afrikaans. I could not understand what he was saying, so I said nothing, and suddenly he hit me with his fists. I let him. I stood there as my grandfather did before Baas Koos, the blows raining down. They didn't really hurt as he was not that strong. He was smaller than me. While he hit me, I remembered my grandfather saying to me, "If you hit a white man, you create much more trouble." After a short while, the boy stopped hitting me and left. I felt a burning in my chest which wasn't pain, it was an anger so strong that it felt like there was a force in my chest. Walking home, I was so disappointed and ashamed of myself, I began to cry.

'On that farm, we were always hungry. There was never enough food. We had pap at night and in the morning we would eat the brown layer of pap at the bottom of the pan. It was hard like a biscuit. We never had meat except if we killed birds and rabbits with a catapult.

'The only other time we would have meat was when a cow died. Then Baas Koos would give the dead cow to my grandfather. That man gave us nothing unless it had no use for him, we were always hungry and we lived in fear of him and his sjambok.

'Koos was one of the reasons I left the country. As I grew up, I never forgot him, and I promised myself that when I was much older, I would get trained in MK and come back and kill him. I hated him for what he did to my grandfather, for making him beg like that. Man, it marked me. Even when I started my training, I thought of Koos. I could see his face. He was first on my list when I got back.'

'Once we discussed my anger during a training session. The instructor was firm. He said that the weapons we'd been given and the training we were getting was to liberate the country and not to settle personal scores. "Look at this discussion," he said. "Already, a number of you have talked of the grudges you bear. Imagine if you all started running off to settle them, you would never get to fulfil your mission." He was tough on us, telling us that this was not a struggle against white people but a struggle against oppression, a repressive government. He told us that whites had supplied our guns. He spoke of Bram Fischer, Ronnie Kasrils, Joe Slovo, Albie Sachs and others who had joined our struggle. If we were caught, he said, we would possibly be defended by white lawyers. It impressed me, I had not thought about it like that. Over the years that I spent in Angola, I realised that Koos was just a terrible man, perhaps even a bit mad, but he was an individual, not a people or a nation. Even if I saw him now, I don't think I would hate him. I would be angry, yes, but I wouldn't waste my time killing him.'

THE BOMB

A lot of thought has gone into the bomb Japie Kok is building. The planners have to consider many factors. It is known that the target is in another country and is heavily guarded, and so a special-forces operation is out of the question, although the sovereignty of neighbouring countries has long been treated with contempt. The problem is that the specific location of this target is unknown. This presents a conundrum: how do you get the target to meet the travelling bomb?

The address of the person to whom the bomb is to be sent in Lusaka comes from a letter written by that person. A letter intercepted by the security police. This was a lucky break. Weeks of listening to the occasional telephone calls of the target have been fruitless. He has carefully kept his location a secret. In the words of a senior policeman '… his telephone security [is] very good' – there is nothing to be gleaned. But now there is an address. A personal address, a private post box. Appropriately so, for there are some very personal scores to be settled.

16

Driving through the suburb of Milpark in Port Elizabeth, or PE as we call it in the Eastern Cape, the houses seem so much smaller than my child-hood memory of them. Where are the wide green spaces that I played on? The parks neat and trim with spinning roundabouts? Now they're lonely places amidst lifeless houses struggling to lend this east coast city some respectability. A windswept town in slow decline after much of its industry has left for greener pastures in the Transvaal. Once thriving with a busy port and a motor manufacturing industry, now largely bereft of both and with a massive unemployed population. The local tourist authority calls it 'The Friendly City'. Believe me, this is a city that needs friends.

The black people who live here stay to the north of the city in New Brighton and Kwazekele, areas of sprawling matchbox houses. These are tough places where those lucky enough to have jobs are the elite.

The Eastern Cape is often viewed as the frontline of our politics, and with good reason. The traditional heartland of ANC support is embedded in this province, with Fort Hare University as the graduation school of choice for ANC leaders. This is counterbalanced by the toughest security police in the country who know they have a blank cheque from Pretoria, which is why any activists detained in PE will have to dig deep within themselves if they are to survive. Some don't. Politics has few rules in the Eastern Cape. Removed from the glare of the foreign camera crews, street protests have become an art form in guessing whether police will open fire before or after they give their warning to disperse. In these bar-ren townships, the ANC does not need to organise and recruit; it is in the blood of the people. They drink it from birth in their mother's milk.

None more so than Govan Mbeki. The Rivonia trialist had been released from Robben Island in late 1987 after twenty-three years. Although he was 'free', he was under a restriction order that confined him to the Port Elizabeth magisterial area and he could not be quoted in the press.

I have secured an appointment with him through Boy Majodina, an attorney in PE who represents Mbeki.

Entering the New Brighton township, I drive past two yellow Casspir armoured vehicles and a police van parked next to each other on the left-hand side of the road. I wonder if they have seen me, a white boy, because if they have, the van will follow me and when I stop they will want to know what I am doing here. The questioning will take up valuable time. If I am unlucky, I will be detained and maybe lose the whole day. In the rear-view mirror, I see that the van hasn't moved, nor the 'Mellow Yellow'. The farther I go into the township the more potholed the road becomes with broken cars littered along the roadside.

The houses are packed together and have tiny gardens. Children kicking a tennis ball in the dirt scatter the chickens and scrawny dogs that range these dusty spaces. No green parks here. I recall the holidays of my childhood lying at the beach with my friends. Kings Beach and Pollock Beach where the surf was much better, endlessly baking in the sun and drinking Coke, the sun and salt bleaching the hairs on our arms to a golden yellow. Watching the lifesaver competitions. Or waiting in the surf for that perfect wave.

About me the wind whips up dust and I know I am in a poor place.

I've met Boy Majodina a number of times and he's done a lot of work with our firm. He's played a key role in torture cases, and established a reputation as a tireless human-rights lawyer. It takes a brave man to do this work in this area where 'disappearances' are often the security police's answer to troublesome individuals.

I stop outside Boy's house. It's bigger than the others in the neat row. He has built an extension so that the house now covers the entire property. The effect is odd, like a giant in a Mini. A brown and mangy dog runs across the road to bark madly at me. Yet it keeps a safe distance, darting in occasionally, feigning attack. He probably doesn't see many white people. I once heard tell that in the white areas the dogs bark at black people and in the townships they bark at whites. Even if we change people's attitudes, I wonder what we're going to do about the animals, with generations of rabid racism in their veins. Who is going to change the dogs?

Boy comes out to meet me, probably conscious of the stares of the children and people standing in the street. He is a tall and handsome man, always well dressed. Today he wears dark well-pressed trousers, polished black shoes and a white shirt. He beams, courteous and friendly, never revealing the hardship of the work and the risks that he takes. We go inside. Boy has positioned his legal practice in the front of the house. In this room the decay of the township vanishes; we are in solid legal quarters. The rooms are small but professionally furnished. We go through the reception area to a fully equipped legal library and boardroom. Like most legal libraries, the room is sombre and quiet, the walls panelled in dark wood with shelving stretching to the roof. Rack on rack of leather-bound law journals. The whole set-up wouldn't be out of place in a big law firm in Johannesburg or London for that matter. A proper law office in the middle of New Brighton! I admire Boy for creating something professional in conditions where most people would despair. His legal life outside this office, in the deprivation of the township and in the cold hostility of the courts in which he practises, may be a constant battle to achieve even the most basic of rights for his clients, but at least here, in this haven, he can reflect peacefully on his work and conduct his preparations for trial.

Govan Mbeki is seated in the library. Boy, friendly and accommodating, introduces me to this grand old man of the struggle and discreetly leaves us alone. Govan Mbeki is a stocky man with silver-grey hair. Moving slowly and with great dignity, he rises and we formally greet one another. I am conscious of being in the presence of a living symbol of resistance. Small talk with such a person is petty. I get straight to the matter in hand.

I tell him about the accused, their families, the charges they are facing, and their decision regarding the trial. 'They have decided to follow the prisoner-of-war option,' I say, 'and will reject the jurisdiction and authority of the court. This means that they will not participate at all in their own trial and will, in all likelihood, receive the death sentence. The accused hope that such a stand will bring a new dimension to the way the ANC approaches treason trials. They will also place into question the legitimacy of the entire judicial system.'

I add that they do not want to take this path without consulting with the leadership of the ANC.

'When are you going to Lusaka?' he asks.

I tell him at the end of the week.

Mbeki nods.

'Well,' he says, 'you must see what they say, I will be interested. I must tell you, I have some sympathy for their position, that whichever way they turn, they will be playing the game of the Boers. Even by admitting that they are guilty, they are making criminals of themselves on charges which only the enemy has formulated. You know, we found ourselves in a similar position in the Rivonia Trial when we did not want to plead guilty to acts which we knew we had committed, and yet we also were not prepared to plead not guilty. For us, it was also about moral guilt.'

I know Mandela's speech from the dock well. In fact, it influenced me to become a human-rights lawyer. It changed the course of my life. But I've forgotten the intricacies of the Rivonia Trial and since recent political trials have adopted different legal strategies, the parallels hadn't sprung to mind.

Mbeki continues. 'In our trial, we had resolved that even if we received the death sentence, we would not appeal. Are they prepared to see this through to the end, even if they get the death sentence?'

'They say so, but it is a different thing when an accused is sitting on Death Row. That is not for me to say. It is for them and the ANC. I will give them legal advice, but ultimately, it is their decision.'

He nods slowly. 'You can tell them that I also say that this is their decision. I am not telling them to take this position, what I am saying is that I have no problem with their position. But ultimately Lusaka must decide if it wants them to do otherwise. They are clearly very brave, but they must also act in a way that reflects on the history and dignity of their movement. They must never behave like hooligans. They are soldiers and professionals.'

I tell him that I will convey this to them and to those in Lusaka. We have the tea that Boy's secretary has brought in. We talk about the inaccessible places that the State chooses for big treason trials. We finish our tea. I say goodbye to Govan Mbeki, now frail and old, passing his final years in the crumbling poverty of the Port Elizabeth townships. As I drive to the airport the knowledge of what this country has lost staggers me. Such a waste.

17

Neo Potsane had never been so cold in his life. Thick snow covered the military camp at Teterow, some fifty kilometres from the German Democratic Republic's Baltic Sea port of Rostock. The clothing the East Germans had given him was good but provided little barrier against a winter that the instructors described as the coldest in years.

About forty MK soldiers had arrived at Teterow in January 1981 for specialist training in guerrilla warfare and tactics. At first, Neo had been excited, honoured at being among a select few chosen for special training. The flight from Luanda to East Berlin was an adventure, a hell of a long time in an aeroplane, but worth it to get to Europe, to the Eastern bloc, places he had only read about.

After a few months in Teterow, Neo felt less inspired, mainly because he and the others were stuck out on an isolated farm miles from anywhere. There was no relief. They were under orders not to leave the camp.

For all that, the training was absorbing, if demanding. Physical, but also intellectually stimulating. Classes on the theory of guerrilla warfare, and lectures on South African history and politics by Pallo Jordan. Neo enjoyed Jordan's quiet presentations, the thought-provoking debates he initiated.

Throughout their training an MK representative was present, a veteran of Teterow who spoke fluent German and would act as their liaison officer whenever difficulties arose. Not that there were many. The food was good and plentiful – five meals a day including tea and cake. Lots of mashed potato, although Neo longed for pap.

What irked Neo, however, were the drinking sessions. Drink, for him, was a relaxation. The instructors turned it into a chore. Made them measure their intake so that they never lost control. Drinking was part of their training. They'd drink only on weekends: vodka, beer and a local brandy, brown vicious stuff that made you ill-tempered and depressed the next morning.

The instructors drank with them. Occasionally, when the recruits were relaxed, slightly intoxicated, they would call an emergency. This meant changing into full combat uniform, pack and helmet, standing there, swaying, the liquor fogging their brains. The instructors would time them. Chastise them for being slow. Neo hated this. Drinking was a social occasion. Something to be enjoyed, not a task to be monitored.

Nevertheless, after hours in the warm house were generally relaxing. Their instructors were billeted with them, friendly men, always helpful and courteous. In the long evenings, the recruits shared stories with these men as they sat around watching television.

Exhausted by the cold and the day's training, Neo would collapse in front of the TV, not minding that it was in German, even thankful for the foreign language, letting it flow over him. Of general interest was the coverage of the Winter Olympics with the men marvelling at the speed of the downhill racers and gasping in horror at the accidents. Neo was amazed that anyone could survive such spectacular falls.

Although he was absorbed by the training, and, despite the cold, enjoyed his time on the shooting range, Neo often found himself thinking of home. This place was so completely different to his house in Dube, Soweto, where he shared a room with his four brothers. For one thing the Dube house could have fitted into the living room of this grand house. Often he wondered about his mother, a domestic worker in the white suburbs of Johannesburg. Wondered what she would think of this huge house sunk in the snow, filled with men training for war. Each of them with their cleaning duties. There were no servants here.

When the cold ached in his feet, he remembered the heat and humidity of Angola, the thick green bush alive with snakes, insects and animals. Here the land was dead: no movement, no life, no leaves, just snow and ice. The cold throbbed in his wounds, an ache deep inside him that stiffened his leg and ankle, made them tender to the touch.

He'd been wounded in a firefight while travelling in the back of a big Mercedes truck from the military camp to Luanda. It'd happened in late 1979. He'd been selected for specialist training in East Germany. Only that time he didn't make it. Nearly didn't make it full stop.

There were a bunch of them in the back of the truck. Not talking much, tired from their training. Without warning, they drove into an ambush. Intense gunfire from all sides, bullets ricocheting off the truck. A Unita ambush. Blindly, they returned fire. The truck came to a halt and then backed into the bush. Neo and his comrades jumped out and hit the ground running. A short distance off they dropped to the ground. Neo felt a numbness in his left hand and saw it was covered in blood. As was his arm. He'd been shot above the elbow, the flesh around the entry wound a pulp of blood.

He bit back the pain. About him Neo could hear his wounded comrades moaning. Their cries for help carrying through the gunfire. He could see a man twenty metres away, his chest gushing blood. As the gunfire became more sporadic, Neo decided he had to help this man. Get him into the hollow out of the crossfire. Don't risk it, the others told him. Wait. Unita never stayed long in a contact. Neo shook his head.

He remembered going to church with his parents, singing in the choir.

He recalled the vlei where he'd played near his home. He wondered if he would die in this foreign jungle. He shouted at the man that he was coming. As he rushed into the open, the injured man, fear and panic in his eyes, swung his AK-47 on Neo, a bullet smashing into Neo's left leg above the knee, another hitting him in the right ankle. He fell. Thought that he was going to die in Angola.

Neo lay still, the firing from the injured man had drawn fire from Unita. His face pressed into the ground, Neo heard the zip of the bullets, prayed that he would not be hit again, that the contact would end before his life had bled into the soil. He knew that a full hit from an AK-47, in most areas of the body, would result in the victim dying of shock. Lying there, he couldn't believe that he'd been shot by both the enemy and one of his own comrades. If that guy survived, he thought, he was going to wish he hadn't.

Two years later in Teterow, Neo hated the cold and the memories it brought and sought refuge in the well-stocked library. The books were mostly political although there were novels from the Soviet Union translated from the Russian, but they were long and boring, lacking life and colour. He read them anyway to pass the weekends. You could only watch so much East German television.

When spring came the vibrancy of the countryside bursting into leaf, the sound of birds and insects, enthralled him. It was a magical transformation. In a few short months life had returned.

In June 1981, Neo was taken to East Berlin for vaccinations and a medical check-up. It was a welcome break from the training camp. Although this was his first outing in civvy street since arriving in East Germany, he was under strict instructions not to speak to anyone. As it happened there was little chance of contact with civilians as he was driven straight to the hospital and escorted to the doctor's rooms. On the way he stared at the people in the streets. As much an outsider here as he was in the white cities of his homeland.

After the check-up, Neo waited in an anteroom for the medical report. A middle-aged man and a young woman entered and the man took a seat next to Neo. Neo kept his face blank, looked straight ahead.

The man turned to him, said in English, 'How are you?'

Taken by surprise, responding to the English, Neo answered, 'I'm fine.' Then remembering his instructions, he kept his eyes averted.

'Where are you from?' the man asked. The woman was leaning forward, looking at Neo, hair golden and soft, falling gently over her face.

'Kenya,' said Neo.

'Oh, really,' said the man. 'I have just spent six months there. What part are you from?'

Neo had never been to Kenya. Knew only that the capital was Nairobi. 'Nairobi,' he replied.

'Lovely city, which part?' the man probed, sensing something.

'The eastern part,' Neo stammered. He noticed the man shoot a glance at the woman. 'What is your favourite club?'

Neo was stuck. 'Jazz,' he mumbled, looking down at the floor.

The man and woman turned away, irritated at his lies.

And suddenly he was angry that he had to play this game, that he couldn't be himself.

His medical report arrived and he left the room, nodding at the man and the young woman. He was tired of this place. Tired of not being able to speak to people.

When he'd arrived, he'd been told not to drink the water. Not a problem, he'd thought. He enjoyed fizzy drinks. But the drinks like Coke and Fanta carried other names and tasted different. Now, six months later, he longed for the taste of pure water. Tried to remember its crystal sweet taste. It was time to go home.

18

I am wondering which is worse: the highway to Pretoria, or flying to Lusaka on Zambian Airways. Tough call. I need to get to Lusaka as quickly as possible and the first available flight is on Zambian Airways.

The reason they can take a last-minute booking becomes apparent the moment I get on the plane. The steward says brightly, 'Sit anywhere. Except in the toilets.'

I am travelling with one of my partners, Thabo Molewa, who has done some work on the case, but on this occasion is consulting the ANC on another issue.

Thabo is not a good flyer and I can see that the steward's request not to take his seat in the toilets has rattled him. Me too, for that matter.

My meeting with the ANC has been arranged through Penuell Maduna, deputy head of the organisation's legal department in Lusaka. I am taking whisky and chocolates. These are always appreciated by those on low stipends.

On my left Thabo grips the armrests and looks decidedly unhappy. I wonder if I should crack open the whisky now. Then at least if the plane goes into a terminal tailspin, the descent will pass in a golden haze of Johnnie Walker. Initially the flight is bumpy but smoothes out, and I fall asleep. I am jolted awake by the plane smacking into something hard and Thabo's screams next to me, as he lunges forward in his seat, madly clawing the air. We are all screaming now as the overhead lockers open and hand baggage and duty-free purchases rain down. Outside, I see lights flashing past as the ice-cool voice of the captain tells us that we have landed and are most welcome in Zambia. No warning about beginning our descent, putting our seats in the upright position and extinguishing cigarettes, just straight in. But I don't care. I'm grateful to be alive.

Penuell Maduna meets us at the airport. A large and friendly man with bull shoulders and a barrel chest, he fires off a dozen questions on the drive into the city. What is the latest on the state of emergency? How many people are in detention? Is the money coming through for the trials? When was I last on Robben Island? Who had I seen? Did we know anything about a police death squad operating outside Pretoria? Why was soccer such a shambles? What was the weather like in Joburg? Was the attorneys admission exam difficult? How much did a Castle beer cost?

I notice he doesn't stop at red traffic lights. This worries me.

'Bandits,' he explains. 'Please keep your doors locked, there have been a number of incidents in Lusaka and nice cars like these attract attention.'

After our experience on the plane, I am alarmed that we cruise through the red traffic lights like a presidential cavalcade, but the coward in me confirms that it is probably preferable to risk instant death by colliding with another vehicle than to be hijacked by an AK-47 wielding armed gang. My fearful thoughts are interrupted by Maduna.

'By the way, we have arranged for you to see someone about the trial. I'm not sure who it is but it has been arranged. We are very keen to get news of Masina and the others. There is a lot to discuss.'

We check into the Pamodzi Hotel, the best and most expensive hotel in Lusaka, but clearly a tired establishment. The grand entrance with the sweeping drive seems out of kilter with the run-down exterior and the unkempt gardens. Inside is tatty and dated but busy. The room rates are ridiculously high given their bland utilitarianism, the stained bath and cigarette burns in the threadbare carpet.

Maduna leaves us in the lobby saying that we will be called after breakfast with the details of our meetings.

Thabo and I have a drink at the bar overlooking the patio. The whisky, warm in the soft heat of the African evening, the sweating darkness outside and the lit foliage on the patio rustled by the lazy turning fans give the drinkers an aura of seedy glamour. Here in this lush city of gutted roads, wide neglected avenues and decaying buildings, the ANC has been allowed to make its headquarters in exile. A grand gesture of generosity and solidarity from the Zambian president Kenneth Kaunda and one which has cost his country dearly as the unforgiving South African government does its best to strangle Zambia's economy.

The next morning I am in my room working after a good breakfast when Penuell calls to say he is in the lobby. We take the elevator to a room on the third floor. I still do not know who I am meeting. Penuell knocks and we enter to be greeted warmly by Chris Hani and another man who does not give his name. I haven't met Hani before. Here is the Nationalist government's public enemy number one. The Chief of Staff of Umkhonto we Sizwe and a senior figure in the South African Communist Party. He is responsible for a number of MK attacks. He has been demonised as an assassin. My first impression is of a mild-mannered and softly spoken man who seems more interested in listening than talking. Penuell orders up some tea and coffee, and leaves us alone.

Hani is dressed in khaki trousers and a flowing white open-necked shirt, African style. A tall, balding, well-built man with long arms, he relaxes into the far corner of the couch. His face is composed and relaxed, not smiling but open and almost friendly. The other man perches on the table near the door, almost behind me. Clearly the room has been hired for this meeting. The curtains remain closed.

Hani asks if this is my first time in Lusaka. I reply that I have been here a few times and get down to business. I outline the situation. He nods, says nothing.

I take out copies of the charge sheet and give them to him. He reads. I wait for him to finish, then talk him through the likely sentences on each charge. I outline the options for legal defence. It takes some time and we order more refreshments. He doesn't have many questions.

When I'm finished he leans forward, sips his coffee and says, 'I am glad that they are still alive. At one stage after they went silent and there was no communication, we thought they had been killed. We saw nothing in the press and so we thought that they had been captured and executed. It was a great relief when we received word that they were alive and being brought to trial. It is a big thing for the police to have captured a squad of this calibre.'

'They also thought that they would be killed,' I say. 'After their capture they underwent interrogation and torture for a long time. I think the State wanted to show the public that they had caught an ANC assassination unit and they also wanted to get the credit and exposure for having caught them. Also, if they did not bring them to trial and simply killed them, the public would think that the killers of those policemen had got away. Their capture was too much of a coup for them to just disappear.'

'There was a fifth member of the squad who was not arrested, Justice Mbizana. Did they mention what happened to him?' Hani asks.

'Yes,' I say, 'Ting Ting drove him to the Botswana border and he climbed through the fence. They think he is still in Botswana.'

'No.' Hani shakes his head. 'He went back in and we have heard nothing from him. We are worried about him.'

I promise to make some enquiries.

'How are their spirits?' Hani asks, changing the subject. 'Do they know what they are facing?'

'Their morale is good,' I say, 'and they are very calm. Each time I see them they seem strong. And yes, we have worked through their legal options in great detail.'

'Tell me how they were captured,' he says.

I reply that they do not know who informed on them. It may have been a woman they knew but they're unsure. Hopefully it will emerge during the trial, although often the State will keep the identity of the informant a closely guarded secret. The circumstances of the arrest suggest that they were betrayed. I go into the details of their arrest.

Hani nods slowly and says, 'And that is what Jabu told you?'

'Yes, it seems to me that their capture was more than just good luck or good policing. From the number of cars involved and the high level of the security police who were present on the scene at the time, it strikes me that this was a lot more than coincidence.'

I do not want to go too deeply into this aspect as it is beyond my scope, so I tell him of my visit to Govan Mbeki. He is interested and asks after the health of the old man. Our conversation drifts. We are not getting to the point. I look at my watch and Hani notices.

Suddenly businesslike, he says, 'It is important for these men to act in a manner which is consistent with their own principles and those of the ANC. At the same time, when cadres depart from the principles of the ANC, we need to have understanding. These men have done an enormous amount. They have already suffered and they will suffer more. While I may not agree with a particular type of defence taken by our people at a trial and may even feel a sense of betrayal when they deny loyalty and allegiance, we in the movement have to understand what it is like to be a prisoner when you are alone and totally in their power. If we have humanity, we must understand the prisoner's situation. In this case, these comrades are like my family because the ANC is our family here in exile. We have left our blood families at home. Within this family in exile, these men reported directly to me and I ensured that they had proper training, amongst the best that we have to offer. They have done what we have asked and so, in my view, we should not and will not ask anything more of them.'

Hani pauses.

'So, and this must be emphasised, this is their choice. And if they have made this choice, which I personally believe to be a correct one, we are behind them. I happen to agree with them, and it also seems to be your assessment, that there is every chance they will get the death sentence, even though we know that miracles happen. But the experience of the ANC is that the water does not turn to wine in South African courts. I understand that they cannot deny that they have committed these acts, and not just because of their confessions, which you say you can challenge anyway, but because they are soldiers of MK and those were their orders. However, I am worried at their stance on not participating and challenging the jurisdiction of the court. Politically, it is correct but it is playing for high stakes to make that statement and test that

79

proposition in a case of this nature, where the death sentence is likely. To take that position in a case where the potential sentence is five or ten years or even life is one thing, but to do it in a death sentence case is Russian roulette.'

High stakes indeed. There are none higher from a personal point of view.

I reply. 'You are right, there is a strong chance they will get the death sentence anyway. The State has a strong case and so there is an element of "If I am going to go anyway, then let it be in the manner of my own choosing". At the same time, they feel that they were driven by history to do what they have done and they want to give that exposure. They don't believe they are criminals and they refuse to be tried as criminals, and while this is not a conventional way to handle a trial, these are not conventional times.'

'You know,' Hani says, speaking with the softness of a man who knows that he does not have to raise his voice to be heard, 'these are special men, that is why I chose them for this mission. These men are not killers, they are not criminals, and in a different time they would be normal citizens. It is the country that has criminalised them, it is not their fault. So please tell them that we respect their choice and that we will support them every way we can.'

'Okay,' I say, facing the abyss, thinking that now the accused will never move from their position. I am already wondering how the case will be handled and how the judge will react. Probably he'll be furious that his jurisdiction is being rejected and his court used as a political stage.

'Tell them that we will be following the case closely and that they have done more than we asked of them.'

Rising, we shake hands and Hani wishes me luck. The door is opened by the man who has remained silent throughout the meeting. I return to my room. I have taken no notes during the meeting, believing that it might upset Hani and also wanting no documentation that the security police at the airport could confiscate.

I have often wondered to what extent a person's status, in terms of their power or wealth, influences our perception of them. If we stripped away the trappings and met them afresh, would we regard them as we had when we knew their status? While we are all susceptible to the influence of high office, it is always sickening to watch normally rational people become sycophants before powerful politicians or the very rich. This degrades both parties. With Hani, I realise that the power comes from the man and not the office.

That night, Thabo and I eat at the hotel restaurant. He has concluded his consultations and we have agreed to meet Penuell Maduna later. Thabo is one of the busiest people I know, and over the past few months we have had little opportunity to chat. He tells me about his family and the excitement of the new house he has bought recently in Spruitview to the east of Johannesburg. It is a new suburb with decent-sized houses and proper amenities that has attracted a lot of black professionals. It is a suburb, not a township. Thabo talks about how his political involvement began when he became president of the student council at the University of Turfloop and he wonders if he might not have ended up in MK if he had left the country as did so many of his fellow students. He tells me about his father who went into exile a long time ago and from whom he has not heard in years.

The red wine relaxes us as he talks about always having wanted to be a lawyer. This is the reason he stayed in the country. We joke about his straightened and oiled hair which is seriously in fashion among black male professionals in Johannesburg, and how he would have battled to maintain that in the camps in Angola. Not to mention his perfect suits. Thabo is far and away the slickest dresser in the office. His charm, combined with his great skill as a conciliator, has led to his being a popular choice as a mediator in many major disputes. A tenacious lawyer, Thabo has represented detainees and run trials in places far away from the comforts of the profession in Johannesburg.

A large, portly man approaches the table and Thabo jumps up and hugs him. He introduces Mzwai Piliso. I recall that he is the head of the Security Department of the ANC. A man from the older generation. Thabo suggests that we have drinks in his room. On the way up, we change the venue to my room. It turns out that Mzwai Piliso is a good friend of Thabo's father and this is the first time in a long while that Thabo has had news of his father.

I pull out the Johnnie Walker Black and pour generous tots. Piliso refuses the whisky and takes a soft drink. Soon we are joined by Penuell and Ronnie Kasrils, the Chief of ANC Military Intelligence. Penuell continues the line of questions started in the car, and the conversation becomes animated as we give updates on other trials, on what is happening in the Eastern Cape, on the effects of sanctions and the sports boycott. We are all sports fans. Politics and more politics, laughter, jokes and commiserations. By two in the morning others have joined us and the room is a haze of smoke and alcohol as we order room service. The whisky that Thabo and I brought is gone. Ronnie starts to reminisce about his home town and soon the talk is of the smells of home, the smog over Joburg in winter with the orange sun burning the dusk. We talk of music, cooking meat on an open fire, watching sport on a Saturday afternoon, driving through the Karoo, the noise of downtown, the lions roaring at night in the zoo in Johannesburg.

I am struck that there is no maudlin self-pity from the exiles. Instead, they are convinced that victory is inevitable. They are optimistic. I am silent.

At about three-thirty, people leave. There are hugs and greetings to pass on, each one saying how lucky we are to be going back. For them there is no going back in sight.

A bizarre event happens at the airport the next day. It's a Friday. Thabo and I check in, go through customs and settle at the bar in the departure lounge. There are a number of other passengers enjoying a pre-departure drink. On the tarmac is a single plane, our flight.

With about thirty minutes to go before our boarding time, I look out and see the boarding stairs have been moved away from the plane. Not registering this, I idly watch as the ground staff push the stairs to one side. I take another sip of my beer. I see the door of the plane shut and then the man next to me says, 'Do you think that is our plane leaving?' There is silence as everyone in the bar becomes alert. The plane moves slowly forward, and the bar erupts as everyone grabs bags and runs madly along the long tunnel to the tarmac. We make it outside in time to see the plane gather speed and take off. There is stunned disbelief. Our luggage is on the plane and at this time on a Friday afternoon, Lusaka is not the place any of us want to be.

A man says, 'Fantastic! Every other airline gets delayed, only Zambian Airways is different, we leave thirty minutes early!'

Thabo and I get back to Joburg late that night, after catching connecting flights back via Swaziland.

19

In April 1986, four men climbed through the border fence with Botswana at Ramatlabama and made their way to Mabopane. They were Joseph Makhura, Neo Potsane, Justice Mbizana and Rufus Kekana. Some weeks earlier they'd set out from Angola but had been arrested while entering Botswana and the ANC had had to negotiate their release. This had taken time. Now finally they were joining up with Jabu Masina and Ting Ting Masango at a safe house that belonged to a traditional healer by the name of 'Mokgalabe' ('Old man'). The unit was complete.

Mokgalabe knew that the unit was on an MK mission and, at great personal risk, offered them accommodation. People often stayed with him temporarily while they received treatment, so four visitors would not have drawn attention.

The four members briefed Jabu and Ting Ting on the orders they'd been given by their commander, Chris Hani.

The men shared a special camaraderie, partly instilled through their training, partly born of their years in exile and the time in the Angolan camps and war. And, Neo and Justice were close friends. When Justice told Neo that a special unit was being recruited, he'd applied to join the group.

The men didn't spend long together at Mokgalabe's. While Neo and Rufus remained with the healer, Jabu and Ting Ting headed for Winterveld and Joseph and Justice for Soshanguve. They agreed to rendezvous after the weekend.

That Saturday night Rufus, bored, went to a local shebeen for a drink. The shebeen was at a nearby house and well patronised. Carelessly, Rufus pulled out his bulging wallet, paid for his drink, and sat down at one of the plastic tables. He finished the beer, bought another. After that he went to the toilet. While standing at the urinal he was mugged. A heavy blow knocked him to the floor. Dazed he looked up to see three men standing over him. They kicked and beat him and removed his wallet, leaving him bleeding on the floor.

Slowly Rufus got to his feet. He found his way out the back door and returned to the healer's house. Armed with two Russian hand grenades he went back to the shebeen. His attackers were drinking beer at a table, laughing, unperturbed.

He went up to them. The men stopped laughing, watched him. Rufus said either they could talk outside or he would accuse them of robbery in front of the other patrons. He turned and walked out the door. The three men followed.

In the yard he waited until they'd gathered round him, then pulled out the hand grenades and told them to give him back his money or he would explode the grenades. He held the grenades at shoulder height, one in each hand, the pins upwards.

The three men stared closely at the objects in his hands, unsure. A stand-off.

Suddenly they rushed at him, punching and kicking, and Rufus fought back, hitting out with the grenades in his balled fists, taking the blows and kicks. He fell to his knees and dropped a grenade. With his free hand he pulled the pin of the other grenade and it exploded. Rufus was killed instantly as was one of his attackers. Another lost his leg and the third thief suffered severe shrapnel wounds.

The security police were quickly on the scene, followed by police explosives and forensic experts.

THE BOMB

The final decision on the nature of the bomb has been taken after carefully weighing all the options. At first a case of poisoned wine was suggested, but rejected because the target might not like that particular wine and choose not to drink it or, worse, give out the bottles to those around him. Also there's always the possibility that a dishonest official at customs might steal the wine and drink it with friends, leading to a number of deaths. A set of Parker pens loaded with explosive and exploding on use has also been discussed, but dismissed as too obvious. A manuscript or letter that would explode on opening, an option that has been successfully used before, has been discarded because the target is a clever and suspicious individual and would not fall for such a ruse.

20

The accused walk into the surgery followed by the warder. I'm seated behind the doctor's white consulting table. I can see they're eager for the warder to leave. He looks around, takes his time, then walks out. Not a word is spoken until the metal door crashes shut. In prisons, doors don't shut, they crash. Warders don't close doors, they slam them. This is about power and noise.

Jabu starts, his excitement palpable. 'How were the trips? Who did you see in Lusaka? Did you see Chris Hani? What are they saying?'

Ting Ting interrupts, calmer, 'Okay, okay, one at a time.'

Joseph and Neo have their eyes fixed on me.

I start with the visit to Govan Mbeki and mention the position taken in the Rivonia Trial. They nod, asking few questions, and Ting Ting says, 'It is important to us that Comrade Mbeki confirms our position. Now tell us about Lusaka.'

I take my time on the Lusaka trip and am not surprised that they want me to describe in great detail everything that Hani said, often repeating a statement two or three times. The relief on their faces is visible when I relate how Hani reacted.

'I must also tell you that he agreed with me that the stakes in this case could not be higher and so this must be a rational, worked through decision and not a rushed decision that you will later regret. He leaves this to you, it is your choice. He also said that he agrees with your choice to act as soldiers rather than criminals. One more thing, he said that he was worried about Justice Mbizana. Apparently, he came back into the country after your arrest and hasn't made contact since then. Have you heard anything?'

'No,' says Jabu, 'we didn't know he was back. He must be in hiding somewhere. If they had caught him he would be here with us or, at least, we would have heard something. No news is good news.'

Normally, I would not have spoken so openly, preferring to use jargon or jot down key phrases for them to read. These jottings would leave the prison with me. But such subterfuge seems superfluous under the circumstances, even childish. Given the decision that's been taken it does not seem important that the authorities might hear of a conversation in Lusaka or with Govan Mbeki. In any event, as soon as the judge is allocated I will have to see him, explain our position, and then bear his wrath for not giving his court the recognition he thinks it deserves. Soon, there will be few secrets.

There is silence as they ponder what I've said. 'Have you had further thoughts about your attitude to the trial? Is there any change?' I ask.

'There is no change from our side,' Jabu says. Affirming nods from Ting Ting, Neo and Joseph. 'Now tell us how the trial will proceed so that we can prepare ourselves.'

I give them details. How this will be a conservative judge, antagonistic towards them, who will not go lightly on sentence. I explain that in high-profile political trials the State favours hard-line judges.

I watch for their reaction to these words. There is none.

'We should soon know who the judge will be. Then I will explain to him your position. I'll ask to play the role of a watching brief. In other words, be present in court but unable to represent you given your decision not to participate in the trial. I expect the judge will be hostile to our approach.'

Neo interjects: 'I think we can cope with a hostile judge, we didn't expect it to be otherwise.'

There is a grunt from Joseph who, as the youngest of the group, follows everything but says very little.

I go on. 'Where they hold the trial will be a real issue as it can cause us serious inconvenience. In addition, if they hold it somewhere far from Pretoria, you will be moved to the closest prison. You may end up in tough quarters with warders who may try to prove a point with you. But we will deal with that when it comes.'

'Where do you think they will hold it?' asks Joseph. 'Because if it is far away, it will cause problems for our families and friends. How will they get there?'

'Guys, that is exactly their intention. They don't want the press there, and they certainly don't want family and supporters there. Also they choose small courts, which means only a few people will watch the trial.'

I can see that this bothers them. They want their trial to make an impact. How can this happen in a backwater?

'Is there nothing we can do about this?' asks Jabu. 'I mean, can we not influence it in some way?'

I tell them I could approach the Judge President but the security police and prosecution will argue that the security in a small town will be easier to manage. The treason trial where Terror Lekota and Popo Molefe were among the accused, and where I was cited as a co-conspirator, along with many others, had been heard in the small town of Delmas.

I try to reassure them. 'Wherever we end up, I will make sure that the trial gets the exposure it deserves and we will also make arrangements for your families and friends to get there. If this means we have to hire taxis or buses, we will do it. You mustn't worry about those issues. And frankly, I think this trial is going to arouse so much interest that journalists and the diplomatic community will make sure they are there, even if it is held in Pofadder.'

There is a rattling of the keys in the metal door and the warder barges in. Our time is up.

21

In Mamelodi, black members of the police kept a low profile. Some were embarrassed by their employment despite a level of acceptance in the community that they were economic recruits rather than political adherents to a cause.

Seun Vuma was an exception. He let it be known that he had chosen his side and took a ruthless approach to his work. The activists he arrested emerged with the scars to prove his vehemence. Vuma knew he was a target and rarely stayed at home, sleeping at other houses and in the male quarters at police stations.

On the night of 16 March 1986, Jabu and Ting Ting retrieved their AK-47s from their weapons cache and drove to Vuma's house in a beige Mazda 323 that they'd rented from a car hire company. They felt that their Audi was being used too much.

The unit had received information that Vuma would be at home, and had decided that this was the moment to assassinate him. Jabu and Ting Ting were appointed to carry out the killing.

They had reconnoitered the policeman's house some days earlier. The house, with a garden, was large by Mamelodi standards. They knew that he normally parked at the back so that no one could see if he was home. After parking he'd walk around the house and enter through the front door.

The plan was to arrive at nightfall, wait for Vuma, and shoot him while he walked from his car to the front door.

Jabu and Ting Ting parked the Mazda a few blocks away and walked back, their AK-47s hidden beneath their overcoats. Vuma's car wasn't there, so they settled down to wait out of sight. From next door came the sounds of loud music and laughter. It was a Friday night, always a good reason to celebrate. The men hoped the noise would cover the gunfire.

One problem. A number of tin roofing sheets were scattered around the yard and Jabu was worried about tripping up. Vuma had a reputation for using his gun quickly. It was also well known that on arriving home at night he would fire a few shots into the air in a show of force. Jabu and Ting Ting had no doubt that if he were alerted to their presence he would shoot to kill.

At half past eleven, Ting Ting wondered aloud if they'd been given the right information. No sooner spoken than they heard a car approaching, the headlights swinging into the driveway, stopping close to the front door of the house rather than at the back as he usually did. Vuma, dressed in civilian clothes, got out, looked carefully around, and walked briskly towards his front door a few metres away.

Taken by surprise, Ting Ting and Jabu were too far away to act. They remained hidden, then slowly circled the house to see if they could get a clear shot of him inside. The lights came on. They watched him move from room to room. He had a gun tucked into the back of his pants, detective style.

Ting Ting readied his AK-47. Jabu was facing outward down the driveway, his AK-47 out and ready. Vuma walked into the sitting room. He sat down on the sofa and then slowly, as if sensing something, raised his head and looked straight at the window where Ting Ting's AK-47 pointed between the burglar bars, the barrel obscured by the lace curtains.

Ting Ting fired. Short, deafening automatic bursts. He saw the explosions of blood on Vuma's chest as the policeman was spun off the sofa. The music and laughter next door stopped. In the silence, Ting Ting fired once again at Vuma and then he and Jabu ran down the driveway, concealing the weapons under their overcoats as they went.

22

It is always good to handle big cases with a partner, not just because of the assistance that is needed but also because at times you doubt your own sanity and judgement. I'm deeply grateful that Thabo Molewa has agreed to help me on the case. Thabo's not only more than competent, but has an exuberance and energy that I've always admired and which is needed for the up-coming trial.

Handling a major trial can be a lonely experience. The hostility of the court, from the judge to the prosecution to the officials to the police, all contributes to a David and Goliath atmosphere, but one without a triumphant ending. And while solitude is something I normally relish, I know that in this case it is essential for me to have a partner. I have never handled a death sentence case before.

I think of the Messina trial in which I took instructions from two MK fighters. On a cold blue winter's day I flew up in one of those small and, in my view, very unstable planes to Louis Trichardt and then drove to Messina. I saw the accused in a small, neat jail surrounded by beautiful trees in red flower.

The men were quiet at first but eventually opened up and told me they were part of an MK unit deployed to attack the farms that had been militarised as part of the border defence against infiltration. While camped in a hollow on one of these farms they'd been surprised by the farmer and captured. That case was handled eventually by another partner at the firm, Azhar Cachalia. The proceedings were long and traumatic, and took place in that small border town. It was a death sentence case. Although accompanied by an advocate, Azhar told me afterwards that as an Indian representing two MK operatives in an ultra-right-wing backwater he had known long hours of isolation and depression. Sitting alone in his hotel room every night had been an ordeal.

Travelling on that terrible highway to Pretoria with the sun bright above us, I feel a great warmth towards Thabo. I'm pleased that we'll be able to handle this together, wherever it may go.

True to form, the warders mess us around and deny us access. I have explained to Thabo that this is part of the process and that it's pointless getting upset by it. Rather, we should take a perverse comfort in giving pleasure to a gang of deprived prison warders who have found an activity more satisfying than making the lives of their prisoners a misery. Slim pickings indeed for those who wait in the midday sun outside a maximum security prison, but you take what you can.

It is Thabo's first time inside Maximum Security and he looks apprehensively at the great steel doors opening, probably wondering what it would be like to spend time here, which is what I'd thought on my first visit. We enter. The door bangs closed. Thabo goes quiet.

The accused arrive in the surgery in good humour. As if, now that the decision is made, they are less stressed, even looking forward to the change and excitement that the trial may bring.

We go through the ritual of weighing ourselves. Jabu, Neo and Joseph are in perfect physical shape, and sarcastically chide Ting Ting and me for putting on weight. Thabo is in good shape and acquits himself well in the ritual. Ting Ting glares at him resentfully. We get down to business. First Thabo introduces himself and I notice the men are quickly at ease with him.

I go through the basic format of the trial, mentioning that the prosecution will call witnesses.

'What kind of witnesses?' asks Jabu. 'There were no witnesses to what we did. No one saw us. Who can they produce?'

'Well,' I explain, 'they may produce witnesses who you mightn't have seen, but who will say they saw you. Or they may have witnesses that saw you leave the area. However, the critical evidence against you will be your confessions and the record of your visits to the scenes where you pointed out where you did what.

'They will also produce forensic witnesses who will connect the projectiles or bullets that were shot at the various scenes with the weapons that were found on you and which you led them to. In all likelihood, they will produce forensic evidence connecting you to the weapons used in the actions – your fingerprints on the weapons, for instance. They may also have statements from the people who gave you accommodation.

'But the main evidence against you will be your own statements. They will say these confessions were freely and voluntarily given, and we do not have sufficient evidence, either medical or forensic, to prove they tortured you. Given that you signed under oath before a magistrate, even if we were participating in this case, we would have difficulty in challenging their admissibility.

'Anyway, this discussion is academic. So the confessions will be admitted as evidence unless the judge decides otherwise.'

'He's hardly likely to do that,' says Neo.

Unfortunately I agree with him.

I continue outlining the trial procedure: the calling of the security police, their presentation of the confessions. After that a denigration of the ANC as a gang of bloodthirsty revolutionaries by so-called experts. On top of this may come evidence from askaris wearing balaclavas, given in camera to protect their identities. They will talk of how they left the country, their training in the same military camps in Angola or wherever. They will talk about the type of training, the political education, and their evidence will describe an ANC hell-bent on destruction. Finally they will identify the accused. It is all predictable.

'But that is ridiculous,' exclaims Jabu. 'I mean, even if we were contesting this trial how could we attack their evidence if we cannot see who they are?'

I shrug. 'In essence, the prosecution is painting a picture, not only to show the horror of what you have done, but also to show that your actions are consistent with the aims of the ANC. In other words, to violently overthrow this government and replace it with a revolutionary government.

'They will argue that this undemocratic ANC government, if it comes to power, will then exact terrible retribution on whites and govern according to the wishes of their Soviet masters. This is crude, but it's the message they will want to convey. Wait until you see the types of prosecutors they put on these trials.'

'Go on, Peter,' says Jabu. 'What else will the prosecution do?'

'They will bring in people affected by your actions. The injured, those who lost loved ones. When the daughter of an assassinated security policeman gives evidence, she speaks not as a member of the security forces but as a child who has lost her father. The prosecution knows this and will make much of it.'

There is silence in the room. I go on quickly to describe the adjournment, the reconvening of the court and the judgment. I think we are under no illusions what it will be.

'Will we get a chance to speak or make a statement before we are found guilty, or will that contradict our position?' Jabu asks.

'No,' I reply. 'I don't think so. After the sentence has been passed, you would normally be given the opportunity to present evidence and argument in extenuation. If you choose to do so, the judge and his assessors will decide if what you have presented amounts to extenuation. If it does, then it is not mandatory for him to pass the death sentence. If he finds no extenuating circumstances, he is compelled by law to pass the death sentence.

'Again, this is academic, as you have chosen not to participate and will therefore be unable to present an extenuation case.'

After that I tell them the judge will read the sentence. It is the best way I can put it, avoiding the words 'death sentence'. But I can feel those words present in the room, cold and unsaid.

Suddenly, I feel exhausted. Working it through to the end point has drained me. Glancing around, I see everyone looks tired, deep in thought. We have been there for more than four hours.

23

After two operations in successive months, the unit decided to lie low. Jabu and Neo stayed in a safe house in Mamelodi, Justice in another house in the same township, and Joseph and Ting Ting rented rooms in separate houses in Winterveld.

They seldom met up and spent most of the time indoors, changing their accommodation every few weeks.

In May 1986 the unit met to discuss a number of potential targets. High on their agenda was a proposal that a small section of the KaNgwane homeland be incorporated into Swaziland. ANC policy firmly called for a unitary and non-racial South Africa. There was to be no hiving off bits of the country. Especially not to a neighbouring state.

The unit decided to investigate a politician called Mabeleke David Lukhele who supported the proposal. They learnt that Lukhele had called for the army and police to remain in Mamelodi and was also campaigning for the resignation of Enos Mabuza, the chief minister of KaNgwane who had publicly stated his opposition to the proposed incorporation of the territory into Swaziland. Enos Mabuza was turning out to be less compliant than Pretoria might have wished. He was even rumoured to be an ANC supporter.

As MK instructions to the unit regarded homeland politicians as legitimate political targets, the unit decided to kill Lukhele.

Although they didn't need specific authorisation for such a mission, they advised the MK command in Botswana of their intentions, and two weeks later received an order to proceed.

Ting Ting kept Lukhele under surveillance for almost two weeks. He established that the man worked during the week in KaNgwane and returned to his home in Mamelodi on weekends. He also travelled frequently to Swaziland and often returned late at night on the weekends. He drove a Mercedes Benz which he parked in the yard. He was vigilant, always looking around before entering his home through the front door.

The attack was scheduled for the Friday night of 6 June 1986. Jabu and Neo would undertake the mission.

At about seven o'clock that evening, Neo, armed with an AK-47, and Jabu, carrying a Makarov pistol and a hand grenade, approached Lukhele's house in the Audi. They drove past and parked a few blocks away. It was dark. A crisp winter night. They walked back to Lukhele's house. His Mercedes Benz was in the yard. They decided to carry out the attack immediately.

Jabu stayed in the street as look-out while Neo walked up to the house and knocked on the door. Jabu saw the door open and Neo walk in. The door closed. Seconds later came gunshots and screams. The front door of the house opened, and Neo stepped out, carefully closed it, casually walking across to join Jabu.

They walked off, Neo not saying a word. In the car, Neo let loose, angry, cursing himself, almost shouting as he asked over and over why he had not moved to get a better angle, then he could have avoided the others.

'What others?' asked Jabu.

Neo told him that Lukhele had opened the door. He'd told the politician he had a message for him. The man invited him in. They walked through a room where a television was on. Sensing Lukhele behind him, Neo had turned, taken out the AK-47 and opened fire. Simultaneously he saw a woman sitting in a chair slightly to the right of Lukhele, almost directly behind him.

94

'I saw that she was in the line of fire, that I'd shot her in the head,' said Neo.

Then another woman ran from the room.

'I think she was shot too,' he said dully, 'but she should be okay.'

The two men drove back to the safe house. The next day a newspaper report said that David Lukhele and his sister Elizabeth Busisiwe Dludlu had been shot dead the previous night.

24

We don't tell the attorney-general (AG) that the accused refuse to participate in the trial. In fact, we do the opposite: we give the impression that we are preparing for a lengthy trial. I want the State to think they will be facing a rigorous defence and will therefore need to prepare their case in great detail. In meetings with the AG's office, we intimate that we will be challenging the confessions of the accused. We give every indication that all the State's allegations will be tested and attacked.

Were the State to know of our true intentions, they would spend little time in preparation. The effect of this would be to bring the case to trial quickly. The less time these men spend in prison and on trial, the less time there will be for internal and international campaigns to take effect. On the other hand, the State will be courting the publicity of having caught such a high-profile MK unit, and they want a speedy resolution of the trial.

To give effect to this subterfuge, we brief two advocates to 'represent' the accused. Dennis Kuny is briefed as senior counsel, with Hans van der Riet as his junior. Dennis is a veteran political counsel in high-profile cases. A softly spoken man in his fifties, he avoids the glare of publicity, competently and with great integrity going about handling the hard cases of the resistance. The ones that others often refuse.

His junior counsel, Hans van der Riet, is a huge man with a jocular manner that belies a serious nature and acute intellect.

Thabo and I discuss the case with them. At first, Dennis finds it difficult accepting our clients' refusal to participate. He would prefer mounting a defence that would stretch out for as long as possible. Hans understands the men's position. Ironically, perhaps the struggle of his own people for their independence from the British gives him a better insight into the minds of the accused. Anyway, after discussions, both agree to play their part. It reassures us to know they are there. As backup.

By maintaining this facade of a defence, we manage to buy time before the start of the trial. The accused first appear in court in Pretoria on 15 May 1987. After a number of remands and postponements, we are told by the AG's office that the trial will start in March 1988. Unfortunately, our counsel are not available at that time for such a lengthy trial. They need to clear their practices to ensure that once the trial starts, it can proceed uninterrupted by constant postponements.

We have known for some time that the State prosecution team will be headed by Advocate Harry Prinsloo, a senior counsel, and Advocate Louisa van der Walt, both from the AG's Pretoria office. These two tend to work together as a team and are well-known figures in the prosecution of political trials. They are known as rightwing prosecutors who take more than a purely professional interest in their work. Probably a bit like we human-rights lawyers, except on the other side.

There are meetings at the AG's office on Church Square. In an office overlooking the square onto which the Supreme Court faces, I meet Louisa van der Walt for the first time. I have a preconceived image of Louisa, tough, hard and blow-dried. I am not disappointed. Medium height, slim, black grey hair coiffed severely back, ten thousand volts through each strand. Skin burnt by a cruel sun, a thick layer of make-up broken by a slit of red lipstick.

Louisa van der Walt achieved some notoriety through her behaviour in a recent ANC case in which she had prosecuted. After the accused had been sentenced they had jumped up and shouted 'Long live the ANC, viva!' Louisa, incensed by their defiance, had screamed out 'Long live the AWB!', naming the ultra-rightwing organisation that has a doctored swastika as its emblem.

It was also known that she brought a gun to court in her handbag, a fact she was not shy to advertise. That was Louisa.

It was also suspected that her co-prosecutor Harry Prinsloo shared her political views, but he was clever enough not to shout about them in the court in front of the international press.

These are the prosecutors my clients will face and here I am, in Louisa's office on Church Square, her words like bullets spattering around me.

She speaks Afrikaans to my faltering Afrikaans. We work through the formalities. Louisa gives nothing that she does not have to, clearly despising my clients, the enemy.

In the square below stands the great statue of the bearded President Paul Kruger. The man who stood up against the invading British forces. Whose bands of guerrillas, mounted commandos, outnumbered and outgunned, roamed the countryside, striking at the British forces who, under the orders of Lord Kitchener, burned farmhouses and crops to deprive the commandos of sustenance. It was Kitchener too who ordered the Boer women and children into massive concentration camps where they died in their tens of thousands. Murdered by disease and starvation. The British won the war, but they lost the country nine years later. I wonder if Louisa believes, like the British, that sovereignty and rights can be denied a people by sheer force. Would Kruger himself see the irony of this situation, some eighty-five years later?

Louisa's officiousness jolts me back. Frustrated by the prospect of more delays, she says my request for another postponement needs to be taken to her boss.

I tell her that I'm sure the AG realises the necessity for these men to be represented and that I am sorry, but my counsel are unavailable to run a lengthy trial in March 1988. Perhaps much later in the year.

Louisa is not stupid, she knows this is a tactic, but there is nothing she can do about it. She knows that the judge will not allow a death sentence trial without proper representation.

I am able to tell my clients that we have bought more time and they had better get used to life at Maximum Security because they will be there for at least another year.

And a very long year it is. Waiting for a trial date seems interminable. The stress of life in Maximum Security compounded by the probable outcome of the trial takes its toll on the accused, manifesting in squabbles with the perpetually sullen warders. Slowly Jabu, Ting Ting, Neo and Joseph settle into a routine of dull monotony, with each visit from Thabo and me a highlight. They miss scents, the scent of flowers, of perfume, of animals. Mostly they miss the moon which they can't always see from their cell windows. On the rare occasion that the moon's trajectory brings it into view, they watch it wistfully, cherishing the sight until it is gone.

The frustration of their prison life is tempered by the knowledge that this time is precious and that one day they will look back and savour every minute of it, boring as it was. Yet it is not all tedious. Among their fellow prisoners are Terror Lekota, Popo Molefe, Moss Chikane and others taking part in the 'Delmas Treason Trial' which, although it is now being heard in Pretoria, still retains its original name. They're able to spend time together talking politics. Every morning, they gather in the exercise courtyard and Lekota gives them the latest news. He has a tiny radio hidden in his cell. My clients also receive newspapers but these are heavily censored, so Lekota's briefings are eagerly anticipated. Afterwards the men participate in a rigorous regime of exercises.

Thabo Molewa and I take it in turns to see the four men. We have other ANC clients in Maximum Security and I feel I am getting to spend too much time on the highway and inside those grim walls.

While it is quiet and dull for our clients in Maximum Security, all hell is breaking loose as the country moves closer to open conflict and the state of emergency takes its toll on resistance organisations. The security legislation becomes stricter and even, at times, bizarre. Outdoor gatherings may only be held with the permission of a magistrate or the minister of law and order, and indoor gatherings for the purpose of organising boycotts are also banned unless permission is granted. The obsession with gatherings extends to funerals.

In January 1987, emergency regulations restrict, in certain areas, funeral ceremonies including memorial services, commemoration services, funeral processions or burials of any person who has died in or during any security action or unrest or of wounds sustained by him or her in or during any security action or unrest. Given that most parts of the country and certainly the areas where black people live are in a constant state of unrest, this restriction proves onerous for the relatives of the numerous deceased. In reality, funerals are defiantly held anyway, attended by tens of thousands of people. Inevitably this draws the police and there is more violence and more deaths.

On 6 May 1987, a general election for the House of Assembly is to be held in which only whites can vote. To highlight the inequality of the election, one of the biggest clients of the firm, the Congress of South African Trade Unions (Cosatu), as well as the United Democratic Front

and the National Education Crisis Committee, call for a two-day stay-away. At the same time, there is a railway strike, a post office strike and a complete rent boycott in Soweto. The leader of Cosatu is Jay Naidoo. Jay, tall and with an easy smile, is a quietly spoken man who, in an unassuming way, is aware that he leads the most coherent and well-organised internal resistance force in the country, and of the obligations associated with that burden. Jay is an exceptional leader, a strategist. He knows how far to push matters and when to pull back and regroup. He is supported by a strong leadership team including Jabu's old school friend, Cyril Ramaphosa, the general secretary of the biggest union in the country, the National Union of Mineworkers.

Over the years of being Jay's lawyer, he and I have built a close bond that goes beyond the strict lawyer–client relationship. It is also cemented by the unfortunate fact that Cosatu is the subject of unrelenting attack by the government. In the past few years, the offices of Cosatu and the United Democratic Front have been firebombed and vandalised. The day after the election, Jay phones to tell me there has been an explosion at Cosatu House. I head off to pick up Jay. This is big news.

At Cosatu House the police tell us two large bombs exploded in the basement and now the building is unsafe and could collapse at any moment. Despite this we enter the basement. It's chaos. Mountains of shattered concrete and skeletons of twisted steel. As we leave we're accosted by the forensic team who want us out in case we contaminate evidence. But we know all too well that they're the sweepers – there to destroy evidence, not find it.

Later that day the Johannesburg city engineer declares the building unsafe and condemns it. The police issue a statement that the bombs are the biggest 'devices' used to date on the Witwatersrand. Prior to this, the attacks on the offices of resistance organisations have been firebombs, grenades and small explosive devices. This bombing of an eleven-storey building signals a new phase in the conflict. More are to follow.

Yet in Pretoria Central Maximum Security time stands still for Jabu, Ting Ting, Joseph and Neo. Thabo and I tell them of the mounting chaos, the continued occupation of the townships by the army, the mass funerals every weekend, and the bombings. They're interested but the malaise of their crushing routine weighs on them.

We have long completed our preparation for the trial and so our time together is spent discussing politics, domestic and family issues, girlfriends past, and what they miss most, which includes the girlfriends past. During one of the consultations Joseph tells me that he'd celebrated his birthday recently. It was the first birthday he had celebrated ever.

'In my family we were just too poor, there was no money for presents or cake so the birthdays passed like any other day,' he says, without self-pity. 'When we were in Angola in the camps, you had to keep your birthday secret for security reasons. All personal particulars had to be kept strictly to yourself, so no birthdays there.'

I wonder at getting to the age of twenty-six before celebrating your first birthday, and then being in Maximum Security facing charges that carry the death sentence.

'Ja, man,' says Joseph, 'Jabu and the unit and Terror, Popo and Moss organised a cake. I don't know where they got it from.'

I look at the others inquisitively. Neo raises his empty hands in that classic 'don't ask me' gesture.

Joseph continues. 'There were no candles on it and they all sang "Happy Birthday" to me. It was great, man, I haven't felt that good in years. It was the best birthday I ever had.'

We all laugh, enjoying the sudden warmth in the cold surgery. No one talks of the future, of after the trial.

The attorney-general's office keeps up the pressure to get a date from our counsel, even if it's eighteen months ahead. We delay, change our minds, change them again, change our counsel and then revert to the previous ones. It should be obvious what we are doing and I nervously wonder what the reaction from the AG's office will be when I tell them that there is no counsel and that the trial will not even be contested.

Eventually, it cannot be drawn out any more and we indicate late 1988 or early 1989. Within two weeks, we receive notice from the AG's office that the trial will start on 1 February 1989. It will be held in Delmas, about an hour's drive from Johannesburg. The judge is a man by the name of Marius de Klerk.

THE BOMB

In constructing any bomb, the right amount of explosive is critical. Too much will cause the blast to disperse and lose direction. Too little will not do the job and kill the target.

Innocuous on its own and looking a bit like Prestik, the explosive material that Japie Kok uses on this occasion is a white putty-like substance. In the trade it is known as P4 – Pentaerythritol Tetranitrate or PETN. PETN is a military explosive that can lie dormant for years and still retain its power.

Originally manufactured in Czechoslovakia, P4 has become the stock-in-trade of assassins and bombers all over the world. PETN has all the qualities required for this particular killing. It is durable, travels well and can be compressed into small compartments, rendering it easier to disguise. It also has no metal component and will not be picked up by the standard detectors.

Importantly, P4 is enormously powerful and you don't need to house it in a bulky casing. The casing, however, is extremely important as it has to be the correct shape in order to direct the blast in the direction where it will do the most damage. This is known as the 'Monroe Effect', meaning that the explosive charge must follow the path of least resistance. Such an effect can be achieved by creating a charge in the shape of an inverted cone. The estimate is that five grams of P4 properly directed will eliminate this particular target.

25

There was a feeling among some in the unit that they needed to address the call by the ANC to take the struggle into white areas. From the beginning, the unit's targets had been in the townships and the men felt a need to broaden their approach. Also the accidental killing of Busisiwe Dludlu had been demoralising. The suffering was in the black areas. Roadblocks. Search and seizure raids. The presence of the army. Casspirs stationed at street corners. Yet in the city and suburbs of Pretoria there was peace and calm. As if everything were normal.

On a visit into Silverton one day, Ting Ting sat in a park and ate a KFC takeaway, the winter sun warming his back. The park was so tranquil he dozed off. In the township such moments were impossible. No peace. No parks.

The regret of the unit, particularly Neo, about Busisiwe Dludlu was tempered by their view that, as soldiers, they had operated within accepted ANC policy. At the ANC's Second Consultative Conference at Kabwe, Zambia in July 1985, the leadership had abolished the distinction between 'hard' and 'soft' targets during MK military operations.

This decision was influenced by repeated cross-border attacks by South African security forces on targets in neighbouring Lesotho and Botswana. A raid in June 1985 by the SADF on a number of homes in Gaborone left twelve dead, including a six-year-old child from Lesotho, two Lesotho citizens, a Somali and eight South Africans. Five of the South Africans were ANC members but not members of MK. The attack had caused Oliver Tambo to comment at a press conference that '[w]hen the regime sends its army across the border to kill people in Botswana, including nationals of other countries, they are hitting soft targets – very soft and not even in their own country'.

In May 1986, the SADF had attacked the Makeni Refugee Centre in Lusaka, resulting in the deaths of two civilians, one a Zambian, the other from Namibia. Simultaneous military missions occurred in Gaborone and Harare.

In their discussions, the members of the unit agreed that the security forces were indiscriminate in their attacks in the townships, targeting

black people as a group and making little distinction between activists and ordinary citizens. Conflict, the men believed, had reached a point where the lines were blurred, where all that mattered was the extent of the damage inflicted.

Given this escalation in violence and their desire to hit where it hurt most, the unit decided that an attack in the white suburbs was appropriate. Whites must be made aware that there was a bloody conflict taking place, and in their suburbs not just in black areas. With mounting anger and bitterness, the unit talked about the funerals that took place every weekend in the townships and that white people didn't know what it was like to bury their children. The innocence of whites was discussed. Could they be innocent when their sons were the soldiers manning the roadblocks, driving the police cars, carrying out the raids, arresting and torturing detainees?

White parents inculcated superiority in their children, supplied the votes that supported the ruling National Party and bolstered apartheid. Where did complicity begin and culpability end? Sure there were whites who supported the struggle and opposed apartheid, but they were a minority.

The unit's discussions took place over a number of days as they focused on how best to take the war to the white areas. Driven by anger, it was no longer a question of whether, but where.

They decided to target a peaceful Pretoria suburb, one that was popular and regarded as beyond the reach of violence. In this way, the unit hoped to send a message that there was no safe place in the country. If Pretoria, the heartland, could not be protected, no city was secure. While the security forces may be attacking elsewhere, in the townships and in other countries, there were ANC soldiers striking in their backyards in Pretoria, the seat of government and of the nation, a few kilometres from the Union Buildings and not far from defence headquarters at Voortrekkerhoogte.

Preferably, the unit felt, the target should be 'hard', but if civilians were injured or even killed, that was collateral damage, regrettable but unavoidable. Future violence, they decided, would no longer follow apartheid lines and be restricted to the townships. They decided that the middle-class white suburb of Silverton would be the target. They would set off a bomb. Any other form of attack would be suicidal.

A few days later, Ting Ting and Joseph visited a shopping area in Silverton. It was pleasant strolling through the busy streets taking in the sights and well-stocked stores. How quickly everything had returned to normal after the recent nationwide strike. A strike so acrimonious and violent that eventually the managing directors of the stores hardest hit – Checkers, CNA, Gallo, Frasers, Garlicks, OK Bazaars, Pick 'n Pay, Woolworths – had met with minister of law and order Louis Le Grange and senior police officers, requesting police restraint. Instead, the detentions increased. In the end both management and the unions issued a joint statement to announce negotiations and call off the strike.

Walking slowly down Pretoria Street, the main road through Silverton, Ting Ting and Joseph stopped at a Checkers supermarket. A number of policemen stood at the bus stop outside the store. Two hundred metres away was a large, well-protected police station.

As it was lunch time and the two men were hungry, they bought fish and chips from a shop called 'Something Fishy' opposite Checkers. They sat on a nearby bench eating, discussing potential targets and where the bomb should be placed.

A refuse bin next to the bus stop and about fifteen metres from Checkers seemed ideal. If a bomb were timed to explode during the lunch hour, there was a good chance that policemen would be injured or killed. There were cars parked along the road, and some people standing around, but the area couldn't be described as busy. A whites-only bus arrived, and the policemen got on. Ting Ting and Joseph hoped that injuries would be restricted to the policemen at the bus stop, and that if civilians were injured there would not be many of them. The target met the unit's criteria.

Some days later, on 4 July 1986, Ting Ting and Joseph took a taxi to Silverton, carrying in a small bag a SPM-2 limpet mine with its detonator. Ting Ting had his Makarov pistol stuck into the back of his pants, covered by a loose shirt. They sat down on the benches where they'd eaten their fish and chips. Joseph reached into the bag and prepared the mine, setting the detonator to explode in an hour. He slowly pulled the pin. The mine was armed and ready.

While Ting Ting remained on the bench, the Makarov digging into his back, Joseph sauntered across the road with the mine in a plastic bag. There were two policemen at the bus stop. Ting Ting moved the pistol to the side so that it would be easily accessible. Joseph was approaching the bin.

The bin was metal and square. At exactly midday, Joseph carefully placed the limpet mine into the bin. The bomb was primed to explode at one o'clock.

He rejoined Ting Ting on the bench. They watched the activity. The policemen had moved off. Civilians waited at the bus shelter.

Then Ting Ting recognised a Mamelodi man standing at the bus stop. His name was Star Masango (no relation), a professional pickpocket. Star was obviously working the bus stop and Ting Ting decided to warn him off. He went over, took the pickpocket aside and told him that he should immediately leave the area. Star was delighted to see Ting Ting, wanted to chat. Ting Ting told him to move away, it wasn't safe. What was so dangerous? Star wanted to know.

'Move away now or you'll be hurt,' Ting Ting replied.

Star, puzzled, shook his head, and eventually drifted away. Relieved, Ting Ting rejoined Joseph and they caught a taxi back to the township.

The unit heard on the news that the bomb had exploded at five during the rush hour peak when people were leaving work.

They looked at Joseph accusingly.

Joseph held out his hands in a gesture of frustration.

'It was set to go off at one,' he confirmed. 'The detonator must have been faulty.'

The news report said no one was killed but eighteen were injured and there was extensive damage to property. The unit later learnt that Star Masango was among the injured.

26

I am apprehensive as I drive to Delmas. It is a week to the start of the trial and I am to meet Judge Marius de Klerk in his chambers at the court. It is our first meeting and I wonder how he will react to the news of my clients' non-participatory decision. I wonder if it won't be best to leave informing him until the day we start and then deal with his anger. Even though the mood of the judge can be unsettling, I am not too concerned as I have long since come to realise that hostility and antagonism from the bench is the lot of human-rights lawyers in political trials.

What really worries me is that he may not let me sit at the attorneys' and counsel's table in the front of the court. If he is hostile, I will have to sit in the public gallery behind my clients. This separation will prevent easy access to them and make it impossible for me to provide help should it be necessary. Technically, he's entitled to do this if the accused refuse counsel and choose not to be represented.

Many judges tend to regard their court as their personal fiefdom. Anything that insults it or shows a lack of respect draws immediate retribution. Unable to distinguish the office from the person, criticism can be regarded as a personal insult.

The key in my meeting with Judge de Klerk is to persuade him that my clients' stand is an attack on the entire State, on history, and not focused particularly on the judiciary or him, personally. I don't know much about de Klerk, but I've clear expectations of how he will respond to my request to be present at the front table.

Sadly, I do know Delmas. The East Rand of Johannesburg is home to a variety of tough places, foremost among them the industrial towns of Benoni, Boksburg and Springs, along with the massive black ghetto townships of Thokoza, Vosloorus and Katlehong. In and between these towns are great yellow mine dumps, artificial barren mountains of rock and soil concentrate taken from the deep shafts of the many gold mines in the area. Most of these mines are dormant and deserted now, leaving only their effluent to mark the already ravaged landscape. Beyond these towns, on the right-hand side of the freeway, is Modder B prison. Ugly and squat, a square spider of concrete blocks and barbed wire. And just beyond Modder B is Delmas.

Apart from its residents, not many people are familiar with Delmas. The town goes quietly about its business as a small agricultural centre with a predominantly Afrikaans population that is conservative and introverted. Had the State not held one of its major treason trials in Delmas, the town may never have achieved a recognition it neither deserved nor desired.

The reasons for the State's decision to use Delmas are various. There's the proximity of a high-security prison. Limited access to the town makes control simple. A few roadblocks can determine who comes into town and who goes out. So even if a support committee manages to bus supporters to the trial, the buses may be turned back at the checkpoints.

Similarly, if there are protests inside or outside the court, the instigators can be picked up at the roadblocks, away from the interfering gaze of reporters and photographers. Troublesome journalists can also be denied access or even detained at the checkpoints.

The distance from the major urban areas makes it too costly for supporters to use public transport, which minimises the chances of large crowds. It's also a major inconvenience for journalists from the city papers and may deter some from covering a trial.

The court buildings, situated in the outlying suburbs of Delmas, are small, designed to serve the modest legal needs of the town and its surrounding area. They are certainly not large enough to accommodate a major treason trial with the families and supporters of the accused, let alone the large local and international press contingent that these trials attract. Nor can they cater for substantial legal defence teams. Which is exactly why Delmas is the State's choice.

I went to the circuit court in Delmas a number of times when the big Delmas Treason Trial started there in 1985.

In all the years that the trial ran, there was only one proposition on which the prosecution and the defence agreed: let's get the hell out of Delmas. They moved the trial to Pretoria. A decision no doubt supported by the residents of the town. They must have resented the invasion that the treason trial brought. Suddenly, their town was on prime-time news in London and New York as a typical white town in South Africa, the subject of sniggering journalists conducting their interviews in front of their garden gates and trim lawns. All to show the incongruity of holding one of the country's most important political trials in a one-horse dorp. And now a new treason trial, the State versus Masina and Three Others, was to be Delmas's next major attraction.

As I find my way through the suburbs to the court I wonder if not knowing anything about the judge is a good sign. Usually the judges assigned to political trials are well known. Some of them have reputations for passing sentences so heavy they've made the gallery gasp, never mind the accused.

What I do know of de Klerk is that he handled commercial cases at the Pretoria Bar before being appointed to the bench, and has the reputation of being a good lawyer. It's some consolation that he hasn't got his appointment for faithful service to the State in political trials. Although there is a rumour that he's related to the cabinet minister, F W de Klerk.

To ensure no slip-ups, the judge will sit with two assessors. The people chosen for this role normally come from the ranks of retired magistrates and civil servants, who can be relied on to support the judge and whose presence suggests the weight of legal opinion.

Courthouses are generally depressing, soulless places. Cold, dry and functional like the people who run them. You might ask, Why should they be otherwise? They're not meant to be cosy places of warmth and laughter. Here is where justice is dispensed, and in this country that can be a brutal business.

The judge's chambers are spacious. De Klerk rises from behind his desk to greet me. Tall and slim, tanned and patrician, he comes round the desk and we shake hands. He is dressed in a dark well-tailored suit. At ease, he sits down again and leans back in his chair.

I thank him for his time and tell him that I want to explain the position the accused have taken so that there is minimal disruption to the proceedings. He nods.

I acknowledge that it's unusual for an attorney to be meeting with him but that there is no advocate as the accused have chosen not to participate in the trial. They have rejected the jurisdiction of the court.

The judge listens without interrupting, his eyes narrowing, the beginnings of a frown. Then he says, 'I know that this is a political trial, but this is a very unusual approach. Are your clients convinced they want to follow this course of action?'

'Yes, Judge,' I reply, explaining the process we have been through. I add, 'They see themselves as soldiers fighting a just war and not as criminals to be tried in a criminal court. They believe they are prisoners of war and do not accept the legitimacy or jurisdiction of the court.'

Waiting for the anger and the reprimand, I am surprised when he says, 'If they want nothing to do with the court and will not participate, then I will have to enter a plea of "not guilty" on their behalf.'

'Yes, Judge,' I say. 'They understand the trial process.'

'And you have told them that they will be severely prejudiced if they do not take part?'

Again I confirm their position, adding, 'They do not mean this as a stunt, and they mean no disrespect to you.'

Gazing at me intently, he asks, 'Are they going to behave in court or is it their intention to disrupt the proceedings?'

'Judge, I have had no indication that they intend to disrupt the court. My sense is that they view themselves as soldiers and not as hooligans.'

Nodding sceptically, he says, 'We will wait and see.'

I am now at another potential sticking point: will he allow me to sit at the legal representatives' table? I put the question.

A long silence as Judge de Klerk stares at his desk and moves some papers. Then he says, 'It seems I have no choice in this. I certainly cannot influence your clients even if I think that what they are doing is wrong. This case will be difficult to manage for all of us. I have no problem with your being in court although you cannot be heard. I must thank you for coming to see me.'

I can go no further. The meeting is over.

I sit in my car, thinking over the judge's comments, yet unsure of his concessions. He was reasonable. Not aggressive or hostile, but also not friendly or too accommodating. Playing it by the book. I've seen this before, judges behaving impeccably throughout the trial, giving away no grounds for review or complaint. And then, at sentencing, blowing your client away with a shocking sentence. Implacable.

27

The unit assembled regularly to report on intelligence issues and to discuss potential targets. They decided it was important to undertake an action that would signal to township residents that the ANC was not powerless against the occupying defence force.

While the unit had wanted to make a statement about taking the war to the white suburbs, the faulty detonator had resulted in more damage than was anticipated. The intended target, policemen, had escaped, and instead civilians, black and white, had caught the blast. The unit had qualms about involving civilians. The pictures of the injured after the Silverton explosion were disturbing and detracted from any sense of victory. This was not a war on a population, a point they made to one another after the Silverton mission. But they were acutely aware that whites continued to live a life of privilege and peace in protected suburbs while black townships were battlefields.

The unit resolved there should be no mistakes and no civilian deaths.

They would place a landmine in a part of Soshanguve that was used only by the SADF.

The unit agreed that Ting Ting, Joseph, Neo and the less frequently used member, Justice, would carry out the operation.

At a little after ten o'clock on the evening of 18 July 1986, Ting Ting drove the unit to the intersection and parked the Audi a short way off. He remained in the car while the three others laid the mine, a TM-52 landmine and detonator. They were carrying the hardware and a hand grenade in a small sports bag. The men wore dark tracksuits and coats. They were each armed with an AK-47. Joseph dug the hole with a trench spade. All of them were aware that if an army Casspir arrived they would be forced to fight.

Joseph placed the mine in the hollow, and inserted the small detonator about the size of a salt cellar into the mine, screwing it into place. The pin lay beneath it. The weight of a vehicle would drive the detonator onto the pin, igniting it and the encasing TNT.

He covered the mine with sand, smoothed the area around it and walked away to where the others stood. The street was deserted, the state of emergency had seen to that.

While standing at the intersection, they noticed a small car parked outside a nearby house. The car was close to where the mine was planted.

On the spur of the moment, the men decided to warn the owner of the car. Neo crossed the road, knocked on the door and told the man who answered that he should move his car inside his yard as it was parked in a dangerous place. It could be damaged by armoured vehicles turning at the intersection. The man looked at them intently. He got his keys and they accompanied him to his car.

This was dangerous. They should have completed the task and got out. At any moment a patrol could appear.

The man got into his car.

'Hurry up,' said Neo. 'We haven't got all night to help you.'

The man turned the key without taking his eyes off the group, clearly scared. The engine swung without catching. He tried again, the engine grinding slower and slower until there was merely a click each time he turned the key. The man looked at them, helpless.

Neo, irritated and realising that they had jeopardised their entire mission, told the man they'd push the car into the yard. Which they did.

The driver set the handbrake and got out. He turned to the men, his arms dangling limply.

Joseph, worried at the man's behaviour, asked, 'What is your job, my brother?'

The man didn't answer.

'We're asking you what job you do?' said Neo aggressively, his right arm beneath his coat on the butt of the AK-47.

'I am a policeman,' said the man.

They looked at him, his fear obvious. Neo broke the silence, quietly telling the man to leave his windows open. They left him standing in his front yard next to his car.

Two days later, when the landmine had still not been detonated, the unit became worried that the detonator might be faulty. Like the Silverton one. They decided that it was too dangerous to leave the mine where it was and that it should be removed. However, there was the policeman in the house across the road. By now he might have notified his superiors and the area could be under surveillance. There was a risk, but the mine had to be removed. The operation was scheduled for the next evening.

On the afternoon of 21 July 1986, the unit made contingency arrangements in case the police were waiting for them. It was decided that the same team would carry out the removal.

And then on the six o'clock news Joseph heard that a landmine had exploded in Soshanguve, detonated by a large caterpillar road grader from a private construction company. The driver, James Nkosi, had been injured in the explosion.

28

A few days before the trial, the accused are moved from Pretoria Maximum Security to Modder B Prison. I sense that the change of scenery will be welcomed, but also worry that the new routine and circumstances will upset the delicate equilibrium so critical in prison life. At Maximum Security they'd reached an accommodation with the warders. Now they will have to start again.

The warders in Modder B will be different. Not necessarily worse, just different. Getting to know them will require work and energy. These relationships are based on power and territory: points have to be made, boundaries drawn, and respect established. My other worry is that Modder B is not accustomed to dealing with serious political prisoners. Detainees, yes, but a high-profile MK assassination unit facing the death sentence might provoke even the most unassuming warder into rash behaviour.

As it turns out, the accused are placed in reasonably acceptable cells adjoining the prison's sanatorium. This is at the rear of the prison, and, in a sense, separate from the main block. Next to their cells are the doctor's consulting room and a number of other rooms with flat beds, steel wash basins and white cupboards.

I am to consult in a large rectangular room with a ping pong table. While my continued inclusion in the penal medical fraternity in the form of the sanatorium is welcome, my relegation to the games room from the status of the surgery in Pretoria Central disappoints me. I am, however, happy to hone my table tennis skills, although not with much success as Ting Ting and then Jabu fast emerge as the champions.

We reserve the end of each consultation for a tournament, characterised by remorseless needling and psychological power play. These are fantastic contests watched by a crowd of three, their heads swinging with each shot, their shouts and applause ringing through the passages. Occasionally, the disgruntled loser calls for 'order' or asks the crowd to 'settle down' in a vain effort to recover some dignity. ·

Dignity is not easy to find in Modder B. The warders are tougher and more aggressive than at Maximum Security. In fact, I have to threaten the prison commander with a legal interdict against his warders if the harassment doesn't stop. This produces results. Meanwhile preparations for the trial continue.

It is agreed that the four will wear dark suits, white shirts, sombre ties. They like the idea of dressing conservatively. If they cannot wear their own uniforms, this is the next best thing.

My new colleague Bheki Mlangeni takes their measurements for the suits, shows them ties, and organises good black shoes. We all agree that they should look like respectable citizens, far removed from the image depicted in the police press statements and amplified by crime reporters in the newspapers. 'Maybe,' Jabu says, 'in a different place and in another context, we might have worn dark suits and carried briefcases, instead of guns.'

Bheki and I spend a lot of time with them, talking and bringing news of what is happening outside. They soak up the information, occasionally commenting and expressing approval.

Bheki has joined the case because Thabo Molewa has taken on a major trial in the eastern Transvaal. Bheki started his articles with the firm in January 1989 and has proved himself a major asset. I'm grateful to have someone of his calibre with me. As his principal, I'm to mentor him and ensure that he receives the necessary training and experience during his two years of articles. He's a short, well-built man in his early thirties, with a premature sprinkle of grey in his hair. His hairstyle is quiet, he's avoided the glistening Afro favoured by the fashionable set.

Bheki had started a BA degree at Fort Hare University in the Eastern Cape but was expelled for 'political activity'. Thereafter, he moved to the University of the Witwatersrand (Wits) where, interrupted by frequent stints in detention, he continued his studies. He wrote his final BA exams while detained in solitary confinement under the state of emergency legislation. Thereafter, he completed his LLB. He was deeply involved in UDF politics and resistance work in Soweto.

The oldest of four children and the only one to make it through university, Bheki had told me with pride during the job interview that his father was a labourer for a swimming pool company. His mother, Catherine Mlangeni, was a machinist in a factory. For a black family from Jabulani, one of the poorer areas of Soweto, sending a child to university for seven years was a monumental achievement. There were very few black law students, and of those who did make it to an institution like Wits, even fewer got through their undergraduate degree, let alone the rest. The obstacles were too great. Bantu education had achieved its objectives. Bheki was the exception.

Soon after he'd started at the firm, I had taken Bheki for a drink and he'd told me how much his family had sacrificed to save the money for him to study law. They had invested in him totally. He also told me that despite his commitment to being a human-rights lawyer (salaries weren't high), he would nevertheless earn more money than the rest of his family put together and be able to pay them back many times over. Even now, on the meagre salary of an articled clerk, he delights in buying items for his parents' house that before they could only have dreamt about. Despite the different worlds we come from, we soon establish a good working relationship.

Bheki makes all the logistical arrangements for the families of the accused. He arranges for them to be taxied from their homes to court each day. He phones their employers, explains the circumstances and gets them granted unpaid leave. He disburses funds so they can buy lunch and cash to make up for their lack of income. Everything possible is done to ensure the families are prepared for the trauma of the trial.

We are helped in all this by the various support committees. In any major political trial, the internal resistance organisations establish support committees for the accused and their families. They're a great help, but one thing they cannot do is ease or remove the pain of seeing a loved one go on trial on a charge that carries the death sentence. They do what they can, offering material and emotional support.

The support takes the form of financial assistance as well as social care and counselling. Networks are set up around the parents, partners and families of the accused to look after their needs and ensure that they do not face this ordeal alone. The churches give pastoral support and advice, doctors are on call to minister to the health needs of the family, and psychologists give counselling where necessary. Others who have gone through similar experiences spend time with the families, sharing experience and comfort. Max and Audrey Coleman of the Detainees' Parents Support Committee spend much time with the parents talking them through the trial process and supporting them however they can. People from contrasting worlds sharing a common loss, their arrested and detained children.

Saki Macozoma of the South African Council of Churches plays a leading role in this case, coordinating the support groups and ensuring that the families receive support and care. Softly spoken and always in the background, he enables us to focus on the trial and the accused.

My clients prepare a statement to be read at the beginning of the trial. We work through it line by line. It explains that, as soldiers under military orders, they should not be tried in a criminal court by a minority government. The statement gives some context and politics to their actions and the trial, and challenges the 'terrorist' tag the prosecution will seek to hang on them.

Exposure for the ANC is also a key objective. Bheki and I debate each word with them. Given their non-participation stance, it is unlikely that the judge will allow their statement. Undoubtedly the prosecution will oppose the reading of their statement on the grounds that it is political positioning. If this happens, I will not be able to argue on behalf of my clients as, in the court's eyes, I don't represent them. It's a difficult situation. But even if they are denied the opportunity, there might be another occasion later in the trial. At worst, the statement could be used by the press.

Jabu, Ting Ting, Joseph and Neo are excited. They have been in custody awaiting trial for two years and four months. Even though they know where the trial will lead, they want it to start. The waiting is over.

THE BOMB

The vehicle or casing that Japie Kok uses for the P4 explosive is one that can be found in any department store and one which has battery-powered circuitry. Due to the distance involved, this device cannot be detonated by remote control and needs to work without being plugged to an electrical socket. Battery power is the only alternative. However, batteries are fallible as they have a limited lifespan. In this case, it has been calculated that the batteries will last the duration of the time that the explosive device will travel.

29

At nine o'clock on the evening of Friday 13 September 1986, Ting Ting, Neo and Joseph left the safe house in Block H Soshanguve by car. They'd been discussing their latest orders from their MK commanders over a few beers and were in a relaxed mood. As they passed a filling station, a car accelerated from the garage's forecourt and pulled in behind them. In the rearview mirror Ting Ting watched the headlights, kept his speed constant. Soon they were leading a cavalcade of five cars, and he pulled over to let them pass. But they wouldn't.

'We're being followed,' he said. Neo and Joseph turned to stare into the glare of headlights. Ting Ting drove on, hoping the cars would turn off into side roads or even stop at one of the shops along the street. At Winterveld he went right onto a dirt road, the dust swirling up behind them, blurring the headlights of the following cars.

'If it is police,' he said, 'they'll have to move soon before we're too deep into the houses where they might lose us if we run for it.'

The car behind them accelerated and drew level. Ting Ting looked right. The car's windows were down and three passengers were pointing R4 automatic rifles at them. Ting Ting braked to a slow stop.

'Stop the car. Out! Stand there,' the man in the front shouted in Afrikaans and English. The barrels of the R4s were close to Ting Ting, almost touched him. He could see the men were ready to fire.

Ting Ting was not too worried. He, Neo and Joseph were unarmed. There was nothing incriminating in the car. They got out. The car was quickly surrounded by men in plain clothes, carrying handguns and R4s.

The three men were pushed to the ground. Held fast there under rough boots.

'Where are the other two?' someone asked.

'There are no others, we are just three friends,' Ting Ting replied.

'What are your names?'

The three gave false names. Ting Ting calling himself Thabo Selepe. He could see men searching the car.

'Who is Ting Ting here?'

Ting Ting didn't answer. Hands hoisted him to his feet to face the man who'd been asking the questions. The man gestured at a kombi. Ting Ting was forced into it. Eight armed men followed him in.

'You think we don't know who you are?' one asked and suddenly they were shouting at him, hitting him hard in the face and in the stomach. He fell to the floor and they kicked him, the blood pouring from his nose and mouth onto his chest.

'I tell you, my name is Thabo, I don't know what you want.'

At Soshanguve police station the three were left in an office for about thirty minutes. Then they were separated, Ting Ting being taken to a police station in Pretoria and locked in a single cell. He was relieved that two weeks earlier he had taken Justice to Botswana to report and get further instructions from the ANC. At least he was safely out of the country. Jabu was currently sleeping at a safe house in Mamelodi and would know that if they did not make contact something was wrong, and he would immediately leave the country. Worried, but convinced they would not break his cover, he eventually fell asleep.

He woke at six the next morning, hungry and thirsty. He'd had nothing to eat or drink since his arrest. At about ten o'clock, he was taken to an office. Inside was a tall policeman with a black moustache. 'My name is Captain Hendrik Prinsloo,' he told Ting Ting. Together with two other policemen, Ting Ting was driven to Compol, police headquarters. On the way, he thought about leaping from the car, but the doors were fastened with child locks.

In an office at Compol, Ting Ting was ordered to sit on a chair. His hands were handcuffed behind the chair's back and his feet separately cuffed to the chair's front legs. Sweat beaded on his forehead and dripped into his eyes.

Captain Prinsloo walked in and closed the door quietly. 'Ja, Commissar Bells,' he said, 'I know your journey. Every camp you've been in and what you've done. First, I will speak and then you will speak, okay?' But he didn't expect Ting Ting to answer.

'Before that,' he said, 'you need to eat and drink. What do you want?'

Ting Ting told him and a policeman was instructed to get the food.

'When you've eaten, we'll talk,' said Captain Prinsloo, leaving him alone.

In due course his meal arrived and Ting Ting picked at the food, forcing it down. When he'd finished, Captain Prinsloo and another policeman returned. The other man, white and short with an athletic build, positioned himself in a corner. Ting Ting thought he could be Portuguese.

Captain Prinsloo spoke clearly but softly, his voice deep. He summarised Ting Ting's military training, concluding with the exact route that Ting Ting had taken to infiltrate the country. At this point he stopped. 'Now you continue, Bells,' he said.

Ting Ting did so, giving details about his equipment and weaponry and the address of the house in Winterveld where he'd stayed. He mentioned a gun, a Makarov, that was still there. And then he hesitated as he searched for information that would satisfy them. He saw Captain Prinsloo nod at a large black policeman. Picking up Ting Ting's empty Coca Cola bottle, the man smashed it down on Ting Ting's kneecap. Ting Ting yelled in pain. The policeman hit him again, harder. Then again and again. The pain was excruciating.

Ting Ting tried to describe the shooting of the policeman Seun Vuma, but the beating intensified, the policeman hitting him in the face with the bottle. In a haze, he noticed that the Coca Cola cop, as he now thought of him, was smartly dressed.

He needed a reference point, something on which he could focus. He seized on the long grey pants of the Coca Cola cop, recognising them as 'Dobbshires', noticing also the neat golf shirt worn by the man. The trousers had turn-ups. Again the bottle was slammed down on his kneecap. Ting Ting shouted in agony. Surely his bone must have broken.

If they would stop beating him, Ting Ting shouted, he would talk. But the beating didn't stop until the bottle slipped out of the policeman's hand. Captain Prinsloo held up his hand to stop the assault.

'You know, Ting Ting,' he said, 'we don't want to use the third degree on you. But we will if we have to. You must cooperate fully. You are not helping me. You are not talking to me. Why are you ignoring me? Another thing, we know where your mother lives, maybe we should detain her? Let's go for a ride, Ting Ting.'

The handcuffs around Ting Ting's ankles were unlocked and he was taken from the room, down in the lift to the same kombi with the seats along the side. He was pushed in. The Coca Cola cop sat opposite, stared with intent, but said nothing.

Other policemen in full combat gear and armed with R4 rifles took their seats in the vehicle. They drove to the house of Ting Ting's uncle in Winterveld, the house where Ting Ting had been staying. When the kombi stopped, the blindfold they had put on him was removed and a black balaclava with eye slits was placed over Ting Ting's head and he was led into the house. He saw his cousin Sarah, his uncle Japie Sindani and, to his horror and surprise, Jabu. Jabu was up against the wall, his hands above his head. Their eyes met.

30

At midday on Saturday 14 September 1986, Jabu and a friend called Thabo took a taxi from Naledi in Mamelodi to the safe house in Winterveld to meet the other three members of the unit. The house was owned by Ting Ting's uncle and the unit had stayed there from time to time.

Jabu and Thabo arrived at about three o'clock to learn that the others had slept elsewhere the previous evening. This was contrary to their arrangement and Jabu worried that something had gone wrong. The unit had strict rules about sleeping arrangements and he had to be notified of changes. This was an unusual situation. It had never happened before that any members of the squad had gone missing – three missing was ominous.

Jabu decided to leave immediately. Something was wrong. While gathering his belongings he glanced out a window to see a policeman in combat uniform jumping the wall. More police followed and positioned themselves behind it, R4 combat rifles at the ready.

Was this a routine search and seizure or was the unit the target? Was this the day they'd spoken about?

What perplexed Jabu were the defensive positions taken by the policemen. They faced the street, as if they were expecting an attack on the house.

Apart from Jabu and Thabo, Jabu's uncle and a young woman named Sarah were the only people in the house. Jabu told them not to panic. He would do the talking but if the police questioned them they were to say that he was a family friend from Soweto. Jabu's uncle didn't know what operations the unit had conducted but he knew the men had been trained outside the country. Much to Jabu's relief, he wasn't carrying a weapon and there was nothing in the house to give them away.

The front door banged open and the police rushed in, guns at the ready. Jabu and the others put up their hands. The police took up positions at the windows, again facing outwards. Two white policemen entered, pushing a black man, his hands cuffed behind his back and a balaclava over his head, only the eyes showing. It was Ting Ting.

The policemen went into the bedroom in which Ting Ting slept. Jabu, facing the wall, his hands above his head, listened to the sounds of them searching the room: overturning the beds and rummaging through the cupboard. They emerged prodding Ting Ting before them. To Jabu's surprise one of the policemen held a pistol that Ting Ting must have left hidden in the room. Ting Ting was then taken outside and the white policeman turned to Jabu and Thabo.

Jabu explained who they were. The policeman asked if they knew the blindfolded man. Jabu replied that he didn't. He knew he was at a disadvantage, convinced that the others had been arrested but unsure if they had mentioned him.

The four of them had often discussed this moment. They'd sworn to hold out as long as possible and then only speak about the acts in which they'd been involved personally. They knew that arrest would be followed by torture and that it might be impossible to hold out for too long. Although two days was a long time under interrogation and torture, they felt that if they could endure this long the others would have time to leave the country. Nevertheless, the prospect of two days of hell filled them with dread.

Jabu estimated that Ting Ting must have been arrested late the previous day. The way the security police were behaving led him to believe that Ting Ting hadn't mentioned him. Then again they could be playing with him. First get the gun, put Ting Ting back in the van and then sort out Jabu. But he knew that it was highly likely that they'd have arrested him immediately if they knew who he was. He was a bigger prize than Ting Ting's weapon. He realised then that the police didn't expect anyone in the house to be dangerous. They were guarding against attack from the outside. So maybe he still had a chance.

The policemen were behind him now, silent, waiting. The impasse became unbearable and Jabu asked if he could lower his arms. No answer.

Eventually came a question: 'Do you live here?'

'No, I live in Soweto, I am a friend of the family, just visiting them,' he replied.

'Where do you work?'

'I sell vegetables in Soweto.'

'Do you know the man we just brought into the house?'

'No, I've not seen him before.'

'Turn around.'

Jabu turned to face four policemen. The one asking the questions was white. The others watched him closely. Thabo remained standing with his arms against the wall.

The questioning continued. The policeman pointed at the young cousin, Sarah, and asked, 'Do you know this girl?'

'Yes, I know her,' said Jabu.

Aggressively, the policeman rounded on the girl. 'And do you know him? Who is he?'

The girl glanced at Jabu and blurted out that she didn't know him. He looked at her in shock, it had been going well up to now.

'Bring them with us,' the white policeman ordered.

Jabu and Thabo were handcuffed and taken to the police station at Soshanguve. Jabu was put in a room alone. No one questioned him; no one spoke to him.

About an hour later, they were transferred to police headquarters at the Compol Building in central Pretoria. Again Jabu was left alone. Soon a tall policeman with silver-grey hair came in to question him. Where did he live? Where did he work? How much money did he make? Where did his parents live? Did they have a phone number? If he only sold vegetables, where did he get the nice clothes he was wearing? The questions went on and on. He answered them, mixing truth with invention. The man with the silver hair became more friendly, said that his name was Colonel Erasmus and that he was in charge of security in the area. He only had a few more questions.

Jabu was relaxed. Things were going well. They spoke in Afrikaans and there was no hitting or shouting. He believed that if he could get through the questions and be released, he would leave the country that night. He would be gone.

The door opened and a man entered. He wore a black hood and at first Jabu thought it might be Ting Ting. But this man wasn't handcuffed. They stared at one another in silence. The policemen arrayed behind the hooded man watched Jabu closely, waiting. With consternation, Jabu realised this was an identification process. The hooded man must be an askari. Calmly, he turned his back on the hooded man and said to Erasmus, 'I don't know what is going on here, but this man in the hood frightens me. Who is he? What does he want from me?' Behind him, he heard the man in the hood approaching. Colonel Erasmus said nothing. The man behind him said, 'Ja, Jabu, and how are things in Viana?'

Before Jabu could reply, the policemen moved in fast, hitting him. Jabu tried to protect himself as he fell, shouting, 'Why were you hitting me?' The blows were hard, he doubled up with pain.

Soon the beating stopped and Jabu was taken to another room. Inside were Ting Ting, Neo and Joseph, their faces swollen, their clothing torn. They looked at him with exhausted red eyes, desperate and helpless. Even if they had not broken, they could not go on for much longer. Ting Ting and Neo were in a particularly bad way, with Neo's right eye blood red and swollen.

'Do you know these men?' asked a white policeman.

'Yes,' Jabu replied.

Roughly, the policemen dragged him off to another room. They closed the door and forced him to sit on a chair. The beating started, blows, kicks. One white man, one black man who took it in turns to assault him. Knew where to hit him on his body and his face. He felt his face swelling, blood in his mouth. The men asked no questions and, in the midst of his pain and confusion, Jabu wondered if they would even be interested in taking him to court or whether they would simply kill him.

He lost track of time, unsure if the beating lasted two hours or twenty minutes. Dazed, he was dragged out of the building to a police van. Surely he was going to be executed. Taken to some desolate spot in the veld, shot and buried.

A short distance off stood a group of black policemen, among them a man in civilian clothes. Jabu recognised the grey trousers and blue shirt as the clothes worn by the hooded man. He remembered the man's name, Fana. They'd been together in 'Viana', MK's transit camp in Angola. Jabu called out to Fana that he would kill him. Fana didn't respond but the black policemen rushed forward and beat Jabu with sticks, forcing him into the back of the police van.

Jabu was taken to the Silverton police station where he spent the night alone in a single cell. He learnt that the others were being held at different police stations as they were regarded as too dangerous to be together. The one consolation Jabu had as the unit's commander was that Justice Mbizana had been sent to Botswana two weeks earlier. At least he was safe.

Early the next morning, Jabu was returned to Compol and taken to a room where four policemen waited. He sat on a chair facing them, his hands cuffed behind his back. He prayed for the strength to get through the coming ordeal.

One of the men introduced himself as Captain Prinsloo and said he was running the investigation. Prinsloo was tanned, his features hard, his mouth emphasised by a thick black moustache. Calm and in control, Prinsloo asked Jabu if he wanted anything to eat. Jabu thought he was joking, but asked for fish, bread and milk. He was going to need his strength and solid food would help, if it was a serious offer. Much to his surprise, Prinsloo sent off one of the policemen.

The questioning started only to be interrupted by the arrival of the food. Jabu was worried that it might be poisoned but felt that he was doomed and might as well eat. Prinsloo watched him while he ate, and when he'd finished the meal said, gently, almost fatherly, 'You have two choices, Jabu. We will make you talk, everyone talks, you know, they really do, trust me on this. Either you can save yourself a lot of pain by talking now, or you can go through a lot of pain and then talk anyway. When it is over, you will know that you have betrayed your comrades and then you will go to jail for a very long time or you may be hanged. We already know what you have done, the others have talked. You can have the pain and the jail, or you can join us. We have a special unit for people like you. We will keep you safe and give you money and food. Of course, you must help us in our work, but you will not be in jail or dead. And you know what, if you are worried about selling out your former comrades, let me tell you, you are going to betray them anyway. You will betray them once my men start to work on you. In the next few hours or maybe in a day if you are strong, but I promise you, you will break and tell us everything. Tell me what you are thinking, Jabu?'

While Jabu had lain awake in his cell at the Silverton police station the previous night, he had decided that he would give them something upfront, almost as a gesture of good faith. This would buy time and give those who had helped them with houses and support time to make their arrangements.

'Ask me the questions,' he said, avoiding a direct answer, knowing that he could never become an askari.

The questioning started. Jabu told them about his leaving the country and joining the ANC, his training and when he had returned. Prinsloo listened quietly, occasionally prompting him. There was no violence. He told them of the Orphan Chapi killing in Soweto and admitted that he was responsible. He felt comfortable with this admission since it was a solo mission and did not involve the others.

Prinsloo told him to write down the events leading to Chapi's assassination. Jabu obliged, writing slowly, choosing his words. When he had finished, Prinsloo said, 'Now tell me about the missions with Ting Ting and the others.'

'I did not have time to undertake any missions with the others,' said Jabu. 'They have just come into the country and we were still in the process of deciding what to do.'

'What were your instructions?'

'We were not given specific instructions. We had to identify the targets and if we were not sure about them, we had to get permission from the ANC. But we were also given the clear authority to identify discretionary targets.'

'You are lying to me,' said Prinsloo calmly. 'Think about what you are saying.'

'That is the truth, I cannot tell you more,' said Jabu.

Prinsloo straightened, turned his back on Jabu and nodded to the policemen standing behind the chair. The beating began. This time there was no control. Most of the hitting was done by the black policemen, although on one occasion a white policeman came close to Jabu and then, very suddenly, hit him in the face with such force that he was knocked to the floor still attached to the chair. The policeman exclaimed, cursing foully as he flexed his fist injured by the impact. The side of Jabu's face was completely numb. He was pulled back into a sitting position and the body blows continued. Although he tried to keep his eyes open, eventually he preferred the comfort of darkness. He tasted the salt of his own blood. Again time lost meaning.

They shouted at him to tell the truth and he told them he knew nothing more. He could hear beatings going on in other rooms. Shouts and screams. The day became a procession of agony and shock, a lonely battered journey down an endless corridor. His body sweated pain. The policemen, now tired, pulled out his hair. They held up clumps of black curls in their hands and said he would never have hair again. They laughed.

Strangely, beneath the pain, his mind was clear and he thought of what he should say. Of how much he should give and when. He wondered how much the others had said. He was sure they were in the rooms along the corridor because occasionally the police would talk among themselves, as if some new information had come to light. That they were still being interrogated and tortured meant that the police believed they had more to give. On the other hand, Prinsloo was often called out into the corridor and would return to taunt him. 'You know, Jabu,' he would say, 'there is no reason to hold out. There is a lot of talking at the end of the corridor. You are being stupid.' Sometimes he would toss in a scrap of information that he could only have got from the others. Or maybe it wasn't from them. It could equally be from an informant, Jabu reasoned.

As the day wore on, he sensed himself withdrawing from the situation, turning inward. He hurt on the outside but at his centre he was clear and clean. While this lasted he felt he would make it through the day.

Emboldened, Jabu told Prinsloo that he had nothing more to tell and that they should take him into the veld and shoot him. Prinsloo, who never participated in the torture and never lost his temper, said, 'Jabu, we must both accept that this is a long and slow process and you must know that it will not stop until I have everything I want. We have all the time in the world, there is no rush.'

'I cannot talk about things I do not know, no matter how much you hit me,' said Jabu, the words emerging thick and viscous through the warm mush in his mouth, his swollen lips slurring his speech.

With complete confidence, Prinsloo slowly walked up to Jabu and, looking down, said, 'You will talk, I promise you. You will talk. You have already started and you will continue. Soon the building will be empty and then we will stop playing with you, then we get serious. Think about it, Jabu. This can stop anytime.'

His eyes swollen slits, Jabu looked at Prinsloo but said nothing. The policemen talked among themselves and Prinsloo and another policeman left the room, leaving two behind to watch over him. Blessed relief.

Jabu spent most of the Sunday with his hands cuffed behind his back on the chair. The only relief was when he needed the toilet. On these occasions, he was taken by two policemen and his handcuffs removed. Back on the chair after these short breaks, he felt strong inside himself, thinking that if he could last most of the day, he could see it through into the night. The pain was still constant, yet he felt in control of his body, especially the untouchable centre that he'd found deep within.

Many hours later, Prinsloo returned accompanied by a man carrying a blindfold and a length of steel chain. Jabu was released from the handcuffs and told to strip. Naked and sitting on the chair, he was cuffed again, blindfolded and his feet strapped with the chain. In this darkness Jabu knew a rising terror. What was going to happen now? A cold object was held against his shoulder and suddenly electric shocks racked his body. A booted foot stood on the chain, forcing his feet to the floor. Great convulsions tore through his body and he screamed. He seemed to explode, and quickly it was over. Sweat poured from him as his muscles slackened and his head rolled forward. He'd bitten a chunk from his cheek and blood filled his mouth. Then his head snapped back as the current rushed through him again. He jerked, spasmed, screamed uncontrollably. This was worse, much worse, as the voltage increased. The shocks came in short bursts, smashing the refuge inside which had been his sanctuary. Obliterating thought and reason. Pain had a colour. It was silver – the blade of a knife.

Jabu heard Prinsloo give instructions to stop. 'Are we ready to have a conversation, Jabu?' he asked. Jabu shook his head.

The attachment to his shoulder was removed and fastened to his inner upper thigh. In terror, waiting for the shocks, he knew before it happened that he wouldn't make it this time. The darkness in his head exploded in screaming light as the electricity convulsed him, his legs contorting. He heard shouts of pain that were like the deep bellows of a dying animal, long and unremitting, echoing through the building.

The shocks stopped and as the blanket of pain lifted, Jabu realised that the sounds were his own. The pain stopped and he heard the policemen laughing. Then Prinsloo said quietly in Afrikaans, 'Put it on his balls.'

From a distant place Jabu heard himself respond in the same language, 'I will talk.'

Late in the afternoon and barely conscious, they dumped him in a cell at the Silverton police station, his body broken.

Early on the Monday morning, Jabu was taken to Compol to face the same interrogation team. He sat dazed and aching, barely able to move, waiting for the first blows. He felt he could go no further. That he'd come to the end.

He was asked what food he wanted. Fish, milk and bread. And this was brought. After he'd eaten, Prinsloo told Jabu that he would be taken to a magistrate to make a statement. 'You must tell the magistrate what you told us yesterday. You will say that you are making the statement freely and voluntarily. If you talk about the shocks or being hit, you will be brought straight back here and you will not sleep for a week, that I can promise you. You will find that I always keep my promises.'

He instructed the policemen to give Jabu fresh clothes and get him cleaned up.

The office of the magistrate was sparse. The man sat at his desk and asked if Jabu was acting under duress or had been assaulted or influenced in the making of his statement. Jabu replied that he had not, and waited for the magistrate to comment on his damaged face. He'd seen himself in a toilet mirror and was shocked at his bruised and swollen face. No one could ignore his state.

In Afrikaans, Jabu told the magistrate that he had been assaulted and that he was sore. Unmoved, the magistrate asked him to sign the statement, countersigned it himself, and nodded to the security policemen. Jabu was manhandled back to the van. He wasn't surprised by the magistrate's indifference. This was how he'd been told the process would work. He could expect no protection from the department of justice.

Back at Compol, Jabu sat cuffed, dreading Prinsloo's wrath. Eventually Prinsloo came in and said, 'I hear you didn't listen to me, Jabu.' Jabu looked up at the policeman without responding. 'It is over. Now I want everything from you. Every single detail,' said Prinsloo. 'I know you will cooperate. I think we understand each other now.'

The police interrogated and beat Jabu throughout the day. Behind their questions and their blows loomed the threat of the electric torture. If they were quieter and shouted less, it was because this was a normal working day. They also took longer breaks between the sessions. For Jabu, the start of each session was the worst. He was ashamed at how quickly he had given the information the previous day once the electric shocks began.

The interrogation and torture continued over the next few weeks, interrupted by trips to the magistrate and to point out places where the actions had occurred. In a spiral of helplessness and desperation, feeling betrayed by his body, Jabu considered suicide. But the police had thought of that and made sure he couldn't take his own life. He belonged to them.

Jabu spent the next eight months in solitary confinement. He did not know if the other members of the unit were dead or alive.

31

Driving to Delmas for the first day of the trial on 1 February 1989, there is little conversation between Bheki and me. The classical music tape that he has brought along plays softly in the background. We are preoccupied with our own thoughts and I am concerned about how the prosecution will react to the accused's declaration of non-participation. Winning without opposition carries no triumph. They will suspect trickery and conspiracy, and certainly question the motives of the accused and their lawyers, and with good reason. They will be furious at having spent more than two years preparing for a high-profile trial against a lethal MK assassination unit, only to find there will be no defence at all. Upstaged in their own court. For the first time, I am looking forward to speaking to Harry Prinsloo and Louisa van der Walt. However, I will leave that to the moment before the judge enters the court.

I turn left off the double-lane highway to Witbank, right over the bridge, around the corner and straight into a police roadblock. Dressed in camouflaged combat uniform, a big florid sergeant approaches the car, a Star service pistol riding easily on his hip. Behind him are two policemen with R4 combat rifles. Looking into the car, the sergeant sees a black man and a white man both in suits, a bad combination. Suspicious, but not aggressive, he asks, 'And where are you going, Meneer?'

'To the court,' I reply. 'We are the lawyers for the accused in the treason trial.' He steps back, looks warily at me, nods and waves us on.

There are a number of vehicles clustered around the courthouse, large buses and mini-bus taxis. On the pavement, six police armoured vehicles – Mellow Yellows – are lined up. Inside them are men in camouflage uniforms, heavily armed. They are predators. The crowd their prey. The key is to avoid eye contact. That would be an invitation. At the end of the road are more police. A big presence for the first day.

Inside the court is a security checkpoint with a metal detector and a bomb detector. Everyone is searched and the police open bags. The police commander, tall and trim with a clipped moustache, ensures his men miss nothing.

We enter the court from a door on the left reserved for legal representatives. A thick Perspex screen has been erected between the dock where the accused will sit and the public gallery. The front of the court is in quarantine and the accused and the lawyers are cut off from everyone else.

'You like the security, Peter?' says a deep voice behind me. Turning, I see a man of medium height, thick black moustache, dark brown eyes and black hair, his face lined and weathered. He wears a dark grey suit and black shoes, not the light blue-grey suits and matching shoes favoured by most security policemen.

Ignoring the question, I say, 'How are you, Captain Prinsloo?'

'Ag, busy, Peter, busy,' he says with the serious air of an accountant after a hard day at the office.

If Prinsloo is busy, then someone somewhere is in trouble. Hendrik Prinsloo is one of the most experienced investigating officers in the security police. Unlike others, he never appears to let political malice cloud his judgement. He may feel it but he doesn't show it. He's an impassive professional who approaches each case with the grim calm of a gunfighter. But, I know that despite the professional demeanour, he won't hesitate to use any means to build his case. Severe torture is one of those means.

'Captain,' I say, 'I see we have the normal problem of your policemen taking up the first two rows of the gallery. They're making a small court even smaller. You have got enough police here and outside, why don't you just leave the gallery for the public, for the families?'

'Security, Peter,' he says with a shrug and wanders away.

I feel the frustration of the powerless. The police always fill the first two benches on the opening day of a trial. It puts a buffer between the accused and the gallery – although in this case there is already a screen. Also it means fewer members of the public and press can attend. This minimises potential disturbances and maliciously deprives the accused of an opportunity to see their family and friends. Given the huge tension on the first day of a political trial, these small acts of spite often explode into violence between the police and supporters of the accused.

At the public entrance to the court, I find Mrs Masina. A pushing crowd has blocked the door. She is upset and angry and has been told that the court is full and there is no space for her inside. Taking her by the hand, I push my way through to the young white policeman at the door.

'This is the mother of one of the accused,' I say. 'Let her through.'

Strong and arrogant, he replies, 'There is no more room.'

I can see at least three rows of empty seats. 'Rubbish, man, there are lots of seats left. There is space for her and many others. What are you up to here?'

'Those seats are for the police,' he says.

Starting to lose it, I say, 'Are you mad? The police have already taken the first two rows. What do you want to do, fill the whole court with police?'

He looks at me smugly but doesn't respond.

Red mist rises behind my eyes. I shout at him so loudly he jumps. 'You think this is a bloody game, you idiot! This is a treason trial in which men are facing the death sentence. You want me to call the judge here right now? You want the press to write this down and make you famous as another stupid policeman? You want me to start this trial by bringing an urgent application to get access to the court and a costs order against you personally? Now do your duty and let these people in. Now, constable, now!'

While I'm shouting, fury in my throat, I suddenly realise the crowd has gone quiet. The policeman drops his eyes, his power stripped from him, a youth in a uniform confused by my reaction. He steps aside to let the people stream in and I stand there exhausted and taut, feeling guilty for having gone for a soft target.

My next priority is to meet with Judge de Klerk. He is in his chambers with two other men, whom he introduces as his assessors, a Mr de Kock and a Dr Botha. I introduce Bheki and de Klerk greets him and shakes his hand. The others merely nod.

'Have your clients changed their position or not, Mr Harris?' asks the judge.

'No, Judge, they have not. Nothing has altered since we last spoke.'

The assessors exchange glances. 'I should mention, Judge,' I add, 'that the accused have prepared a short statement which they want to read out. I believe this statement explains their position.'

The judge nods.

We head back to court. I see that Louisa van der Walt and Harry Prinsloo are setting up their papers and books at the prosecution stand where Captain Prinsloo is also seated.

At the entrance to the dock, a policeman guards the stairs leading up from the cells. Bheki asks to see the accused. The policeman glances at Captain Prinsloo, gets the nod, and Bheki disappears below.

I greet the prosecutors. 'By the way,' I say, placing my notepad on top of the case file, 'the accused have decided not to participate in the trial.'

The two stop arranging their books and look at me blankly. 'What do you mean?' asks Louisa van der Walt.

I repeat myself, adding, 'Just go ahead and do what you have to do. This is going to be an easy one. Another notch in your gun.'

'That's why there are no counsel?' says Harry Prinsloo.

'Correct,' I say.

'Are they mad?'

I shrug.

'The judge won't accept this,' says van der Walt.

'He doesn't have a choice, and neither do you, Louisa. This is their decision.'

She slams down the books on the table and the retort draws attention. 'This is totally unacceptable, to be told this on the morning of the trial!' Her voice is shrill, angry. I can see her point. Harry is also upset, but keeping a grip on himself. He can see the politics moving away from them, and there's nothing they can do about it. The focus will now be on the unusual stance of the accused, rather than on their activities.

Captain Prinsloo, grasping it far quicker, shakes his head. 'Clever,' he says to himself.

Returning to our desk in the middle of the court, between the dock and the elevated judge's podium, I am joined by Bheki. He lets me know the accused are fine. Struggling in a morass of hate, and tired from the constant conflict, I just want the trial to start.

'All set then,' I say, looking at Captain Prinsloo.

The policemen lining the walls of the court stand erect and tense as

Captain Prinsloo turns to the policeman at the top of the stairs leading to the cells below and says in Afrikaans, 'Bring them.'

One by one they move into the dock behind us. Jabu turns to the gallery, raises a clenched fist and shouts, 'Amandla!' The gallery returns the call. The police lurch forward to restrain the accused, but Captain Prinsloo waves them back. Jabu, Ting Ting, Neo and Joseph turn to face the front. Immaculately dressed in dark suits, white shirts and ties, they look like businessmen rather than 'terrorists'. The prosecutors are surprised at their dress, clearly thinking it carries meaning but unsure what that is.

The judge is called and the orderly intones the time-honoured instruction, 'Staan in die Hof! Stand in court.' Judge de Klerk and his two assessors walk in. We are in session.

THE BOMB

Japie Kok is sent on an out-of-town mission for a few days and hands over the operation to his brother, Captain Kobus Kok, who is also an explosives expert based in the technical division.

Kobus Kok knows that because the P4 explosive is very stable, he will need a stronger detonator than usual. He chooses a military detonator of Eastern bloc origin that has the necessary strength and power. He likes the idea of using an Eastern bloc detonator as it opens the door to blame the bomb attack on the ANC and its Soviet allies.

Kobus Kok removes the wiring from the machine that will carry the charge, replacing it with wiring from an obsolete piece of equipment imported from England. The purpose of changing the wiring is that the wires must be capable of carrying a particular level of charge to detonate the explosive material. In this case, three amps is more than sufficient.

As with most bombs, the electrical charge activates the detonator when a button is pressed on the device and the electrical circuit is connected.

The difficult part is ensuring that the recipient of the device is not suspicious of the package that he (in this instance the target is a male) will receive, and that he will want to press the button that will activate the explosive device and kill him. An entrapment device is needed, something alluring. Easier said than done when your target is himself an experienced killer.

32

Captain Prinsloo was a patient man. He chose to let others cover the ground, moving in for the final moments. He was on the trail of Justice Mbizana, the fifth man in the unit. Captain Prinsloo had positioned askaris at the train and bus stations in Johannesburg and Pretoria on the off-chance they might spot the fugitive. To no avail. He had combed the streets of Mamelodi where Justice grew up. He had tortured the other members of the unit, and all he had learnt was that Justice had gone to Botswana two weeks before the unit was caught. It was a great pity that he had slipped through the net. For Captain Prinsloo, he was the one outstanding piece of the puzzle.

Then in early 1987, just over three months after the arrest of the unit, an informant revealed that a man thought to be Justice was hiding in a house in Eersterus, Pretoria. The informant had other news. This man planned to avenge the arrest of his comrades.

The arrest of Justice Mbizana took place shortly before nine o'clock in the evening at the house in Eersterus. The police team was led by Captain Prinsloo. It was swift and efficient. Justice was alone in the house and within minutes he was handcuffed and bundled into the back of a sealed van and driven to police headquarters – Compol. He was taken straight to an office on the first floor, where his interrogation started immediately.

The questioning continued through the night and into the following day, mainly by Captain Prinsloo assisted by constables Mathebula and Matjeni. Captain Prinsloo concentrated on the interrogation with single-minded attention. It was known that he hated disruptions, and those who slipped in to learn from his meticulous approach did so quietly, fearing the captain's wrath.

Oblivious to those around him, Captain Prinsloo laboured into the night, taking food and smoke breaks from time to time. Throughout he ensured that Justice also received sustenance, including coffee when he wanted it. Captor and captive even smoked cigarettes together.

With daylight breaking, Captain Prinsloo and Constable Mathebula took the manacled Justice to the washing area set aside for black policemen on the fourth floor. With a hand towel, Captain Prinsloo washed the sweat and grime from Justice. To his prisoner he remarked, 'You know, Justice, this is the first time that I am bathing a terrorist.'

The interrogation of Justice had been interspersed with punches, slaps and kicks, but there remained areas in which it was clear that Justice was holding back. At one stage, Constable Matjeni held Justice on the floor while a rubber tube was drawn around his neck. Captain Prinsloo stood back, silently watching. The tube was slowly tightened until Justice choked. He jerked and pitched, Constable Matjeni restraining him. Then the rubber tube was released and Justice gasped for air. The procedure was repeated. Then again and again. All through the next day and into the night Justice held out on the essential information Captain Prinsloo required.

It was clear that the interrogation needed to take a different form in a different place. Here Captain Prinsloo had in mind a farm in the Hammanskraal area where the interrogation could continue unrestrained. The farm was a venue he'd used before, both for reconnaissance and for interrogation. As everyone on the team knew, when a subject was taken to the farm for further questioning, it was serious.

The farm, named Klipdrift, presumably after the well-known brandy, was made available courtesy of its owner, a Mr Pretorius. Mr Pretorius was well disposed to the security police and friendly with Captain Prinsloo. The police were free to erect their tents and Mr Pretorius saw to it that they had water and braai wood. The primary facility that the farm offered was its isolation.

The difficulty of removing a severely beaten Justice from Compol was solved by forcing him into a metal trunk and carrying him to the waiting police van. It was imperative that no one saw the captive, for his arrest and detention had not been recorded in any occurrence book or in any police record. In fact, apart from the policemen who had participated in his arrest, there was no record of Justice ever having been in police custody.

It was a struggle to get Justice into the trunk. It could be closed but not locked. Nevertheless, the trunk was carried to the lift and then to the kombi parked directly in front of Compol. Not far off was the Supreme Court at the far end of Church Square. Once in the vehicle, Justice was pulled from the trunk.

At the farm, constables Mathebula, Matjeni and Kruger were assigned the task of guarding Justice. That night he was tied to a camp bed so that his guards, Mathebula and Matjeni, could get some rest.

The next day the interrogation of Justice continued. Captain Prinsloo ensured that there was no violence, and, blessed with the luxury of time and space, he prodded and probed Justice for the information he sought. Justice gave but also held back, mildly irritating his interrogators although Captain Prinsloo knew it was just a matter of time before Justice broke.

Another reason for a more 'gentle' approach was Captain Prinsloo's belief that Justice could become an askari. To turn someone so well trained, and who had reported to Chris Hani, would be a coup.

Over the next few days, a strange rapport developed between the two, with the captain sometimes asking questions, on other occasions sounding out Justice on his attitude to joining the police. Invariably Justice would say that he needed time to consider the offer. Nodding, Captain Prinsloo would confirm that there was no rush.

Justice gave more. He told of an occasion in July 1986 in Mamelodi when the unit was trailing a police armoured vehicle, a 'Hippo'. They'd been on the trail for thirty minutes and Justice was waiting for the right moment to fire the RPG. Suddenly the armoured vehicle accelerated, turned a corner and simply vanished. Just like that. Both men laughed at the anecdote.

There were times when Prinsloo was absent from the farm, sometimes for days, but he kept strict control of the process, knowing the danger of having different points of authority in an interrogation process. Varying styles confused the subject, leading to resistance and the loss of valuable information. It was important to keep the bond between captor and captive.

The other members of the team were aware of Captain Prinsloo's interrogation technique and stayed in the background, giving support only. But issues arose. The presence of Captain Sakkie Crafford, recently transferred from the detective branch and nominally more senior than Prinsloo, became problematic. Captain Prinsloo regarded him as a novice and would not be distracted by the captain's blustering. In fact, Crafford had been assigned to the team by their commander Brigadier Cronje precisely because he had much to learn in this delicate area of security police interrogations. And who better to learn from than the master, Captain Prinsloo.

Captain Prinsloo suffered the presence of Captain Crafford. Often Crafford tried to assert his seniority. Questioned methods. Wanted more force. Missed the bigger picture. The other members of the team – Captain van Jaarsveld, Lieutenant Roodt and Warrant Officer Strydom – sensed Captain Prinsloo's irritation but could not intervene between the two men.

As the sessions proceeded, the flow of information from Justice diminished, and then, as Captain Prinsloo pressed further on names and details, it dried up. The real prize that Prinsloo sought was the MK operational commander in Swaziland. Known by the MK name of 'Gebhuza', he was responsible for the entire Northern Transvaal machinery of MK. The infiltration of MK guerrillas and their sphere of operations, including all instructions and information, flowed to and from MK high command through Gebhuza. The man had a reputation for fearlessness and efficiency. Captain Prinsloo knew that if Gebhuza could be eliminated, it would be a major blow to MK.

It was imperative that he got the correct information from Justice on Gebhuza. Cooperation was critical. He needed details of routine movements; receipt, flow and storage of weapons; modes of communications; safe houses; sleeping arrangements; vehicle descriptions and registration numbers; guards and security; but, unlike other areas in which he had been cooperative, when it came to Gebhuza, Justice held back.

After six days of questioning, it was clear that Justice would not reveal the details needed. Finally, Justice refused to talk. Captain Prinsloo spent time with his stubborn captive, at first talking, then threatening, but nothing was forthcoming. In frustration, and with the weekend approaching, Captain Prinsloo left the farm, consigning Justice to Captain Crafford and the rest of the men. They were under strict instructions not to question Justice until his return.

On Saturday, at about half past six in the evening, Captain Crafford, Captain van Jaarsveld and Warrant Officer Strydom went to buy food in Pretoria. While they were gone, the constables gathered wood and lit a fire, as the evening was surprisingly chilly. Justice was bound to his bed in the tent.

At about ten thirty Captain Crafford, Captain van Jaarsveld and Warrant Officer Strydom returned. They'd been drinking heavily. Their speech was slurred and Warrant Officer Strydom held a bottle of J&B whisky. Captain Crafford ordered that Justice be brought from his tent. When he emerged, he was instructed to strip. Naked, he was led to a tree and tied tightly to it, his arms outstretched above his head. The men began their 'interrogation', except this was not an interrogation, it was drunken fun. Again and again, Justice was hit in the face and on his head. Captain Crafford pulled out his pistol and put it against Justice's head, the barrel

pointing upwards, and emptied the magazine, the shots loud and cracking, echoing and chasing each other over the silence of the dark veld.
He shouted at Justice, 'You terrorist, you terrorist.' Frustrated, Crafford
drew a burning log from the fire, the flaking orange heat fierce in the
cold night air. He pressed it against Justice's head, yelling at him. Justice
cried out in agony, his flesh searing.

Warrant Officer Strydom stood nearby still clutching the whisky bottle. Constables Mathebula and Matjeni watched appalled from a distance.
Constable Matjeni had been in the police for twenty-three years. He had
witnessed much brutality, but nothing like this. When he could bear it
no longer, he went to his tent. Yet he could still hear the man's pain, and
wished it would end.

The bottle of whisky passed between Crafford and Strydom and they
drank deeply. Again Crafford put his slurred questions. Demanded answers but wouldn't give the bound man time to respond. Crafford thrust
the flaming log into Justice's genitals. Justice screamed. And his screams
had no sooner quietened, than Crafford forced the log between Justice's
buttocks and held it there, burning his anus. Beyond torment, Justice no
longer cried out, but keened softly, a sound that wasn't human.

Strydom, in a craze of violence, grabbed a glass bottle lying on the ground
and smashed it into the side of Justice's head above the ear. Justice lost
consciousness, his head flopped forward. But the beating did not stop.

Constable Mathebula looked on aghast.

Captain Crafford and Warrant Officer Strydom stood exhausted,
swaying, their bodies illuminated by the flames of the dying fire. All the
other policemen had stayed in their tents, only Constable Mathebula
watched.

When Captain Crafford and Warrant Officer Strydom drove off, he
too went into his tent, leaving Justice Mbizana, comatose, tied to the
tree, naked.

33

The judge looks hard at the accused, these men who have chosen not
to participate in his court. Harry Prinsloo springs to his feet, a study
in controlled anger. Plaintively he voices his grievance to the judge and

assessors. The four accused, Prinsloo says, have been represented since 14 May 1987 – coincidentally my birthday – and they have their lawyers in court now. At the end of the trial they cannot contend that there has been no due process because they were not represented. If later they change their minds about representation and want to recall witnesses, the State will oppose them strongly.

The judge stops him, saying he understands the position. Addressing the accused, he urges them to accept counsel as it is in their interests.

Jabu stands to reply. 'I choose not to be legally represented.' The rest follow suit.

'I am sorry about that,' says the judge. 'I think you are making a mistake and if at any time you decide to change your plan, you must tell me immediately so that we can arrange counsel for you. I have also invited Mr Harris at any time to indicate to me if he requires an adjournment so that he can speak to you, or if he needs to talk to Mr Prinsloo or Mrs van der Walt. In such a case Mr Prinsloo or Mrs van der Walt can, on his behalf, indicate that an adjournment is required.'

Harry Prinsloo and Louisa van der Walt glare at me, not happy about having to assist me in such a matter. I smile at them, nodding my gratitude. I turn to look at the other three in the dock. Their faces are impassive but I can see the elation in their eyes. The people in the gallery shift in their seats, then go quiet as Jabu unfolds the document that has been prepared.

It is agreed that as the accused have had the charge sheet for some time, the lengthy process of reading out the charges will be dispensed with. The judge asks the accused how they plead, guilty or not guilty. Jabu replies, 'With due respect, Sir, there is an explanation.' The judge indicates that he should move to the microphone in the witness stand to read his statement into the record. This is more than we'd hoped for. The prosecution look at each other, puzzled that an unrepresented accused is making the opening address of the trial. The day is running away from them.

From the witness box, Jabu looks straight at the judge and continues in a slow, clear voice that carries over the screen to the back of the court. 'With due respect, Sir, there is an explanation I would like to put forward. This is not aimed as an insult to you. We respect you as a person.

'I refuse to participate in these proceedings for certain reasons which I desire to place on record. In this regard I speak on behalf of comrades Ting Ting Masango, Neo Potsane and Joseph Makhura. The charges against us are that we, in effect, allegedly committed certain acts with the intention to eradicate the apartheid system so that the majority of South Africans could participate in the making of this country's laws. Our refusal to participate in the proceedings stems from our belief that this court and this judicial system is founded on injustice and oppression. We state that such a judicial system cannot operate independently from the political system within which it functions.

'Furthermore, all of us were held in solitary confinement without access to legal representation for eight months. During this period all of us were tortured and brutally assaulted. In the process, information has been extracted from us by the security police which will in all certainty be used against us. We, as members of Umkhonto we Sizwe, the military wing of the African National Congress, are involved in a war of national liberation; this is true. Also true is that the South African government and defence force leaders constantly state that South Africa is in a state of war. We, as soldiers, cannot and should not stand trial in a civilian court. As trained soldiers and freedom fighters we have taken up the struggle on behalf of our people to rid this country of a system which is evil and which degrades and dehumanises people on the basis of skin colour.

'We do not stand in isolation in our perception of South Africa and its political system. The international community has repeatedly condemned apartheid as a crime against humanity. In doing so, it has recognised the legitimacy of the struggle of the oppressed people of South Africa in pursuance of their human and political rights as detailed in the Charter of the United Nations and the Universal Declaration of Human Rights. In particular, the International Court of Justice has ruled that racial discrimination is a breach of a country's obligation to the international community. Church leaders have declared that apartheid is a heresy. In conclusion, we reiterate that as MK soldiers we do not recognise this civilian court and accordingly we refuse to plead to the charges. We thank you, Sir.'

There is silence in court. Jabu remains in the witness box as if lost in thought. The judge, taken aback, breaks the moment. 'Thank you. Thank you, you may go back.'

Addressing Ting Ting, he asks, 'Accused number two, are you prepared to plead?'

All three of the remaining accused stand and confirm that they refuse to plead. Suddenly the silence is broken by loud applause from the public gallery.

The judge raises his hand and the gallery falls silent immediately. He says, 'I will appreciate it if the public keeps the applause of solidarity to a minimum. I realise that there are special circumstances here and it is because of this that I gave the accused the opportunity to make a statement that is of a political nature, which would not normally happen. But I make an appeal to the public to ensure that the proceedings are disturbed as little as possible.'

Turning to Bheki, I say, 'This judge hasn't put a foot wrong yet. He didn't have to allow Jabu to make the statement. Maybe it's because he knows there are a lot of press and he wants to make an impression. Still, to refer to the special circumstances of this trial is an acknowledgement that we are dealing with something different, and not just a normal criminal trial.'

Bheki replies cynically, 'Give it time, this is just the first day.'

The judge, as he must do when the accused refuse to plead, enters a plea of 'not guilty' on their behalf. Our time is over. Now it is up to the prosecution to build their case. I wonder which witnesses they will start with. Tactically, you always want to make an impression at the beginning and at the end of a trial. The chronology of events doesn't matter. I know they will save the bomb for last. If I were them, I would lead with either the Lukhele killings or the Soshanguve landmine.

Harry Prinsloo announces that Mrs Lukhele will be the first witness. Louisa van der Walt leads the witness as she tells about the killing of her husband.

We hear how David Lukhele had just returned home from Swaziland with his sister, Elizabeth Dludlu. They were watching the seven o'clock news when there was a knock at the door. Mr Lukhele got up and opened the door to find a man in an overcoat standing there. Mr Lukhele asked the man to take a seat while the family watched the news. The man refused, walked to a corner of the room, and stood there. Mrs Lukhele could see he was holding something under his coat. A small child ran out of the kitchen and stood next to Mr Lukhele. Feeling there was something wrong, Mrs

Lukhele told the child to ask for ice cream in the kitchen. Once the child had left, the man pulled out a weapon and opened fire on David Lukhele. There were shots and smoke and he fell down. In the chaos that followed, David Lukhele and his sister were both killed.

Watching this woman slowly relate how her husband died in front of her and seeing her clear inability to understand the politics which lay behind the murder, I feel anguish for her visible pain and sorrow. This is not about scoring points, legal or political. Maybe it is about a war, but it is also about a woman who lost a loved one and cannot understand why. Despite the context it remains simply loss, and there is no forgetting.

'Who made this decision?' Mrs Lukhele asks, as she points out Neo Potsane as the man who changed her life forever. She tells how she was shot in the lower left leg in the spray of bullets that ricocheted around the room. The high-velocity projectile, tumbling as it entered her leg, splintered the bone and blasted a gaping hole on exit. She tried to run, but her leg collapsed under her. Frantically crawling, dragging her leg behind her in the thunder of gunfire, she made her way along the passage to the back door where she fell down the stairs into the safety of the night.

'At that moment, as I crawled away, my sister-in-law was in a chair … she was covered in blood from the head down. My husband lay on the floor and I never went back.'

At the end of the day, I meet the families of the accused outside the court. No one speaks as we shake hands and part. Driving away, I see Mrs Lukhele being helped into a car. She looks up and our eyes meet. She does not drop her gaze until I've passed. That stare has never left me.

34

The next day Bheki and I arrive at court together. There are many more policemen about. The door to the court is guarded by policemen carrying R4 rifles. The one who received the brunt of my ire yesterday smiles grimly as if to say, Now there's trouble. I ignore him, pushing my way into the court. Armed police line the walls, some standing near a table in the centre of the court. I can see why.

On the table is a large pile of weapons. To be exact: two 9 mm Makarov self-loading pistols with magazines, four AKMS light automatic combat rifles and three AK-47s, two of these with folding butts, and many magazines. Very serious weaponry. Thank goodness the prosecution has not put their entire cache out here, complete with grenades and mines.

This bit of theatre will have a profound effect on the judge and the public. Smart, if it pays off. Real and shocking, these ugly black and grey implements kill people. These specific ones have killed, and they belong to my clients. Everyone is staring at them, from the police to the public to the accused. People talk to each other, but their eyes are on the weapons.

The judge and assessors enter the court. They stop short when they see the weapons. They have clearly not been forewarned. Excellent shock value, I have to give it to Harry and Louisa. There is a long silence after the judge and assessors sit down. They, too, are transfixed by the pile of guns, the malignant AK-47s, the stuff of horror and legend, wielded by heroes, terrorists, murderers and bloody revolutionaries. Right here in this court, the tools of my clients' trade. Ugly stump-nosed pieces of functional metal, shining and polished from use.

In this grim clinker-brick little court there is a dreadful sobriety as we all stare at these guns that have murdered. The accused look at them and I know that from now on, when the judge and assessors look at the men in the dock, they no longer see them in their suits and ties, but in overalls and overcoats, black balaclavas, carrying these weapons.

In a moment everything has changed. This is no criminal trial. Not with that quantity and type of weaponry. Those weapons speak of war, and every person in the courtroom acknowledges this with a jolt. Those weapons beg the question: are these men soldiers or terrorists?

Louisa van der Walt, on her feet, breaks the spell and leads the first witness on the assassination of the Mamelodi policeman, Seun Vuma. Dr Jacobus Albertus Malan is the state pathologist. He confirms that the body of 'an adult non-white male with extensive gunshot wounds' was brought to him at the Medunsa Forensic Medicine Laboratory on Tuesday 18 March 1986. He states that there was extensive bruising on Vuma's body and that the deceased died of massive blood loss as a result of the gunshot wounds.

The journalists in the gallery lean forward as Louisa van der Walt asks, 'With these injuries, what do you say, would death have come quickly?'

'There is no evidence that death came quickly,' replies Dr Malan, 'as none of the main arteries of the heart were pierced, which would cause rapid bleeding. Therefore, I am sure that the bleeding did not take place quickly and that a lot of time passed before he died.'

The wife of Seun Vuma is next. Showing little emotion, Busisiwe Dalene Vuma relates that she had moved out of their family home in Mamelodi East some time before the shooting as it had often been the target of attack by unknown persons.

'Frequently, people bothered us, bombs exploded at this house and it was damaged and had to be repaired,' she says. She went to stay with her parents.

The next witness is clearly ill at ease. He fixes his eyes on the floor and never looks at the judge or the accused. His name is Walter Vilakazi. He lived next door to Vuma.

'On that Friday evening, can you tell the court what took place at your house?' asks van der Walt.

'I and my family were already in bed,' he begins. 'We heard a noise. As I woke up, I heard something like a bang on the door and I thought that the person was maybe fearful as he knocked on the door very hard. I got up to see what the noise was. My kitchen window is opposite Mr Vuma's house. As I was standing there in the kitchen, I saw pink smoke rising. I then went back to bed as I thought that it was perhaps Mr Vuma firing into the air.'

Van der Walt goes on to question Vilakazi about the days after the shooting. 'Was there anything strange about the house of Constable Vuma on that Saturday or Sunday?'

The witness replies, 'Yes, normally in the morning when I go to work, I hear him trying to start his car. Sometimes, I go to the sports fields and when I returned on the Saturday or Sunday, I asked my wife if she had seen Vuma. She said no.'

'Why did you ask your wife if she had seen Vuma?' van der Walt wants to know.

'The noise that I heard on that day was the first time I had heard such a noise,' says Vilakazi. 'Normally, Vuma had a habit of firing into the air [when he came home], but the noise of shooting into the air and the noise I heard on that day was different.'

Assessor Botha asks, 'The shooting at Vuma, describe it to the court? Was it an explosion or one or more gunshots?'

'I think it was a shooting,' says Vilakazi.

145

It is clear that Walter Vilakazi is unwilling to add much more and is anxious to get out of the witness box as soon as possible. He doesn't want to be asked the obvious question – but then the prosecution also doesn't want to ask it. That question hangs there: why, even on Sunday night, when no one had seen Vuma since the sounds of shooting on Friday night, had he not gone round to the house or phoned the police to report something suspicious? It is all too obvious.

According to the evidence, Vuma died a slow death. In all probability, Dr Malan suggested, he finally died during the course of Sunday or later. He was only found on Monday, after a fellow policeman, Warrant Officer Booyse, heard that there had been a 'shooting' at his house three days earlier and went to investigate.

35

Justice was still alive on the Sunday morning. The policemen cut him down and rubbed salve on his injuries. They dressed him as best they could. Then they waited for Captain Prinsloo's return.

It was some hours before the captain arrived and the sight of Justice's injuries brought out an intense anger in him. 'Who has done this? Who has done this?' he demanded, raging at his men. Shamefully they told him. Captain Prinsloo turned to Warrant Officer Strydom demanding to know why Justice had been assaulted. Strydom did not answer, afraid that Prinsloo would hit him. Terrified, Strydom jumped into his car and drove off at high speed.

Captain Prinsloo sat with Justice in the tent. Talked to him quietly, told him that he was sorry about what had happened, that he had known nothing about it. For hours, he sat there soothing his captive.

Eventually Captain Prinsloo ordered most of the men to leave the farm. The interrogation camp was packed up quietly and the men drove away, grateful to be spared his wrath. Soon he too left, entrusting Justice to the care of some constables.

The next morning Captain Prinsloo consulted with Brigadier Cronje before driving back to the farm. Whatever Prinsloo had said, Cronje felt it expedient to send Crafford and Strydom on a mission to Swaziland, well out of the captain's reach.

At Klipdrift, Captain Prinsloo ordered the remaining policemen to leave. When the cars had driven off and the dust had settled, he went into Justice's tent. He sat quietly with the injured man, talking. From a plastic shopping bag he took out a can of Coke and offered it to Justice. Justice pulled the ring and drank deeply.

The Coke had been doctored with sleeping tablets. Five tablets had been ground into a fine powder, liquidised and injected into the can. The tiny needle hole was then sealed with wax. The sleeping tablets were from Captain Prinsloo's personal stock. An insomniac, he dosed himself each night, but the medication seldom worked.

It worked gradually on Justice, though. The two men talked about their families. Intimate details. So intimate that Justice, hazed with pain, drowsy from the sleeping tablets, rambled on about his mother's murder. She'd been killed by his father and he wondered if he had ever recovered from the trauma. Prinsloo listened intently.

As the day softly turned to dusk, Captain Prinsloo offered Justice a cigarette, lighting it for him. Before the cigarette was finished, Justice fell into a deep sleep.

Captain Prinsloo gathered the captive in his arms and carried him to the boot of his car. He drove to Compol and in the street outside the building rendezvoused with two security policemen, a Lieutenant Momberg and a Sergeant Goosen. Both men were explosives experts and had been instructed by Brigadier Cronje to assist Captain Prinsloo. The men headed off along the road to Rustenburg with the captive in the boot. Under a bridge, the captain stopped to check on Justice, who was awake, groggy from the tablets. He was helped from the boot and his handcuffs removed. Prinsloo offered him a Coke. This one too was doctored and the drugs worked rapidly. Justice almost collapsed on the road before they could get him back into the boot.

Captain Prinsloo leant over the comatose man and pressed a finger hard into his eye. There was no reaction. The men drove on until they came to a dirt road, more a track than a road, that was seldom used. Lieutenant Momberg knew it well. The track was ideal as it meandered through an uninhabited area. Now he guided Captain Prinsloo to a sandy spot.

The inert Justice was laid on the ground in a foetal position. While Lieutenant Momberg and Sergeant Goosen prepared their explosives in the light of the car's open door, Captain Prinsloo took a spade from the boot and stood over Justice. He was concerned that if Justice regained consciousness, he might dislodge the explosives and botch the operation.

Swiftly, with hard hacking blows, Prinsloo smashed the edge of the spade again and again against Justice's head, cracking the man's skull. Then Lieutenant Momberg and Sergeant Goosen attached six mini limpet mines to Justice's feet, hips and his bloody head. Mines were also put under his hands to ensure no part was left that could later lead to the MK guerrilla's identification. There was a full moon which gave the men enough pale light by which to work.

Once Sergeant Goosen had finished, the men drove off a short distance then stopped to listen for the explosion. Captain Prinsloo switched off the ignition. They waited. About them the veld was alive with insects and far off a jackal howled. The blast came loud and reverberated across the grasslands. Afterwards the veld lay silent. Captain Prinsloo started the car and the three men drove back to Pretoria.

THE BOMB

The responsibility for the implementation of the instruction to eliminate the target is given to a group of men based on a police farm on the banks of the Hennops River to the west of Pretoria. The name of the farm is Vlakplaas.

The farm is home to a number of askaris, the 'turned' MK guerrillas that now work for the police in identifying and tracking their former comrades as well as internal resistance figures. The askaris are organised into squads of four to six men under the leadership of usually one but sometimes two white policemen. Originally, these units were intended to play a counter-insurgency role, but, either by accident or design, they soon degenerated into lawless bands that kidnapped and murdered activists and captured MK guerrillas. Generally this is done on the instructions of police headquarters in Pretoria, but often it occurs at their own initiative. As time passes, the squads go increasingly freelance for private gain.

The picturesque farm wants for very little. It has excellent buildings, new offices and living quarters, garages, a shooting range, soccer field and braai areas. It also has an atmospheric clubhouse with a fully stocked bar. It is here that one night, in an angry blur of cheap brandy and cigarettes, the discussion originally took place on how to eliminate the target, a well-protected, high-profile individual in Lusaka.

36

A few days into the trial, the prosecution leads evidence relating to the confessions of the accused. Louisa van der Walt puts it on record that the accused, freely and voluntarily, indicated to the investigating officer Captain Prinsloo that they wanted to make statements. Captain Prinsloo arranged for them to be taken before a succession of magistrates who took down their statements which were duly signed. On each occasion the men were asked if they were acting under duress. In order to confirm that they had not acted under duress or been assaulted, Captain Prinsloo had them medically examined by district surgeons. At the same time as these confessions were made, the accused were taken to 'point out' the specific places connected to their activities.

This is the point in political trials where the accused contest the admissibility of their confessions by trying to prove that they were extracted under torture or duress. This 'trial within a trial' often leads to embarrassment for the police, as their methods of interrogation and investigation come under scrutiny. In this case, they will have an easy ride. There will be no challenge. Even so, the proceedings approach farce as the prosecution paints a picture of the accused eagerly assisting in their own investigation and enjoying a relationship with their captors that is relaxed, close and spontaneous. From the way Louisa van der Walt leads Captain Prinsloo it is clear they are old partners.

VAN DER WALT: On 15 September 1986 the four accused before the court were handed over to you by Lieutenant Colonel Erasmus for further investigation, is that correct?

CAPT. PRINSLOO: That is correct.

VAN DER WALT: After you received the accused, did you have any conversation with them?

CAPT. PRINSLOO: I introduced myself to the four accused. I asked them if they had any complaints or if they had been assaulted. All four of the accused told me that during their arrest they had been assaulted with balled fists and also kicked. I told them that I would tell members of the detective branch to investigate their complaints … I also told them that they should not fear any assault from my side …

I hear a noise behind me and, glancing back, see the accused, particularly Ting Ting and Neo, slowly shaking their heads. Captain Prinsloo looks at them briefly, turns his shoulders towards the judge and assessors, and calmly continues with his evidence. I look at the judge. He has seen the interchange.

VAN DER WALT: On the 17th September 1986 after investigating [the killing of Orphan Chapi], you had a conversation with accused number one [Jabu Masina].

CAPT. PRINSLOO: That is correct. As a result of information at my disposal, I warned accused number one that I was investigating the death of a Sergeant Chapi of the SAP in Soweto. I asked the accused if he voluntarily wanted to go with a police officer and point out certain aspects of the case of Sergeant Chapi. I also explained his rights to him in relation to the pointing out, should he choose to do it. He understood this and I told him that he in no way whatsoever can be forced to do the pointing out. The accused then said to me that he was prepared to do the pointing out in Soweto in connection with the Chapi case ... I also told him that I was not making any promises to him and that I do not want to influence him in any way.

And so it goes for each accused in relation to each incident. Always this relationship of mutual understanding and spontaneous warmth between the captor and his captives. Until the judge unexpectedly interrupts.

JUDGE: Do you know when each of the accused were arrested?

CAPT. PRINSLOO: No, I only got them on the 15th September from Lieutenant Colonel Erasmus. I was informed that they were arrested on the 13, 14th September, if I am right.

JUDGE: You told the court that as a result of their allegations that they were assaulted during their arrest, a docket was opened?

CAPT. PRINSLOO: That is correct ... I saw the docket after the investigation was complete and it was laid before the attorney-general of the Transvaal who refused to take the alleged complaints any further.

JUDGE: What happened from the time the accused were handed over to you to the time you spoke to the accused number one on the 18th September [in connection with the pointing out]? That is two days after he was handed to you. What conversations and events took place between you and him between the 15th and the 18th?

CAPT. PRINSLOO: There were conversations between accused number one and me as a result of which he was taken before a magistrate to make a statement about certain information in relation to all of the accused.

JUDGE: I want to know what happened between you and him between those two dates?

CAPT. PRINSLOO: There were conversations between us.

JUDGE: You have said that in relation to accused number one that you accept that he is an intelligent person. What is your reading of the other three accused?

CAPT. PRINSLOO: They strike me as the same.

JUDGE: We are dealing with people that claim they are Umkhonto soldiers, intelligent persons. Captain, we can accept that these men are committed to their cause and that they are determined and convinced in this regard?

CAPT. PRINSLOO: Yes, that is so, all four of them are very fanatical in relation to the ideology in which they believe.

JUDGE: The allegation is made, I believe, that they leave the country, get training somewhere and come back to carry out the alleged acts, and that surely shows a degree of determination.

CAPT. PRINSLOO: I agree, your Lordship.

JUDGE: Now what would be the reason why such a person, simply on such a request, would declare himself prepared to make pointings out in relation to circumstances that could lead him to the death penalty?

CAPT. PRINSLOO: Your Lordship, I have twenty-six years service in the SAP, the last twelve of which have been in the security branch where I have dealt with militarily trained terrorists from the ANC as well as the PAC. During these interrogations and conversations with militarily trained members of the ANC, there is one point that has clearly come to the fore, and this is that as long as such trained members commit acts of terror in South Africa, they are man enough; the moment when they are arrested, to realise that it is the end of their terror career and, regardless of their determination, they admit the deeds they have committed.

This is the first of a number of explanations which Captain Prinsloo proffers, none of which appear to satisfy the judge's curiosity as to why such dedicated soldiers should spontaneously reveal all to their enemies. He addresses the same question to Lieutenant Colonel Erasmus.

JUDGE: Captain Prinsloo told us that he found accused number four [Joseph Makhura] an intelligent person. We can accept that he is a committed man in the eyes of the ANC and that he views himself as an Umkhonto soldier. To what do you think it can be ascribed that almost immediately after his arrest, he is prepared to point out things?

COL. ERASMUS: The experience in the past is that this always happens. They are completely prepared to open their hearts and to talk about these things and point out things to the police.

JUDGE: Is it your experience that they are prepared to open their hearts even when they know that this can lead to them being found guilty of a hanging offence?

COL. ERASMUS: Yes, your Lordship, my experience is that they want to get publicity by doing this.

JUDGE: Are they prepared to offer their lives for that publicity?

COL. ERASMUS: I believe so, your Lordship.

It is unusual for a judge in a political trial to take this tack, to question security police with scepticism, casting doubt on their version of events. Is he serious or simply putting up a charade? He knows that these accused have no defence and that they will go down, so what harm is there in being a little critical of the police witnesses? It gives him an air of independence and the result is still the same. The rope. Or perhaps I am doing him an injustice.

The prosecution witnesses start to stumble a little when the court hears that the accused told the magistrates that they had been assaulted. I exchange glances with Bheki. Behind us, the accused and gallery sit quietly.

Warrant Officer Marthinus Ras, stationed at the headquarters of the Security Branch in Pretoria, states that on the Saturday morning, he and other security personnel interrogated Masango, Potsane and Makhura at Compol.

WO RAS: In my presence, there were no assaults and I did not see accused two, three and four being assaulted.

VAN DER WALT: In the afternoon, you went to Winterveld for further investigation?

WO RAS: That is correct.

VAN DER WALT: You went to a certain house. Who pointed the house out to you?

WO RAS: The house was pointed out by accused number two.

VAN DER WALT: Who did you find at the house?

WO RAS: We found accused number one at the house.

VAN DER WALT: Have any charges of assault been brought against you by any of the accused before the court?

WO RAS: Yes, your Lordship, accused numbers one and three laid charges against me. Accused numbers one and three also pointed me out at an identification parade. I do not know what the result of this case was.

VAN DER WALT: Do you know if a docket was opened in this case?

WO RAS: A docket was opened and an identification parade held.

VAN DER WALT: To this date, there has been no follow-up against you, is that correct?

WO RAS: That is correct.

VAN DER WALT: What were the allegations against you?

WO RAS: Accused one and three alleged that I hit them.

VAN DER WALT: When was the assault meant to have taken place?

WO RAS: Accused number three alleged it took place during interrogation when Sergeant Willemse was present. Accused number one alleged it took place in Lieutenant Colonel Erasmus's office while he was present.

VAN DER WALT: Is this on [the Saturday], 14th September ...?

WO RAS: That is confirmed.

After this exchange, the judge pointedly asks the accused whether they want to direct any questions towards this particular witness. 'This is the first time the court has before it someone who is alleged to have committed assault,' he explains. 'Therefore I now emphatically ask the question and specifically give the opportunity to the accused to ask questions if they want to do so.'

But the accused are not prepared to respond.

Sergeant Douw Willemse of the Pretoria Security Branch admits in his evidence that he was in the office of Lieutenant Colonel Erasmus on the Saturday but denies that any assaults took place. He does confirm that when he arrived in the office he '… noticed that [Potsane's] right eye was bloodshot. I pointed this out to Lieutenant Colonel Erasmus and he said that he already had knowledge of that.'

Sergeant Matemele Musimeke confirms that he was present during the same interrogation and also denies that any assaults took place. He admits that accused two and three laid charges against him and that both of them pointed him out at an identification parade.

SGT MUSIMEKE: They alleged I had hit them.
VAN DER WALT: With what did you hit them?
SGT MUSIMEKE: With fists.
VAN DER WALT: Do you know on what part of their bodies?
SGT MUSIMEKE: On their bodies, but I can't say precisely where.

Again, the investigating officer, Captain Hendrik Prinsloo, gives evidence of how the accused consented to make further confessions and point out alleged scenes relating to their activities.

Van der Walt asks, 'What was [their] disposition towards you from 15 September to 2 October 1986, while all these statements were being made?'

'I would say that they revealed a good disposition,' Captain Prinsloo replies. 'They behaved spontaneously towards me.'

The judge intervenes, an edge in his voice. 'This last point, one would expect that someone in your position, so far as I can see, is the personification of the enemy. Why would there be such a good relationship between you, from their perspective?'

'I can describe it thus,' says Captain Prinsloo, 'and this is based on my experience over the last twelve years, that a terrorist is a cowardly person. While they commit acts of terror they are very brave … but when they are arrested, they realise that the game they have played is over.

'During interrogations of terrorists for the last twelve years and also in the case of the accused, it has come clearly to the fore that in the ANC training camps across the borders, certain members of MK are indoctrinated

155

that when they are arrested by the SAP they will be terribly assaulted and tortured. During conversations with the accused, they clearly told me that they had never thought they would be so well treated by the SAP.

'Another aspect that comes to the fore is that it appears to me that the acts of terror that they committed made such an impression on them and that they are such motivated members of the ANC that, for propaganda purposes, they freely admit their deeds as members of the ANC.'

'It does not appear to me that it is the action of a coward to admit deeds that he knows will very possibly lead to the death sentence,' says the judge.

And so it goes between the judge and Captain Prinsloo. The captain, says the judge, has stated that the accused will make admissions and point things out through bravado or to make propaganda. But why were the confessions made one by one? Why not reveal everything at once? 'Someone who speaks out of bravado, in other words, who is boasting or making propaganda, would not hold back, is that not true?'

'Normal persons, yes,' says Captain Prinsloo, 'but in the case of the ANC, in certain instances, you will get people who will make certain admissions for the sake of propaganda right from the beginning, others who will do so piece by piece at a later stage.'

This judge is getting interesting, I think. Perhaps I should give him more credit. Even one of the assessors gets involved.

ASSESSOR DE KOCK: Could you perhaps at this stage just give an indication of how long they were held under Section 29 [of the Internal Security Act]?

CAPT. PRINSLOO: It was quite some time, I speak under correction, seven to eight months in total.

ASSESSOR DE KOCK: After that they were placed under arrest for these offences?

CAPT. PRINSLOO: That is correct.

ASSESSOR DE KOCK: Before they were arrested they could only be visited by officials of the State, is that correct?

CAPT. PRINSLOO: That is correct.

Why don't they just admit that it is solitary confinement, I wonder.

The prosecution is irked but not worried by this unexpected questioning from the judge and the assessor. I'm curious at their behaviour, it is not what I expected. The Judge could have confined himself to the contents of the confession. This deviation from the script is unsettling for everyone, not least the prosecution. Forging ahead, the prosecution calls the magistrates before whom the accused made their confessions.

Brian Andrews is the assistant magistrate for the district of Wonderboom, an area on the outskirts of Pretoria.

Harry Prinsloo hands in the statement made to Andrews by Ting Ting Masango. In this statement, Ting Ting explicitly stated that he had been assaulted. 'On 14 September 1986, I was assaulted by a policeman with his open hand and fists in my face and on my body – hit with an empty cooldrink bottle on my knees. Kicked on my stomach and chest with shoes. I don't know him but will be able to identify him.'

Harry Prinsloo, needing to address this damage quickly, asks Magistrate Andrews if he saw the accused's injuries. 'I looked to see if the accused had any injuries, I could not find any,' says Andrews.

PRINSLOO: What was your conclusion?
ANDREWS: That the accused did not have any visible wounds.
PRINSLOO: Did it in any way appear to you that the accused made the statement to you unwillingly?
ANDREWS: No, certainly not.
PRINSLOO: Was he influenced or anything?
ANDREWS: No, certainly not.

The next magistrate called by the prosecution is Andre Goosen. Before Harry Prinsloo can get into his stride, the judge asks Magistrate Goosen: 'What was your impression from the conversation and answers [of Ting Ting Masango]?'

The magistrate replies: 'I can say to this court that the person appeared to be completely relaxed and he answered comfortably, without any problems.'

On the same day, Magistrate Goosen took a statement from Neo Potsane.

GOOSEN: Do you have any injuries or bruises of any nature and if they are visible, show them to me?

POTSANE: The only one is my right eye.

[Goosen notes that 'the eye is red, no swelling, no other visible injuries'.]

POTSANE: My ribs on both sides are sore.

GOOSEN: Have you been assaulted by anyone?

POTSANE: Yes, the police. I don't know their names.

Giving evidence in court Goosen says, 'At that stage [of taking the statement], I didn't think it necessary to further explore around the injuries that he might have had to his ribs.'

That day Magistrate Goosen also saw Jabu Masina.

GOOSEN: Do you fear such violence if you refuse to make a statement?

MASINA: Yes, if I do not make a statement, I fear that the police will hit me or do something else to me.

GOOSEN: Have you been threatened with violence by anyone if you inform me about those threats of violence to which you may have been subjected before you came here?

MASINA: No.

GOOSEN: Have you been encouraged/persuaded by anyone to make a statement?

MASINA: Yes, the police.

Judge to Magistrate Goosen: 'Mr Goosen, when the accused allegedly said that he fears violence if he does not make a statement, because he fears that the police will then hit him or do something else to him, why did you not ask him why he had that fear? The statement [questionnaire] is not put together to be followed slavishly.'

GOOSEN: As I have already said to the court, as a result of his answer to the question, I did not personally think it necessary at that stage to put further questions to him.

JUDGE: Mr Goosen, I find it strange. Should you not when he was asked if he was encouraged [to make a statement], then have asked in what ways he was encouraged?

GOOSEN: I can just perhaps add the word 'aanmoedig' was not properly translated in the sense that the police did not beg or implore him to go to the magistrate to give a statement, but more in the sense that the likelihood is that there is a procedure that someone can make a statement before a magistrate.

JUDGE: Mr Goosen, issues like that should be immediately followed up.

Other magistrates who took statements from the accused, among them magistrates Hugo Smith and Petrus Venter, take the witness stand. In many cases there are claims of assault and intimidation yet none of the magistrates followed up on these allegations. Even now, when Harry Prinsloo goes through their reports, they gloss over the contradictions, adamant that the confessions were given voluntarily.

Judge de Klerk intervenes repeatedly, asking why the magistrates followed the statement questionnaire by rote and did nothing to establish the veracity of the assault claims. At the end he turns to the accused and, referring specifically to Joseph Makhura, invites them to ask questions, declaring that it is in their interest to reconsider if they want legal representation to challenge the confessions.

Thanking the judge for his concern, Joseph Makhura reaffirms that he is not prepared to participate in the proceedings.

The judge adjourns the hearing until Monday. He leaves the court grimly, apparently upset by the charade. The content of the confessions, unchallenged by the accused, receives scant attention from the gallery and the media, the focus being on the judge and his questioning of the magistrates. The consequences of the refusal of the accused to take part in the trial are becoming increasingly apparent to a fascinated media. These people are different.

Sensing the prosecution's disappointment, the accused are upbeat. For now, the terror of torture and interrogation is forgotten. They smile and wave to family and friends in the gallery, and mouth greetings through the scratched shield of Perspex. The brown Delmas dust sticks to the wet handprints their supporters leave on the transparent surface.

Louisa van der Walt and Harry Prinsloo pack their books. They are not happy.

The investigating officer Hendrik Prinsloo is more sanguine, almost detached. He walks over to the accused and says, 'It's going fast, né Jabu?'

This is not overtly hostile, but the message is clear: 'Enjoy it, because your days are numbered.'

Jabu nods to Prinsloo, acknowledging the comment, and I'm struck by this exchange. They are no longer captor and prisoner, almost equals. Between them lies a mutual acceptance of their differing objectives, a strange kind of respect, without warmth or wrath.

37

Thankfully, the weekend is quiet. No social arrangements, just myself and Caroline at home. Our first child is due in less than a month. Caroline works for ITN/Channel 4 News and her job is a stressful one that often demands long hours especially when a story is breaking. And right now there is a lot of breaking news.

I drive out to Delmas early on Monday morning. In court, Louisa van der Walt looks at me oddly. It's a look I am not unused to, but this time there is a smugness to it, when she has no reason to be. She announces a change in tack. She wants to interrupt the evidence on the confessions and call witnesses in connection with the Silverton bomb. I have dreaded this moment. I know that the security forces have been targeting civilians for years and that since the Kabwe conference, the ANC has blurred the distinction between hard and soft targets. With both sides sliding to war, I feel abhorrence for the activities of the police, which is why I defend their victims.

I support the resistance organisations but the killing of civilians is different, regardless of the provocation. I know what effect this evidence will have on the trial and on the attitude of the judge.

Martha Erasmus, a fifty-nine-year-old woman, tells how she was waiting for the bus to take her home after work. The bus was late. She stepped into the street to see if it was coming and then back onto the pavement. The movement positioned her next to the dustbin. She heard an explosion and realised it was a bomb. When she came round, her one leg had been blown off; the other was a raw wound.

She speaks without bitterness of her loss and of the pain, glancing at the accused from time to time. She spent five months in hospital. There are no tears or recriminations, rather an acceptance of her fate, that fickle thing that cruelly placed her at a bus stop at the exact time the bomb went off. Doing what she always did. Going home from work. Catching a bus. Normal life. If her bus had arrived on time thirty seconds earlier, her life would not have changed. In two weeks, she will be undergoing a major operation on her badly damaged leg. It will be her twenty-third operation on that leg.

Belinda Cochrane was coming back from work in the city on the bus. She got off with two other people and walked towards the Checkers supermarket. She'd waited to cross the street and in that moment the bomb exploded. She saw black smoke. Blood everywhere and pieces of legs. She tried to help until she realised she had a shrapnel wound in her head. The right side of her face still gives her pain and is stiff.

Captain Prinsloo leads evidence about Rebecca Mpofu. When he arrived on the scene, he found her lying on the ground with her left leg blown away below the knee and her shattered lower right leg twisted up beside her thigh. Mpofu had died of natural causes some two years later.

The witnesses come forward and give evidence about that day. Black, white, young, old, all sharing the tragedy. There had been no deaths, thank God. Some tell their story calmly, others are more emotional, the anger rising in their voices. Some are confused, bewildered by what happened to them, still unable to make the link between their context and what the accused did. The connection is too remote.

And should they be able to? Maybe not. The gap between the worlds of the accused and some of their victims is wide. How can the witnesses be expected to understand the desperation that drives an ordinary person to kill, to give up a part of their humanity? Even more so, to take that extraordinary step for a cause and not for personal gain. And should they? The real fault lies elsewhere.

Looking at the accused, I can see that the witnesses have made a deep impression on them. Confronting the results of their work, the damage done to ordinary people, victims of a random attack, they are sober and subdued.

There is a strange moment when Samuel 'Star' Masango gives evidence. He describes walking past the bus stop when the bomb explodes. The next thing he is flat on his face. He says he saw nothing and heard nothing. In frustration, Louisa van der Walt asks him how he could have got hurt if nothing happened. He looks quickly at the accused, sees Ting

Ting staring at him and lowers his gaze, telling the court that his leg was broken in the explosion. He reiterates that he saw nothing. Van der Walt asks him if he is related to Ting Ting. He says no, but they live in the same street. No more questions. Gratefully he scurries from the witness box. Ting Ting shakes his head at the frightened pickpocket.

The judge steps in and tells van der Walt to move through these witnesses quickly and not ask irrelevant questions. He knows she is painting a picture and he has little time for it. It seems he does not want these victims to become props in a stage play where the ending is clear. It is too awful.

I, too, want this to end. I want them to go away, back to where they came from, where I do not have to see them with their confusion and pain. And I wonder if that makes me a hypocrite. Can I represent clients and an organisation capable of such things? In conflict, there are no angels, I tell myself, just violence and death.

38

The following day, the judge finds that the evidence led by the prosecution in relation to the pointings out, as well as the confessions of the accused, is admissible. He confirms that while there is clear evidence that the accused alleged they were assaulted, this is merely evidence of the allegation having been made, it is not evidence of the actual assault.

Short, sharp and sweet, like a lemon, as they say in Durban. Even though I know there is not much else the judge could have done, based on the evidence before him, I still feel let down. Perhaps because he'd been critical of the police witnesses, I'd expected something different. He's also not entirely correct to say that there is no evidence of assault, when at least in the case of Neo Potsane, the magistrate concerned and a number of policemen noted the injury to his eye. In addition, he should have picked up that some of the accused stated that they feared assault if they didn't make a statement.

In the end, though, it is an academic issue, given the stance of the accused. The real question is, would he have found differently if the accused had participated and presented real evidence of assaults? I know from my consultations that we would have had difficulty finding such evidence. When you're interrogated under Section 29 of the Internal Security Act, there are no independent witnesses. But still, it would have been interesting to see which way he would have gone if we'd come up with evidence to prove the assaults.

The prosecution moves on to the discovery of the arms caches, Louisa van der Walt leading Colonel Erasmus through the events. He describes how a convoy of security police cars and a squad from the Reaction Unit were taken by Neo Potsane and Joseph Makhura to a house in Winterveld.

At the back of the house was a locked room. The door was broken down and inside the policemen found a large blue metal trunk with two locks, and under the bed a rucksack. In this were clothes and a Russian SPM-2 limpet mine as well as a cardboard container for the limpet mine detonator and a Russian chart that tabled the delaying times for setting the mine. There were also four time delay mechanisms for the limpet mine. In addition, the security forces found four RGD-5 offensive hand grenades and detonators and eight fully loaded AK-47 magazines and an AK-47 cleaning kit as well as a cocked AK-47 with a double magazine and forty-seven loose rounds. Against a wall lay a rolled-up grass mat containing a rocket-propelled grenade launcher, and an RPG-7, capable of firing anti-tank grenades.

When questioned by van der Walt about the pointing out, Colonel Erasmus claims that the accused 'freely and voluntarily offered to show me the place where they were living'. He then lists the military hardware found in the trunk which includes landmines, detonators, limpet mines, hand grenades, delay mechanisms, pistol rounds. I'm relieved when he finishes. But the witnesses and guns don't stop coming.

Warrant Officer Ras is called and gives evidence that on the same day the police took Ting Ting Masango to another house in Winterveld, the house where he and Jabu Masina had lived. Under the bed in Masango's room they found a cocked Makarov pistol with a full magazine. They also arrested Masina at the house.

Warrant Officer Ras is enjoying himself. In the voice of a mortician, he recounts that later that afternoon Jabu Masina took him and other policemen to a house in Mamelodi. Here they found a haversack containing another cache – AK-47s and magazines, hand grenades with detonators, an AK-47 cleaning kit and a Makarov pistol with two full magazines. In the drawer of the bedside table was a cocked pistol with a full magazine, and in the pockets of a jacket was R1 200.

Jabu attracts my attention. He tells me that the police have got their times mixed up: they only arrested him in the late afternoon of 14 September, and took him first to the Soshanguve police station and then to Compol. The visit to the Mamelodi house occurred some days later.

Frankly, the way the case is going this detail is immaterial, but I can see it bothers him. Implicit is the contention that he talked straight after his arrest. Unfortunately we are powerless to correct this impression.

The forensic experts now proceed to link the weapons to the various acts. The cardboard box that would have carried an SPM limpet mine detonator receives particular attention as it implies a connection to the Silverton limpet mine bomb. Other witnesses give evidence associating the accused with particular weapons. The keys to the trunk were found on accused number four.

But it doesn't stop there.

Captain Hendrik Prinsloo, now virtually living in the witness box, details finding under a tree in the veld near Mamelodi a rucksack containing an AK-47 with a full magazine, ten RG 42 hand grenade detonators in a sealed tin, one SPM limpet mine detonator in a red cardboard box, an optical sight for an RPG-7, six RGD-5 hand grenades and two hand grenade detonators, and two RPG-7 projectiles. On the same day, he unearthed at a rubbish dump in East Mamelodi an AK-47 with a full magazine and various hand grenades and detonators.

I look at the gallery to see how this is being received. Not surprisingly, the accused are gazing gloomily ahead, lost in thought. The press are frantically scribbling notes although I know the prosecution will be only too happy to give them detailed lists. This is a big haul.

Later Bheki and I meet Mrs Masina outside. She grabs my hand and squeezes as if I'm the one needing comfort. The press cluster around her and the other family members asking for interviews and peppering them with questions. The journalists have been soaking up the details of how the unit operated, getting a glimpse into the world of the security police and the soldiers fighting them. They are clearly intrigued by these men who refuse to save their own lives.

I wait while Mrs Masina answers questions. Another day has passed. Another day closer to judgment.

39

I'm standing outside the court enjoying a Camel plain and watching the Reaction Unit lounging around their vehicle, joking and chatting, bored. There is little action here. As I grind out the butt, I hear Mrs Masina calling, 'Mr Harris, we need to speak to you about a serious matter.'

She is with Neo Potsane's father.

'We can see that this trial is going one way,' she says, 'and while it is not our choice and we respect what our sons have chosen, we do not want them to die needlessly. I know they will not change their position and they have told us that, but is there no way that we can help them? Can you not speak to them and tell them that they are now very near the end and they must reconsider their position?'

'As you know, Mrs Masina,' I say, 'they are very firm in their strategy. But I've been thinking about approaching the judge and asking him for time to speak to the accused, to see if we can't somehow arrive at a situation where we can mount an extenuation case. If the court allows this, the judge just might find extenuating circumstances, because without them he is compelled to impose the death sentence.'

'Please, Mr Harris,' Mr Potsane says, 'speak to them before the court starts. Any delay now would be good. Otherwise this will all soon be over.'

I find the accused are in good spirits. They ask after Caroline and want to know when the baby's due. 'Are you looking forward to being a father?' Jabu asks. As excited as I am about being a father, I steer the discussion back to my clients. I reiterate that the trial is proceeding quickly and that it needs to be slowed down. Perhaps we should find a way to present their story. Perhaps we need to reassess the strategy.

They look at me quizzically. Will I persuade them to backtrack? Am I losing my nerve? To be honest, I'm not sure I ever had any. And yes, if not wanting them to die is losing my nerve, then maybe I am.

'I would like to ask the judge for an adjournment of about a week so that we can at least take stock,' I explain. 'If you decide to maintain your position, that's fine, but we must explore all the possibilities. Do you agree there is no harm in a week's adjournment?'

'Peter,' Jabu says, 'we trust you and we know you are with us. You should know that we discuss this a lot in prison and our views are unchanged. We can see exactly where this is going, but we will not participate. We know that our families are desperate and we appreciate that, but this is bigger than all of us and you must help us in dealing with our families. I know this is a difficult thing to ask you, but you and Bheki have to talk to them for us. It is difficult for us to talk to them through the Perspex, and the prison visits are always very tense for us.'

I tell him I understand but that the purpose of the break is to explore what we can do to keep them alive for as long as possible without compromising their principles.

'Then go ahead and speak to the judge,' says Jabu. The others nod.

I don't want the prosecution to oppose the adjournment request and so I raise it with them. Harry Prinsloo has no problem and agrees to accompany me to the judge. He has the confident air of a man who can afford to be generous. We meet Judge de Klerk in his chambers next to the court. As always, he is scrupulously polite. I explain the reason for the meeting. He responds that if there is a chance the accused will change their minds, he will grant an adjournment. In any event, he will need time to write his judgment after the close of the prosecution's case. It is settled.

In court, Harry Prinsloo brings an application to protect the next witnesses by continuing the trial in camera. The witnesses are former MK guerrillas. To support the application, Captain Prinsloo testifies that the witnesses fear for their lives and will not give evidence unless they are guaranteed anonymity.

The judge asks the accused if they wish to oppose the application, and they politely indicate that they have no comment. Having got his first prize, Harry Prinsloo decides to go for the second prize as well. He requests that the order to clear the court should include me as I am holding a watching brief and not representing the accused. He's implying that I might disclose the identity of the askaris to the ANC, who might then kill them. Unable to argue on my own behalf, I sit quietly, an irritated observer. The judge overrules the prosecutor and confirms that I can remain in court.

The court is about to be cleared when it occurs to Harry Prinsloo that the order will also apply to the press. He wants media coverage of his prize witnesses. On his feet again, with a beady sweat on his flushed forehead, he declares that the State has no objection to members of the press being present. The judge agrees and the gallery is cleared of all but the press.

The first witness is x1. He appears in a black balaclava with only his eyes showing. He could be anyone. x1 describes how he left the country and joined the military wing of the ANC. He also details the modus operandi of a typical MK unit. He confirms that he had met Ting Ting, Neo and Joseph in the various camps at various times. The next witness, x2, gives much the same testimony, mentioning that he had met Joseph in Viana Camp and later in the town of Cacuso.

The last witness to give evidence about MK and its activities is Brigadier Jac Buchner, the commander of the Natal Midlands Security Branch. Urbane and silver-haired, Buchner is a good-looking man with sculpted features and a polished manner. A natty dresser and seldom in uniform, he has a reputation for being clever, and projects a more sophisticated and humane face for the security service.

Buchner is well known among political lawyers as a seasoned witness who has given 'expert' evidence for the prosecution in numerous ANC trials. He is also well known among detainees as an interrogator who gets what he wants without bothering about the niceties of his methods. The head of the Security Branch's Investigation and Research Unit into the ANC until 1987, he claims twenty-five years' experience, mainly focused on the ANC. This experience includes, in his own words, '... the personal interrogation of the majority of the [ANC] terrorists that were arrested between 1976 and 1987. I was also involved with the rehabilitation programme for members of the ANC that have been arrested.'

Confident and at ease in the witness box, he answers Harry Prinsloo's questions about the command structure of MK. As he works through the names of the military commanders in the frontline states and unit structures, Buchner appears on top of his subject. Confirming that the ANC has claimed responsibility for the killing of certain policemen, he quotes extensively from *Sechaba*, an ANC publication, as well as from other ANC documents.

Buchner sets out ANC policy as described by Chris Hani on the distinction between hard and soft targets, backing up his assertions with statistics of 'terrorist' attacks and the casualties since 1976. He shows that with each passing year, the attacks increase and become more deadly, and he describes ANC 'terrorists' as being highly trained and well motivated.

Prinsloo leads him to a final question, 'Was there any change in approach by the ANC since 1976 or not?'

'Yes,' says Buchner, 'the ANC definitely changed its strategy and actions, especially after 1979 when the top structure of the ANC did a study in Vietnam on the Vietnamese struggle against the Americans. They started to implement it in South Africa in 1984 by launching the so-called "people's war" concept. Then came the mass mobilisation, the external training of people and the local training of people for a massive onslaught against the State.' Crude but effective is Jac Buchner.

After a few more corroborating witnesses, the State closes its case.

The judge suggests an adjournment. He concludes, 'I have already said to them [the accused] that it is in their interests in case they want to participate … and I and my assessors and the court are of one mind that participation from their side and a defence from their side will be valuable in ensuring that justice takes place in connection with this matter.' The court is adjourned to Wednesday 1 March 1989.

THE BOMB

The Vlakplaas operation is a secret and it is clandestinely supplied with mostly Eastern bloc weapons seized in the wars waged by South African forces in the frontline states. Wars that took place in the then Rhodesia, in Namibia, Angola, and Mozambique.

On various occasions, a fifteen-ton truck, a five-ton Bedford truck and five one-ton bakkies all with trailers travel to Ovamboland in Namibia to collect weapons, ammunition and explosives. The laden convoys bring to Vlakplaas massive quantities of AK-47s, PKM machine guns, RPD machine guns, SKD machine guns, RP-7 missile launchers, 82 mm rocket launchers, landmines, limpet mines, hand grenades and detonators. In the words of the Vlakplaas commander, 'If there is anything you could imagine, it would have been there ... We had six or seven Sam7s – these were missiles which would be fired by troops on the ground.'

These weapons are dispensed by the Vlakplaas commander on receipt of requests from various Security Branch offices around the country. Colonel Taylor, who runs a similar squad to Vlakplaas consisting of policemen and askaris and based on a farm in Natal, is a special recipient of these weapons and explosives.

For the purpose of assassinations, many of these weapons are fitted with silencers, like the HMKs (9 mm) supplied to the Middelburg Security Branch. AK-47s, Scorpion machine guns, and 16 Uzi's are all fitted with silencers, as are a number of .44 Ruger pistols which are also equipped with telescopic sights. All these weapons are for use in covert operations by the security police although some of the new AK-47s are dispensed to selected police officers for their own personal use.

The weapons are kept at Vlakplaas in two large storerooms and in two shipping containers, for which there are only two keys. There is no record or register of any of these weapons. They are untraceable.

In addition to this armoury, the Vlakplaas operation has recourse to the technical division. And Colonel Waal du Toit is always happy to lend a hand when called on, as in this particular matter.

40

The next week I find tense and disturbing. The families are putting pressure on me to 'do something', while the accused remain opposed to participation. I know they will not change their minds. On the other hand, the families want something done. Anything. The challenge is how to present witnesses and argument in extenuation without compromising my clients' position.

Bheki and I soon realise that it has to be the parents who intervene to save their sons from the death penalty. The only problem, in legal terms, is that the family of the accused have no right to be represented in a criminal case. Families may assist the defence team, or even the prosecution if they feel so inclined, but if the accused refuses representation, the family has no right to step in and ask to be represented on behalf of the accused. So, our dilemma is that not only has this never been done before, but that it is not even provided for in the Criminal Procedure Act and the rules of court.

If we can somehow get this representation for the families, we can lead witnesses and develop a sophisticated argument presenting the accused as soldiers fighting a just war. We can also contextualise the historic position of the ANC and explain why it is fighting a war of liberation against an apartheid government. These issues then become extenuating factors if the judge is prepared to listen, and be very brave. Not a combination often found in political trial judges. In short, the possibility of a judge accepting this line of argument and finding extenuation for ANC cadres who have killed policemen is slim. Certainly, no judge has ever found that the 'soldier' or 'just war' argument constitutes extenuation. But it is better than no chance.

Bheki and I agree it is worth a try and put it to our clients. Even if they accept, we will still have to persuade the judge to allow a procedure for which the law makes no provision and for which there is no precedent.

The meeting at Modder B Prison is preceded, as always, by a game of highly competitive ping-pong. This time I play Neo and lose, largely because of my backhand which he and the others have long since discovered is my weak point. I will have to improve my game in this regard if I want to hold the sporting respect of my clients. They are in good spirits, probably relieved at the break in their court routine.

I come straight to the point. 'Look, your families are desperate that we make some kind of legal intervention. I know this may sound strange to you, but they almost need this more than you do. You are their children and they cannot sit idly by while you proceed to your deaths. You must understand this. Have you talked about your position and is there any change?'

'We've discussed this so much we are now exhausted from it, and there is no change,' says Jabu. 'There is not one of us who thinks differently, and while we love our families and we do not want to die, we will not compromise. And even if we did, we have heard the evidence of the prosecution and it is all true, except what they said about not torturing us and what they said about the ANC. Their case is strong because we did all the things they accuse us of and more. You see, we are convinced that the decision we took was the right one. It is even clearer to us that we would have lost this case anyway, even if we had participated and been prepared to deny we carried out those acts. It is sad, but we cannot help our families or even ourselves on this, and we know what the cost will be. But that is the way things are and that is the course we have chosen.'

It is what I expected. Nonetheless, I argue that 'there is a chance, although a very slim one, that we can get the court to agree to let your families present an argument in extenuation on your behalf, but without your participation. Whether such an extenuation case will be successful is another question. But at least your story and that of the ANC can be told properly.'

'That sounds strange,' says Joseph.

'It is and I'm not even sure it's possible,' I say. 'It certainly hasn't been done before. But these are desperate times and that means we must try the unconventional, even if it is refused.'

Ting Ting is thoughtful. Then he says, 'How would our extenuation case work if we are not a part of it? I always thought that for there to be extenuation, the accused had to go into the witness box and give evidence.'

'This is true,' I say. 'But perhaps we can lead evidence from witnesses who know the conditions under which you left the country and from experts on the ANC. This will at least correct the distorted picture presented by the State and will also give the public insight and understanding into what is really happening in the country. It will wake them up.'

They are listening closely now.

I continue, 'At the end we will construct an argument based on your current position, which is that you are soldiers of the ANC engaged in fighting a just war against an illegal government. Look, it will be a complex and detailed argument. But at least, if the worst happens, your story will be known and people will be able to understand why you carried out the actions you did.'

The discussion goes back and forth, the accused becoming increasingly interested. Bheki makes it clear that we don't know if we will be allowed to represent their families. In the meantime we'll talk with their families about this new approach.

Bheki and I leave Modder B cheered by the prospect of possibly doing something on behalf of our clients. I am lucky to have Bheki with me as his interaction with the men is gentle but direct, revealing his humility. He treats them with respect.

Back at the firm, Bheki and I discuss the matter with Halton Cheadle and Fink Haysom. Halton's practice focuses largely on labour matters, although since the mid-eighties he has become involved in commissions of inquiry and applications to challenge state of emergency regulations and expose police use of torture. Fink's practice is almost exclusively political, with a major focus on representing black communities that have been victims of 'forced removals' from white areas. Both men have acute legal minds and an outstanding sense of legal strategy. I ask them if they think Bheki and I are crazy trying to intervene at this late stage. To my relief, they are supportive although sceptical that the judge will allow the family to present evidence on behalf of the accused. I also run it past Charles Nupen, a fine lawyer with whom I worked at the Legal Resources Centre. He agrees that there is nothing to lose.

Our meeting with the families is brief. The parents need no persuading. Bheki explains that the accused have requested time to consider this approach and how it will impact on their position. Mrs Masina worries that her son and his comrades may refuse to exploit even this narrow gap.

I reassure her that we will try to persuade their sons to seize this opportunity. But I also stress that the court may refuse our request, and that even if we are allowed to proceed, this may not influence the outcome. I don't want the families entertaining unrealistic hopes.

'Just do what you can, Mr Harris,' says Mr Potsane.

His voice is weary, and as I look at his lined face, I think of the end point and what he will have to go through. It will surely be too much to bear. In the end, it is about people, mothers and fathers, sons and daughters, and every life is precious and worth fighting for. In itself, this is a battle of its own.

The next day, we are back at the prison. Ping-pong and politics in Modder B. I lose again, this time to Joseph. Bheki leans against the wall, smiling broadly at my defeat.

Jabu starts. 'Peter, Bheki, we have thought about it but before we discuss it, we would like to hear from you. What do you think we should do?'

'I'm not the one on trial with a potential death sentence at the end of it,' I say, and then advise them to let their parents and families tell the court why they should be regarded as soldiers, not criminals.

Jabu replies that if their parents want to get involved, they won't prevent them. But they do not want to compromise the ANC or themselves. He wants me to check this development with Govan Mbeki, and Lusaka if necessary.

Driving back to Joburg, Bheki and I agree that, if nothing else, we have gained a bit more of that rare commodity – time.

41

Again my meeting with Govan Mbeki is facilitated by Boy Majodina in Port Elizabeth. While kids play ball in the dust of New Brighton streets, Boy and I chat about the case in the tranquillity of his library. He tells me that people in the township have been gripped by the way the accused have handled the trial. People follow the trial closely and are proud that these MK soldiers are not prepared to bend. At a time when good news is in short supply, particularly in the Eastern Cape, he says the four accused have seized the popular imagination. These men have become legends.

My concern is that they do not become martyrs.

Because Govan Mbeki is feeling poorly I visit him at his home. We meet in the sitting room of a modestly furnished, newly built duplex. The room is small, as is the apartment, and I wonder if this is where he lives or whether it is just being used for this meeting. I don't ask.

Govan Mbeki is seated in an armchair. He apologises for not rising to shake hands and tells me that his doctors have advised him to rest. I'm grateful he has agreed to see me even when sick.

Like others in the township, Mbeki has been following the trial with interest. We talk about the proceedings and then I tell him of the attempt to mount an extenuation case. He wants to know who will be called as witnesses and the basis for the extenuation. Eventually, he says that if the accused have no problem with their parents intervening, then he accepts their decision. While admiring my clients' stand, he believes they must not be needlessly inflexible.

Before I leave he asks after their welfare, and requests that I convey his greetings and support.

My next meeting is with Dennis Kuny. I like Dennis because he accepts the tough cases and fights them strenuously and with great integrity. Intellectually honest, he carries the respect of the profession and takes his clients' views seriously.

It's six in the evening when I arrive at his home in a townhouse complex in Parkhurst. He is casually dressed and, as always, calm and relaxed. I can't recall ever having seen him stressed or tense, or maybe he just doesn't show it like the rest of us.

I bring him up to speed, speaking fast as the story envelops me. Slow down, he says, slow down, offering a drink which I refuse. Regaining my composure, I continue the briefing, building up to a request that if refused would cause me to jump off his balcony.

'So can you come in as their senior counsel?' I ask. 'We'll get you a junior. Anyone you want.' He is at the window looking out, deep in thought.

Turning, he says, 'I have set aside the next few weeks to prepare for a major trial, but there is a chance that the trial will be postponed. If so, I'll take the case.'

I thank him, relief flooding through me. 'If you don't mind,' I say, 'I'll have that whisky now.'

I hadn't expected him to take the case if the accused still refused to participate and did not give evidence. I need to make sure there is no misunderstanding and he quietly allays my fears. 'I know what you're asking, Peter,' he says.

We discuss the arguments that can be advanced, the evidence and the potential witnesses. The hours tick by and it's past eleven when I finally drive home. The next day Bheki and I start work on the extenuation case.

42

Today is judgment day. The court is due to sit again after the adjournment. A large crowd has gathered and the mood is angry and tense. I sense the frustration that while the verdict cannot be stopped, it will never be accepted. Buses and taxis are parked on the pavements, the occupants milling excitedly around, talking. There's no toyi-toying. Someone has briefed the crowd properly, as demonstrations in and around court buildings have been outlawed. To defy the law in front of squads of Reaction Unit police with attack dogs would not just be folly, it would be suicide. It would also give the police at the roadblocks an excuse to stop vehicles with supporters. So, the crowd shows uncharacteristically good behaviour. Long may it last, I hope.

I am drawing on a cigarette when the families arrive in the minibus taxi arranged by Bheki. Mr Potsane and Mrs Masina and Jabu's sister Busi in her school uniform. They're dressed formally and under the hot blue sky I can feel the desperate worry consuming them.

Inappropriately, I wish we could all be in a place where there is laughter and children playing. Somewhere uncomplicated and warm with joy. I snap out of this daydream, chiding myself for being ridiculous. I must focus on the extenuation case. I tell the families that today is not going to be a good one. I don't want them to have any false hopes about the coming judgment. Surprisingly, it is Busi who says they are prepared. I look down at her, this slip of a girl, and wonder where her strength comes from.

Bheki and I meet with the judge in his chambers before the session starts. He is at his desk and this time does not get up but motions us to sit. This is the wrong time to speak to him. Unfortunately, we have no choice as we have not heard from Dennis about his postponement and need more time to ensure his availability.

'Judge,' I say, 'the families would like to lead evidence in extenuation

175

on behalf of the accused even though the accused will not participate.' He leans forward, interested. I continue, 'We are in the process of procuring the services of senior and junior counsel but availability on such short notice is difficult.'

He looks at us. 'The court will have to give serious consideration to this request, particularly if the accused continue to insist on not participating. You know that you will have to bring an application to the court to participate on this basis. This is completely new.'

I acknowledge that we're aware of the technicalities. There's an awkward silence. He is distracted and somewhat irritated, which is understandable as he's about to give judgment and probably will find my clients guilty of murder, high treason and other serious offences.

The court is equally sombre. The accused dressed in their dark suits, the packed gallery silent. We rise when the judge enters. He sits, arranges his papers, asks the accused to be seated and in measured tones starts reading his judgment in Afrikaans. It takes a long time because each sentence is translated into Sesotho for the accused.

The judge has done his homework. He deals with the accused not being represented and the fact that their rights have been explained to them repeatedly and that, nonetheless, they still chose not to participate. In my opinion he's covering himself, as I would do in his position.

His judgment continues all day. It's detailed and meticulous because he must leave no grounds for review or appeal. He must cover every angle. At the end of the afternoon he is still not finished and adjourns to the next day.

This is a respite, but it also increases the tension. The following morning the conclusion of his judgment comes quickly. The words 'guilty of murder' reverberate around the court, hitting me like bullets as I hear them again and again. I turn to the accused, they stare straight ahead. Then Ting Ting turns and talks quietly to Jabu, who nods. The reporters are frantically taking notes.

The judge finds the accused guilty on all of the main charges. Each time he says 'guilty', a door slams in my mind, until he is finished and there are no more doors to close. Except, I realise, he hasn't found Joseph guilty of murder. Perhaps there is a chance he will escape the death sentence. For the other three the situation is dire, as I'd always known.

Often, in such cases, the accused react emotionally when found guilty of treason and murder. It's an opportunity to shout ANC slogans, even sing. Jabu, Ting Ting, Neo and Joseph remain silent. Dignified. Louisa van der Walt is staring at them, but they ignore the provocation and focus on the judge.

The judge looks at the accused. He finds accused numbers one, two and three guilty of crimes for which the death sentence can be imposed. He tells them that what he has to say applies to all of them, including accused number four.

A low buzz of interest stirs the gallery as he continues. 'The onus to show that there are mitigating factors rests on you. If mitigating circumstances are not shown and the court finds that there are no mitigating circumstances, then the court has to impose the death sentence.' The words 'death sentence' silence the gallery.

'Mitigating circumstances are circumstances that affected your state of mind and influenced you to commit the deeds that you did, and which as a result of that influence make your actions less morally blameworthy. I have understood from Mr Harris that your families are concerned about you and intend to give evidence in relation to mitigating circumstances. The court will welcome that help. I understand that there is not yet clarity about whether you will participate. Clever people like professors and psychologists will possibly be called as witnesses and they will possibly say that they have tried to look inside your heads to see what possibly influenced you. That is not the best evidence that can be laid before the court about what possibly influenced you. Strictly speaking, it is only you who know if something happened and if there are types of influences that worked on you, and it is necessary that you yourselves give evidence if there are circumstances that worked on you, that made you commit the deeds you did. And on many aspects it will only be you who can place the facts and evidence before the court.'

I experience a rush of elation even while I realise that he is making it clear that unless the accused give evidence themselves our strategy mightn't succeed. I'm intrigued that he's dismissive of the 'clever people', but the most important factor is that he will allow the evidence.

Not so fast. Harry Prinsloo jumps to his feet. 'Your Lordship, can we please get from the accused what their position is, as the accused have to give the instruction [to participate]. With respect, their families are not a party to the matter.'

This is dangerous. Harry Prinsloo is right. The judge considers this and then says that he is sure the accused will reserve their rights. Turning to my clients, he asks, 'Will any of the accused say anything about the question of mitigation of sentence?'

The men shake their heads and indicate that they have nothing to say.

In response the judge postpones proceedings to give the accused an opportunity to consider this issue.

As he leaves the court, I sit down, drained. I expected the guilty verdict, so why am I so upset? It's probably because the finding of murder is a big step closer to their final destination. It seems so irrevocable. The reasoning has taken a day and a half. Judge de Klerk has delivered a meticulous judgment. Yes, we can always appeal at a later stage, but I know that on these facts we have no chance of appealing against the findings of guilt. At the same time, I am excited that he has not closed the door on the families presenting evidence on behalf of their sons. He has also dismissed Harry Prinsloo's objection. Then again, we took the prosecution by surprise with this approach. When we make formal application to the court after reconvening, they will be much better prepared.

I go down to the cells. Ignoring the finding of murder, I ask my clients if they're happy on the extenuation issue.

'We have no problem with it,' says Ting Ting, 'but the judge must not expect us to participate.'

We talk briefly and then I head back upstairs as the judge wants to see me in his chambers. He's sitting in an easy chair beside a coffee table. He looks exhausted, yet more relaxed than the previous morning. 'Have your clients given any indication that they will participate?' he asks.

I shake my head. 'Their position at present is unchanged.'

He sighs and gets to his feet. 'Please thank your clients for their professional behaviour.' I am struck by his use of the word 'professional'.

THE BOMB

The askaris at Vlakplaas, like most traitors, are not trusted by their police colleagues. They are all highly trained and experienced in combat and may, in the view of their commanders, defect back to the ANC. In order to prevent this, some of the established askaris are paid to inform on the new askaris at Vlakplaas. Their phones are also tapped, the recording devices being located in one of the offices at Vlakplaas, and listened to on a regular basis. In addition, their movements are strictly monitored.

The askaris are paid from a secret fund according to an official scale of remuneration. This includes incentive bonuses for performance successes. Deserving of merit here would be the identification of members of the ANC, their former MK comrades, the tracing of weapons and, of course, the arrest or killing of members of the ANC or PAC. All members at Vlakplaas have false identification documents, passports along with false credit cards, cheque accounts and petrol cards. The false identification documents are initially supplied by the intelligence service but this proves cumbersome so the Vlakplaas commander speaks directly to the department of internal affairs and arranges to obtain the necessary false documentation directly from them. All this to ensure the total secrecy and anonymity so essential to an assassination squad.

43

We are back in court to argue the application to mount an extenuation case on behalf of the families. This time Bheki and I are accompanied by Dennis Kuny and his junior counsel Elna Revelas. We're all exhausted from the intense preparation that a last-minute extenuation case demands and aware that the prosecution will put up a stronger fight this time. I know that Harry Prinsloo is less concerned about the legal implications than he is about the political exposure that the accused and the ANC will be given. Like most of the legal commentators, he probably rates our chances at zero.

Kuny, in his black gown, stands and says quietly, 'We are instructed by the families of the four accused having regard to the fact that the accused, who have adopted an attitude of total non-participation in the trial to date, are now convicted of the most serious offences. They face the prospect of, or at least three of them face the prospect of, the ultimate penalty if extenuation is not established. Their families are concerned about the fact that they have chosen not to participate and that extenuation may not, in the circumstances, be established. We are instructed by Mr Harris that the accused do not intend to do anything more than to read out a statement to this court, and we have therefore been instructed by the families to lead evidence and to argue the question of extenuation should this court see fit to allow us to do so. I must emphasise that the instructions do not emanate from the accused themselves; they completely dissociate themselves from our presence in this court, and they maintain their attitude of non-participation save for the reading of a statement. Now I know of no precedent for the court allowing appearance on this, the basis on which we seek to intervene, but it seems to us, M'Lord, that in the interest of justice [the court] could and should allow us to take part in the proceedings to the limited extent to which we would want to do so.'

Harry Prinsloo immediately opposes the application. The accused have given no mandate to Kuny to represent them, he says, and the Criminal Procedure Act makes no provision for this type of representation. Like Kuny, he points out that there is no precedent for this application. He ends by emphasising that there are no legal grounds on which his learned friend can present evidence on behalf of the families.

Incredibly, the judge comes at the issue from a different angle. Is there any precedent to the contrary, he wants to know, which says that this cannot be done?

Prinsloo flushes at this unexpected opposition from the judge and refers to the law.

The judge cuts in. The accused have already been found guilty of deeds that attract the death sentence. 'Can it ever be that the court, approached by a parent of such a person, albeit an adult, will slap the face of that parent and say to him, "I am not prepared to listen to you," when the parent of such a person wants to give evidence or lead evidence? Is that just?'

Not letting go, Prinsloo maintains that the parents cannot intervene. He asserts that the accused want to participate on their own terms – after all, they wish to read out a statement. The implication will be that any parent can just walk in and say, 'I now want to present evidence.'

The prosecutor and the judge argue back and forth until Prinsloo, raising his hand petulantly, says that he cannot take it further and abruptly sits down.

The judge asks Kuny if the accused wish to place evidence on record. Jabu responds, 'We are still committed to our stand, although we do appreciate the course which has been taken by our parents. We believe they have the right to show concern, but we do not change anything.'

At the lunch break, the gallery spills out into the corridors, chattering excitedly about this unexpected development in a trial that is already far from conventional. Representatives from the embassies exchange views with the press, talking earnestly to some of the political leaders, sympathetic but keeping their distance.

The investigating officer, Captain Prinsloo, confers angrily with the prosecution, while Harry Prinsloo shakes his head and gestures towards the now vacant bench. If the judge rules in our favour, allowing us to mount an extenuation case on the basis suggested, we will be getting the best of both worlds. In effect, the accused will be participating on their own terms. The prosecution is losing control and they don't like it.

Speaking to the families in the corridor, I sense hope for the first time. Not hope of success, but hope that they will be heard.

Outside the court, the crowd gathers in the street, watched by the Reaction Unit. At present, this crowd is no danger.

Bheki and I enjoy a cigarette in the hot sun. 'You know, Pete,' he says, 'this judge is not behaving as I thought he would. I really expected something else. I don't know if this is his reputation or whether he has been slowly changing during the course of the trial, but he has behaved correctly and with compassion.'

I agree. I've never seen a judge in a serious political trial be so accommodating. It is not that he is sympathetic, but he seems to understand what drove the accused, and that, in itself, is significant. That he is prepared to entertain this application is an indication of his bona fides. I believe that the accused have influenced him through their conduct. He sees them as 'professionals'. The challenge is to make him see them as soldiers.

Back in court the judge is quick and to the point. He summarises the morning's proceedings, adding that the court is concerned with the fact that justice must be done, and that it cannot be done unless the other side is heard.

'Finally,' he says, 'I wish to remark that although the interests of family herein may, as yet, not be founded in a judgment or in legislation, they do have an interest, even if it is based on the blood bond and relationship which binds them. I am unaware of any basis on which it could be said that the family should not be heard and in my opinion, not to hear them in a case like the present would be improper and unheard of. Moreover, it is hard to imagine that, where someone's life is at stake, a court would refuse to hear any responsible person or institution that could make a contribution. The application that the family may present evidence is allowed.' He glances at the accused and leaves the court.

Silence, then an outburst of clapping and cheering from the gallery. The gallery is on its feet, the clapping continues and slowly ends. I see tears on the faces of some family members. Others have bowed their heads in prayer. Jabu's mother smiles at me, nodding her head. I look at the accused. There's a hint of a smile on Jabu's face.

44

The first salvo in the extenuation is the accused's statement. It has to set the scene. We'd spent much time formulating the statement to provide the framework for what would follow in the extenuation argument. And it'd been checked with the internal political leadership. Raymond

Suttner, released in 1983 after seven years in prison for ANC activities, gave valuable input.

Jabu, trim in his black suit, stands squarely, feet apart, military style. He turns to acknowledge the gallery and then faces the judge. From the inside pocket of his jacket he pulls out the folded typed statement. His presentation is not melodramatic, although emotion flows powerfully through the words as they echo around the packed courtroom. Occasionally he stumbles over words, losing his place and taking time to find it again in the way of someone unaccustomed to public speaking. Clearly, at other times, he has memorised parts and he recites whole sentences without referring to his notes. The delivery is that of an ordinary man. An ordinary man in an extraordinary position.

'Thank you, Sir,' he begins. 'It is important for this court and all South Africans to understand that the African National Congress and those that they represent turned to armed struggle as a last resort. If anyone is aware of the true meaning of violence, it is the black peoples of southern Africa. It is we who have been the victims of violence for centuries. Our own experience has taught us to hate violence and it was to terminate the violence against our people, which is inherent in white minority domination, that the ANC was formed. For almost fifty years, and particularly under the extreme provocation that came with the apartheid system in 1948, we resisted the natural urge to respond by resorting to armed struggle. For more than a decade, we continued to proclaim and indeed follow a policy of non-violence in the face of unrelenting and mounting violence against our people.'

Jabu goes on to outline how the non-violent ANC, after the government massacred people at Sharpeville, was forced into embarking on an armed struggle. He mentions the formation of MK and the hopes that it would make the government see sense.

'Let it be remembered,' he says, 'that the onslaught of Nazism ultimately left the people of Europe with no choice but to fight. In the same way, the onslaught of apartheid has ultimately left its victims in South Africa with no choice but to fight.'

He cites the struggle of people in the United States for human rights, and reminds the court of the preamble to the Universal Declaration of Human Rights which states that human rights should be protected by the rule of law. He talks about the ANC's requests over the decades for negotiations and how only when those were stonewalled did the movement turn to armed struggle.

'We are not criminals,' he says, 'we are not murderers. I, myself, am a survivor of the Soweto revolt of 1976, where I suffered the trauma of seeing hundreds of innocent children and young people, including my own relatives and friends, drop dead from police gunfire. That event shocked us all into the realisation that the life of the black person has no value under apartheid, and will have none until the system is destroyed. Indeed the slaughter has continued, and many more have been killed or hanged since 1976.'

Against this background he presents his unit's actions as the actions of soldiers. Their cause is a struggle for self-determination which he likens to the fight against fascism in the Second World War. 'We, as soldiers of a people's army, struggle against a State which continues to deny the people's right to self-determination and which practises a policy of apartheid which has been characterised as an international crime,' he points out. 'The charge sheet refers to the ANC attacking the "state authority". Who gave it that authority? We say that the present South African government has no authority, no moral or legal right to rule over the people of this country. It is therefore our duty to bring this crime to an end, to remove this illegal state. We are soldiers in a patriotic army, struggling to establish democracy and peace. We believe that we are prisoners of war and that we should be treated in accordance with international rules governing such status. The state of war which exists in South Africa is a war of national liberation.'

Jabu then outlines the civil war that exists in the country and the cross-border violations of the SADF into Angola, Botswana, Lesotho, Mozambique, Swaziland, Zambia and Zimbabwe. Actions which the ANC has tried to regulate in conformity with the international laws of war to protect civilians and the innocent nationals of these countries. To no avail.

The sweep of Jabu's statement now includes the war in the townships, the tragedy that civilians are included in the atrocities, and again he compares the violence to the slaughter of innocents during the Second World War and in more recent wars in Vietnam and the Middle East. He reiterates the ANC's policy of not striking at civilians and places the responsibility for the Silverton bombing solely on his unit. There is a war going on,' he stresses, that is of a violent and often arbitrary nature. 'The whole of

South Africa is beginning to bleed,' he says, 'and will continue to do so unless the apartheid system is destroyed and replaced by a democratic system of government.'

He ends by saying, 'To whites in this country we stretch out our arms and call on you to help end the violence of apartheid. You have the power and the opportunity to contribute decisively to redress an historical injustice which has persisted for over three centuries. We know that this court may sentence us to death. If this happens, so be it! We love life, but we love our people and our country even more. If we are hanged, our death will not be in vain. Those who come after us will undoubtedly complete our mission in life: to create a just and democratic South Africa which belongs to all who live in it. The struggle continues!'

The accused rise, turn to the gallery and shout, 'Amandla!' The gallery roars back, 'Amandla!' Normally, this slogan would have been repeated a second time, culminating in a third cry of 'Amandla awethu!' and the crowd's response, 'iAfrica!' But Jabu, avoiding showmanship, quickly sits down after the first 'Amandla'. This immediately silences the gallery. The accused face the judge.

45

Early the next morning, I pick up Bheki outside the office and we drive through to Delmas. I notice that the newspaper billboards refer to the trial and the statement from the dock. Bheki has scanned the major dailies and says that all have carried extensive reports and some have printed the statement in full across the two centre pages. As we drive, he reads excerpts.

He's excited, perhaps invigorated by the exposure the accused have received. He tells me that Jabulani in Soweto is buzzing with news of the trial and that at a political meeting last night he was questioned on every detail about the accused.

The behaviour of the accused in the trial lives up to the legend of how an MK soldier is perceived in the township. There are constant stories in the papers and on TV about the communist demons of the ANC, hell-bent on reducing the country to ashes, committed to the slaughter of whites and the destruction of the economy. Somehow Jabu, Ting Ting, Neo and

Joseph don't quite fit the picture and their statement challenges popular preconceptions. And, as all lawyers do in every trial, we discuss the judge and speculate about what he is thinking and how he will conduct himself in the future.

There is a bigger crowd at the court than usual. For Bheki this is a good thing. 'Even if they can't get into court it shows the kind of support the accused are getting,' he says. 'It's a good indicator of what we will be able to muster in a campaign if they are sentenced to death.' I look at him, shocked at his thinking ahead like that, and then I realise that he's right to be realistic.

The accused are also in a good mood, cracking jokes and waving to people in the gallery. They're excited by the press coverage Bheki shows them. The statement is a hard act to follow. After such powerful words from the dock by men virtually condemned, leading witnesses through their evidence is something of an anti-climax. However, this is not routine stuff. It is about finding details that may save these men's lives.

Kuny begins by outlining our objective, which is to place the accused's conduct in context and to give some idea of what motivated their attitudes and actions.

'We believe,' he says, 'that if placed in context the court may be able to evaluate with a greater degree of understanding the acts which have led to their conviction and, M'Lord, our submission will be at the end of the day that the moral responsibility for the acts committed is diminished to the extent that the court is able to see their conduct in the context in which we propose to place it.'

Bheki and I exchange glances, more comfortable with our role as participants rather than observers. It is a relief to have the security of a full legal team and we are all conscious of the unspoken bond that has developed between us. We have our individual roles. Bheki has taken to communicating with the families, which he does calmly and respectfully. The prosecutors never address him, even when he speaks to them. They answer his queries through me. In their eyes I may be a traitor but at least I'm white. Bheki pretends not to notice their rudeness. I envy him his lack of expectation.

The first witness is Professor Colin Bundy. In his forties, he cuts a boyish figure in the witness box. Oxford qualified and one of South Africa's most eminent historians, he has been used by our firm in a number of treason trials. Based at the University of Cape Town and the University of the Western Cape, Bundy had struck me in consultations as a man of quiet integrity, avoiding the grandstanding that is the territory of so many trial experts and speaking authoritatively on his field as an expert in our history of the nineteenth and twentieth centuries.

Kuny begins by asking Bundy to describe the circumstances that led people like our clients to leave the country and join the ANC after the events of 1976.

Speaking softly, Bundy describes those days of shock, grief and anger. Kuny leads him to comment on how the resistance in those months united black communities and how the conflict with armed police radicalised a generation. The questioning is gently guiding and to the point. I know that in these cases everything depends on whether the judge is prepared to put himself in the shoes of the accused. To do this, he has to cast aside the prejudice that lives in every South African. A tall order. The accused have made it clear that they have no expectations on this front, but despite myself I know that we have to hope and, frankly, this judge has not yet killed hope.

Moving closer to the crux, Kuny begins to examine the conduct of the accused in the context that Bundy has sketched. They have described themselves as soldiers of the ANC. Would Bundy regard this as an accurate self-description?

'Yes. I believe it certainly is that,' says Bundy. He goes on to detail the ANC's move to the armed struggle as civil strife escalated. Then Kuny changes the point of view and asks him to assess if the government regards the situation as one of war. Bundy replies that although the terminology is different, there is a 'striking agreement between the two sides'. He quotes from government documentation that show a doubling of the period of conscription, the massive increase in military budgets and the sort of language that cabinet ministers and generals use. Terms such as 'total onslaught' and 'mobilisation' and even that South Africa is engaged in 'warfare'.

Trying to recreate the state of mind of the accused when they committed the acts, Kuny asks Bundy to comment on the perceptions of the police held by the black community. The historian digs back into research first conducted in 1935 and then refers to the role of the police in the townships and the homelands as administrators and enforcers.

From their statement, says Kuny, the accused regard themselves as fighting a war of liberation.

'That is so, yes,' confirms Bundy, once again alluding to the armed struggle as a strategy of liberation.

The questioning then looks for parallels in other parts of the world and Bundy points to instances, adding that sometimes 'yesterday's guerrillas will be tomorrow's prime ministers'. He cites Mahatma Gandhi, Kenyatta, Nkrumah, Hastings Banda, and a number of other leaders. Equally, it was true of Jan Christiaan Smuts, General J B M Hertzog, General Louis Botha and John Vorster, all of whom were imprisoned for their part in the struggle against what they regarded as oppressive and alien restrictions. He states that the struggle of the Afrikaner for liberation was akin to that of black South Africans taking place today.

Kuny then leads Bundy into commenting on how 'liberation fighters' like the accused are perceived in the black community and the political situation in the townships during the mid-1980s. Bundy's answer paints a picture of MK soldiers being given support by ordinary citizens in their conflict with an invading army. 'Troops out of the townships', Bundy adds, was a slogan frequently heard in those times.

Finally, Kuny asks Bundy to comment on the commitment of the accused to their struggle. Judging by their actions of going into exile, joining a political organisation, undergoing military training and returning as combatants, Bundy believes these actions speak of a distinctive level of commitment and political idealism. As does their attitude in court. It also demonstrates that they are under the command of a military structure.

Kuny sits and we wait for Harry Prinsloo to begin his cross-examination. Bundy appears almost embarrassed at being the subject of so much attention. He peers about, fidgeting. Harry Prinsloo's tack is to request a postponement on the grounds that the prosecution was given no notice of this witness. Bundy's evidence has put him in a foul mood. He gets his request and when the court reconvenes Prinsloo predictably attacks the man and his credentials. He argues that Bundy relies on insufficient sources, lacks intimate knowledge of the political scenario, and is one-sided.

Prinsloo focuses on Bundy's methodology, questioning whether he is able to distinguish between the propaganda and the truth contained in ANC publications. Bundy refers Prinsloo to the standard tests used by social scientists and historians when assessing printed material, tests of consistency, coherence and corroboration from other sources.

Slim pickings for Prinsloo. He enters into the substance of Bundy's evidence and engages the historian in a debate on the causes of the 1976 political uprising.

PRINSLOO: Are you able to say to what extent the public at large in Soweto was intimidated by people to participate in uprisings or aren't you able to say?

BUNDY: Again, I do not think that that operates at any kind of level of accuracy as an explanation for collective behaviour. The explanatory model of the external agitator has been so thoroughly and widely discredited within the social sciences that it really does not bear entertaining.

PRINSLOO: Concerning yourself with the factual situation in Soweto, are you able to say that the uprising in Soweto was not attributable to people intimidating the public at large to start uprisings or would your answer be mere speculation? Can you tell the court, please?

BUNDY: No, I think that the whole pattern of events in Soweto, and I am restricting us here to South Western Townships for the moment rather than a national phenomenon, classically adheres to what one would describe as spontaneous political behaviour. Large numbers of people acting, for one thing, in accord, and for a second thing, without very much formal leadership. Those are the characteristics of spontaneous crowd behaviour and they seem to fit very accurately the events in Soweto in 1976.

PRINSLOO: On what do you base your reply that it was spontaneous behaviour?

BUNDY: I base my reply on the studies that have been made of events in Soweto, the best available scholarly studies of those events and, believe me, given their importance, they attracted a good deal of scholarly attention.

We sit back, although I wonder how long the judge will allow the argument to continue before asking Prinsloo to get to the point. But the

189

judge appears interested. I exchange glances with the accused, who are impassive but attentive. I can see where Harry Prinsloo is going but the movement is cumbersome and slow.

PRINSLOO: Professor, the proportion of people, the percentage that left South Africa as a result of so-called uprisings as opposed to the percentage of people that remained, would you agree that it was only a small percentage?

BUNDY: Evidently.

PRINSLOO: Why didn't the rest of the population leave, or a large number of them?

BUNDY: It would be a very extraordinary phenomenon were that to take place. I cannot think of a reasonable or rational parallel in recent history. I think also that the question reveals some lack of sensitivity or nuance with respect to the action of leaving one's country and going into exile. I think it takes little cognisance of the difficulties of doing so, in many cases without official travel documents. I think, if I may, it seems to me to be not very useful … The arithmetic way is not a very useful way of expressing the difference.

Listening to Harry Prinsloo's meandering cross-examination, I feel grateful that, so far, he has not identified the weakness in the extenuation case. This is the Silverton bomb and whether the accused were acting on orders or within their mandate as soldiers of the ANC. Or was it, as we say in law, a frolic of their own? Clearly, when they set off that bomb, they were not acting on orders – but were they acting within ANC policy?

If they were, it could be contended that this reduced their moral blameworthiness. In their statement the accused had placed some distance between the Silverton action and the ANC. So the issue was debatable. Then again, it doesn't look like we have to worry too much about this, as Prinsloo continues to focus on the 1976 uprisings.

During the adjournment for tea I visit the accused in their cell. Their first question is how Caroline is coping with her pregnancy. This is typical. I respond in kind because I know that whenever we discuss children they become animated, asking for the smallest details. The minutiae of normal family life fascinates them, takes them through the prison bars to a distant place.

Gradually I move the conversation to the topic of Harry Prinsloo's cross-examination. But they're not interested. Joseph, the youngest, talks about an attractive woman who signalled to him from the gallery. Discussion of the people in the gallery is always a good topic.

After the tea break, Harry Prinsloo resumes the fight. Unfortunately, someone's had a few words with him, probably Captain Prinsloo, as he moves off the topic of 1976 to that of the Silverton bomb. Now he is on much firmer ground and he knows it. Boldly, he asks Professor Bundy his personal views on the ANC's policy of violence.

Bundy replies in measured tones. 'I think that the only defensible forms of political violence or perhaps the only explicable forms of political violence are those which are governed by some principle, some policy, some discipline. I think that whether on moral terms or terms of historical efficacy indiscriminate violence is highly undesirable.'

Bheki and I exchange glances – this is getting tricky. The potential disjunction between the views of Bundy and the actions of the accused entices Prinsloo. We have briefed Bundy on this line of questioning so he is not completely at sea, but we are still in deep waters.

And then Harry Prinsloo inexplicably blunders. 'Members of the South African Police and armed forces are also trained,' he says. 'If they had been in the dock would you also testify on the same basis that they had been militarily trained and politicised to kill? Would that be extenuation according to your evidence?'

Bundy replies in a clear voice, turning slightly towards us, our eyes acknowledging the gift Harry Prinsloo has foolishly offered. 'It would depend on the circumstances, but I can see extenuation being made on parallel grounds.'

Harry Prinsloo pauses, looks down at his papers, realising that he has just put our own case to our witness. The court is silent. The prosecutor looks at the judge and tries to regain lost ground, hoping that an expert witness in an ANC trial would never support an SADF soldier. 'If they were members of the defence force, for instance? If members of the defence force were being, were on charges of murder?' Red in the face, he stumbles over the words.

Bundy confirms his answer and lines up Harry Prinsloo. 'You are asking me would professional training, military training, be an extenuating circumstance?'

'Yes,' says the prosecutor weakly, the roles reversed.

Bundy says, 'I can easily imagine such evidence being led, yes.'

Floundering, compounding the damage, Harry Prinsloo, with a rasp in his voice, asks why.

Bundy replies, 'It seems to me to be not too large a logical link. I am describing processes that are in parallel.'

Kuny leans over to Bheki and me and slowly smiles.

The prosecutor returns to the safer ground of the compliance of field operatives with ANC policy. He scores some points, but we all know this cross-examination is over. He sits down. The investigating officer, Captain Prinsloo, glares at him furiously.

Kuny's re-examination is brief, touching up the weak points and driving home Harry Prinsloo's mistake. 'Now, you were asked by my learned friend whether the sort of case that you have put up here today, if one can call it that for the moment, will also apply in respect of actions committed by trained soldiers of, let us say, the South African Defence Force, who might be charged with such an offence.'

'Yes,' replies Bundy.

'And your answer was that you thought that such a case might be made out.'

'Yes.'

Kuny says, 'Are you familiar with an instance which is in fact current in Namibia where certain soldiers of the South African Defence Force received a presidential pardon in respect of a prosecution?'

'Yes, I am familiar with that,' Bundy replies. 'I believe there are six soldiers involved.'

'Are you familiar with the basis on which the pardon was issued?'

'I understand that the basis is that they were acting in good faith in the carrying out of instructions.'

'Yes,' says Kuny.

The judge intervenes, asking questions that focus on the nature of the training of ANC recruits in the camps and also on the extent of political training. Bundy confirms that such training takes place. The judge asks if there is theological training in the ANC camps, to which Bundy replies that he does not know, except to say that one of the twenty-seven departments in the ANC is a department for religious affairs.

Our next witness is Mr Potsane.

46

Mr Potsane walks to the witness stand. His sixty-nine years compel a stiffness of movement as he slowly climbs the three steps onto the elevated wooden podium. Standing there, frail but upright, he has a dignity which silences the court. Even the sniggering Reaction Unit police in their close-fitting light-blue uniforms are more reserved.

Mr Potsane gazes around the court, looking at his son and then at the judge. Kuny clears his throat to attract Mr Potsane's attention, and starts to lead him through his evidence.

Born in Ladybrand in the Orange Free State in 1920, Simon Atoyi Potsane went to Johannesburg as a young man to work as a municipal labourer. In 1949, he got married and in the following years he had five children. The youngest boy is Neo, accused number three.

Mr Potsane tells the court that he joined the South African Army in 1941 to fight in the Second World War. After training, he was posted to North Africa as a member of the 10th Field Ambulance Unit. Captured at Sidi Rezegh, for three and a half years he was held prisoner in camps in Italy and Germany. At the end of the war he returned home and trained as a carpenter.

It doesn't come out in his testimony, but in our consultations he'd told us that he'd joined up because there was talk that if black people fought this war they would return to a country where everyone would be equal. I was fascinated by his experiences in the war and in the POW camps. It was physically and mentally hard but he'd survived. After his release he spent a little time in Germany until the yearning for his family and the rich brown earth drove him home. He was paid some money for his war efforts and returned to civilian life. Nothing had changed but then he expected that it would take time for things to change. In the meantime, he, who had fought and suffered for his country, still had to sit on designated park benches, had to travel in separate buses and trains, could not own land or even a house. But he was patient.

Then in 1948 the National Party came to power and things got worse. It baffled him that those Afrikaner leaders who had supported the Nazis and fascism, and who had been incarcerated for acts of sabotage, were now in power. Whereas he and his family were not even second-class citizens; they were not citizens at all. He was powerless to deal with the great betrayal. Bitterly he realised he'd helped to fight and win a war, only to lose everything.

Potsane joined the Pan Africanist Congress, but after it was banned in April 1960 he had no further involvement in politics. He moved with his family to the Orange Free State in 1961 to work on a gold mine, where he remained until 1974.

A deeply religious man, a preacher in his church, the Gereformeerde Kerk in Suid-Afrika, he represented his community at the church synods. All his children were brought up in the church, particularly Neo, who was a staunch member of the choir. He recalls that he and Neo competed in an inter-choir competition in KwaThema.

With Kuny prompting him, Potsane recalls how Neo was a good pupil at school. While in Form One in 1976, he was unable to sit his exams due to some 'misfortune'.

The judge wants to know what sort of misfortune.

'Well,' Mr Potsane answers, 'it was mainly due to the riots, M'Lord, there was no proper schooling.'

'And what about 1977? Was he able to complete that year in school?'

'Due to these unrests he could not sit for his exams.'

Kuny continues, asking if anything happened to Neo during the unrest.

'Yes,' says Mr Potsane. 'He was shot on his ear.'

'Was he seriously injured?'

'Ja, the ear is made of a certain tissue, the bullet penetrated this tissue and only blood could be seen.'

There is something very emotional about a parent giving evidence on behalf of their child. I have seen it a number of times and it is always moving. Regardless of what the child has done, the obvious love of a mother or a father standing publicly in court, their anguish visible, talking of their child and pleading for understanding and leniency, perhaps pleading for the child's very life, is something which strikes to the soul. It is an act that demands respect. In this case, the entire court listens quietly to Mr Potsane.

In December 1977, Neo left home saying he was going to visit his grandfather in the Orange Free State. Some time later, Mr Potsane received a visit from the police to inform him that his son had left the country. From then until October 1986 when the police told him that they'd arrested his son, he'd heard nothing from Neo. And the first time he saw him was that December. Nine years had elapsed.

Mr Potsane talks of the 'difficulties' in Soweto at the time. Police harassment, unemployment, the poverty. He'd sent two of his children to Lesotho so their education would not be disturbed. He describes the reaction of the public to the killing of the policeman Chapi, whom he describes as a ruthless murderer. 'The news of his death spread like wildfire. The public was jubilant.'

Louisa van der Walt is on her feet, objecting to Mr Potsane's evidence as hearsay. The judge overrules her. 'Madam, I think we must allow this witness to tell what is in his heart. We will decide later whether it is relevant.'

The old man in the witness stand is beginning to tire. He grips the wooden ledge of the witness stand tightly with both hands, but he still stands upright, rigid, showing a soldier's back. Kuny catches my eye and says he is going to finish up. I nod in agreement.

'What is your attitude towards your son's conduct?' Kuny asks.

'While his deeds do not so much trouble me,' Mr Potsane replies, 'as a Christian I was really hurt, because in Christianity no killing is allowed.'

'So could you explain what you mean when you say that his deeds did not really trouble you.'

'I mean him leaving the country, him being trained abroad, his return, that did not worry me, because I knew he had left for training in order to defend his fellow men.'

In her cross-examination, Louisa van der Walt tries to get Mr Potsane to admit that his own son misled him by not telling him he was leaving the country. Her aim is to question Neo's integrity. The judge curtly stops this line of questioning. 'I don't think this question is relevant, next question please.'

Van der Walt moves on to Neo's church attendance as a youth. Again, the judge intervenes and stops the question. There is clearly an empathy for this old man whose son is facing the death sentence. Each time the judge intervenes, the frustration of the prosecution rises. Going nowhere, Louisa van der Walt ends her cross-examination. Mr Potsane slowly returns to his seat.

THE BOMB

The Vlakplaas operation is led by Captain Eugene de Kock. Captain de Kock is a man of average height and stocky build, his jet-black hair falls forward across his forehead to the thick black-rimmed spectacles that he favours. The large glasses obscure his aquiline features and a Roman nose curving down to a strong chin. While handsome in a dark way, there is little striking about de Kock. He is not nondescript, but he is very normal looking.

De Kock had grown up on the East Rand. His father was a senior magistrate. As a child, de Kock was considered a gentle boy with a penchant for classical music. He wasn't thought of as violent. He joined the police in 1968.

De Kock is a quiet man who holds the respect of his men. He is also totally feared and with good reason, for he is one of the most decorated and experienced combat veterans in the entire South African security establishment. A veteran of the elite Special Air Services in the Rhodesian war and later a member of the Koevoet Police Counter-Insurgency Unit in Namibia, legendary for its violence and for a litany of atrocities.

De Kock survived more than three hundred contacts with Swapo guerrillas in the Namibian and Angolan wars. He also survived two landmine explosions. In the first incident his eardrums were damaged. In the second he had to be cut from an armoured vehicle that had been blasted forty metres from the point of the explosion. In total, he spent four and a half years with Koevoet. They were years filled with war and brutality, unaccountable years in which de Kock acquired a reputation for savagery and a merciless attraction to murder in an undefined conflict where there were no boundaries.

At the end of his time with Koevoet, his commander, General Dreyer, wrote in a report on de Kock that he should not be used for operational services again and, specifically, that he should not be used for any operational work of the same gruesome nature that he had been exposed to in Koevoet. He was transferred back to security police headquarters in Pretoria. After a month's leave, he joined the Vlakplaas operation on 1 July 1983. On 1 July 1985, he took over the command of Vlakplaas from Colonel Jack Cronje. Damaged goods. The men he inherited were equally disturbed.

47

The final witness in extenuation is Father Eddie Risi. Ordained as a Catholic priest in 1974, he is currently the provincial Superior for the Transvaal Province of the Missionary Oblates of Mary Immaculate. In August 1975, Father Risi was posted to the Diepkloof parish of the Catholic Church in Soweto, where he remained as a priest until February 1985. Father Risi, a short man with a shock of black hair, is dressed in black pants and a black jacket with a white shirt and the familiar round collar worn by men of the cloth. A wooden cross hangs in the middle of his chest. Although relatively young, his face is weathered and lined, giving him a hardness of aspect.

Father Risi, fluent in Zulu and Sesotho, is a well known and highly respected figure in Soweto. At a time when few whites had even gone near a township, this man lived and worked in Diepkloof. His church was a sanctuary and, like many of the white priests working in Soweto, he was regarded with deep suspicion by the police. He also assisted at the school established and run by the Catholic Church in the area.

On 16 June 1976, he was in his parish. At midday, he met people in Johannesburg for lunch. When he returned after lunch, he was not allowed through a police roadblock. He could see the smoke rising from a Soweto in flames. He went back to Johannesburg and only on Sunday 21 June could he return to his church, hidden in the back of a parishioner's car.

Father Risi, led by Kuny, gives evidence of the change in the attitude of the youth after 16 June and how 'the experience of violence and the violence that they saw in front of them, before their eyes, certainly opened up their consciousness politically'. He speaks strongly and with conviction, no longer a small man in the witness box.

His firsthand knowledge of the daily life of his parishioners and the pupils at his school is incontrovertible. He talks of the massive unemployment and the desperation which drove so many young people to leave their homes and join the ANC in exile. Kuny asks him why they left.

'I think the most common reason was the experience that there was no hope in their situation,' he says, citing the inferior education and the unemployment, while exile and the ANC offered hope and education.

Kuny takes him further. 'I think there seems to be a general perception that people went out of the country to undergo military training. Is that your experience from people that you spoke to and the attitudes that were expressed to you?'

'It is not,' says Father Risi. 'I feel that some did go out for military training, but many went out in the hope of finding something better and it was a very courageous decision to move away from family, friends, situations, to go and find something better, and I would say it was an act of desperation on their part. They felt desperate.'

And then he gives examples of youths he knew who left the country. He is careful to mention no names. Predictably, Captain Prinsloo leans over and speaks to Louisa van der Walt, and I sense that this issue will receive attention later.

Father Risi talks about the community's perception of the police as hostile, of the roadblocks, of the armoured cars in the streets, of funerals for those shot by the police. He likens the conditions of 1976 to those in 1985 and 1986.

Kuny leads him through other issues to the final question: in such circumstances, can murder be understood?

Father Risi says, 'I should make it clear that as a minister of religion my role is one of service in reconciling people in the community. I would not in any way support violence nor the killing of people, whether by people supporting the ANC or the defence force or the South African Police.'

He turns and looks at the accused and the gallery, speaking loudly and clearly as if to his parish. 'I do not support killing from any angle. Yes. And I can say only this, that I can understand the frustration people have and how it leads to anger and therefore to the killing of policemen or other people in politics. After what young people themselves have seen and experienced at the hands of the South African Police and the SADF in the townships. I can understand why they do that. I do not support them, I do not encourage others to do the same, but I can understand what it is that makes a person so frustrated, so angry that he or she would do that. To see one's parents, for example, humiliated publicly, and I have had the experience of being humiliated publicly by the South African Police. There was no sensitivity, no awareness of human dignity, of my [dignity], and therefore I say of anybody else's.'

There is a long silence after this statement, the vehemence of the priest cutting through the court.

The gallery breaks into spontaneous clapping and cheering. The judge looks at the crowded gallery, worrying that this mood could get out of hand, but it calms down and Father Risi continues that while he might react differently he can 'understand why a person can snap or in a blind rage and anger do something like that'.

Harry Prinsloo gets his cross-examination off to a bad start when he forgets or chooses not to call the priest 'Father'. He corrects himself and proceeds to ask if Father Risi personally saw anyone shot in the township in June 1976.

'No. But I buried people from my own parish,' says the priest. 'I buried five people who were killed at that time. One of them was a young girl of twelve and the oldest of those five was nineteen.'

Prinsloo, furious that this evidence has gone on record as a result of his own question, turns on Father Risi. 'Will you please confine yourself to the question I put to you, whether you witnessed any incidents. I never put to you at any stage whether you buried people, Father. Please listen to the question.'

The priest nods.

'Your reply,' says Prinsloo, 'is that you did not witness any incident?'

'No,' says the priest ambiguously. Does he mean 'no, that's not what I said' or 'no, I saw no incidents'? Kuny shakes his head as Prinsloo doesn't seek clarity and moves on.

The prosecutor's questions focus on the partiality of Father Risi, attempting to prove that he is inherently biased against the police. Prinsloo hammers away, his questions becoming increasingly aggressive.

With each question, there are murmurs from the gallery. Many shake their heads, talking openly until their anger is so loud that the prosecutor cannot be heard. They do not like this assault on a man who lives and preaches amongst them. The prosecutor looks at the judge and waits until the noise from the gallery subsides.

More questions about 16 June, and then Harry Prinsloo fulfils my expectation. Shooting a glance at Captain Prinsloo on his left, he asks, 'Father, you told the court you were aware of various people who had left the country and undergone military training outside South Africa under the auspices of the ANC, is that correct? Who were they?'

'No,' replies the priest. 'I do not see it as my role to disclose those people because I was brought here to explain the situation in Soweto as I found it in those years.'

'Father, are you refusing to answer the question?'

'I cannot disclose their names.'

'Why not, for what reason?'

'Because I have not asked their permission first of all to do so.'

'Why should you ask their permission, Father?'

The judge, seeing that this whole cross-examination is getting out of hand, says it is not necessary to disclose names to understand Father Risi's testimony.

Prinsloo tries another tack, looking at unemployment and housing in 1976, and comparing it to the present time. The judge stops him. 'Mr Prinsloo, is the present position relevant? We are dealing with a certain time when these deeds were done. I do not think the present situation is relevant.'

Stone-faced, Harry Prinsloo perseveres. Again the judge steps in. 'Mr Prinsloo, you are still dealing with the present situation and I have already made a ruling on that.'

The prosecutor pushes on, asking incomprehensible questions that clearly irritate the judge. 'Mr Prinsloo, I do not understand the question.' It is rephrased. His patience exhausted, the judge says in a tired voice, 'It is not relevant, Mr Prinsloo, put the next question.' Prinsloo looks at his junior counsel and at his investigating officer, and shrugs his shoulders. He wraps up by accusing Father Risi of being biased against the police, and glumly sits down.

Kuny stands up to present his final argument to persuade the court to find extenuating circumstances.

48

Now we wait. We have reached the point that I've been dreading. Whatever brief sense of influence we experienced in the extenuation case is gone and we are back in a barren place. Everything lies in the hands of the judge and the assessors. I know that I should have no expectation of the judge finding extenuation. Granted, he behaved well in the trial, being considerate to the accused and impeccably polite to Bheki and me. He also had some empathy for our witnesses, even protected them at times. But I cynically ascribed that to the irritation Harry Prinsloo and Louisa van der Walt caused him. His assessors were a different 'bucket of fish', as they say in Delmas. They hardly said a word throughout the trial and for the most part looked bored. To me, they were in the judge's shadow and will probably follow him. So, it all comes down to Judge Marius de Klerk.

Bheki and I meet with the families, sometimes separately and then together. Throughout our meetings there is an unspoken assumption that the accused will follow other ANC prisoners onto Death Row. They will be hanged.

Bheki is magnificent at this time, giving support to the families while also gently counselling them to have no false expectations. He himself either has no hopes at all or disguises them well, for he continues to talk about the accused as if they have already been sentenced to death, remarking that it will be much easier to visit them on Death Row rather than at Modder B. I admire him for his realistic fatalism and worry about my own softer shell. Will it hold if – when – they are sentenced to death?

The fact is that none of my clients has ever been sentenced to death. I've heard from my partner Azhar Cachalia that when his two clients at the Messina trial were sentenced to death a terrible silence followed the pronouncement. He told me how the prosecution watched him and the accused. Not smiling, just watching to see if he would crumble and if the accused would break. The security policemen showed less restraint, smiling openly and nodding in congratulations when the sentence was handed down. At that moment, he said, he lost control of his emotions. Now, every time I play the anticipated moment through in my mind and think about how I might react, I remind myself that I am not the one being sentenced. If the accused can handle it, then I must. When I see the families, I am struck by their strength and their acceptance of the situation. Almost a calmness.

In the middle of this awful time, on the evening of 4 April 1989, my son is born. Caroline, the heart of this miraculous event, brings a perfect child into the world. We name him Simon. Inexplicably, he emerges with a broken collarbone and as he lies there, fragile and helpless on her chest, I pray that I will always be able to protect him. Our time together during the first hours after his birth is precious, poignant, yet always at the back of my mind there is a shadow.

Bheki and I see the accused a few days before the day set for sentence. I give them the news about Simon and they are overjoyed, shaking my hand and clapping me on the back. If we had cigars, we would have smoked them. It is a wonderful moment that takes us away from the coming day as they pepper me with questions. Does he look like me or his mother? How does he behave?

Simon's birth has afforded them a glimpse into a world they have been denied since their capture. It is very rare that, as prisoners, they have access to or even sight of children. In this strange sense of celebration we play ping-pong and Ting Ting keeps his position as the reigning champion. Afterwards we talk about developments in the country and discuss politics.

I ask how they're feeling. Are they ready? They reply, No problem. That's it. I can see that they know this is only going to end one way, and they don't want to discuss it. My mind churns with issues to be handled after the 'day', but it is premature to talk about them.

Bheki and I leave. In the car on the way back to Johannesburg, we again work through the things that will need to be done.

Bheki, in charge of the logistics for the 'day', spends a lot of time with the parents of the accused, arranging transport for relatives and friends, meals, financial allowances, and clothing for the accused. The accused have asked for MK uniforms, but I know this request won't be granted. At no stage has any MK guerrilla ever had the opportunity or been allowed to wear military combat uniform in court. In fact, the security police and prosecutors are so fanatical on this issue, that in previous trials of mine if the accused wore any item of clothing that resembled the black, green and gold of the ANC flag, they were stripped of it before they got to court.

Wearing the colours of the ANC, or even just one of the colours, in the dock on the day they are sentenced means much to ANC accused and to their supporters in the gallery. Often people go to great lengths to wear the colours. In a number of trials, the accused come up from the cells dressed in black with a bit of green in a tie or scarf. Some have been handed yellow flowers by a sympathiser to complete the colours. But those days have gone. Yellow flowers are confiscated at the court door, so obsessive have the prosecution and security police become about the ANC colours. Such symbolic gestures were seen as defiance at a time when the accused should be broken.

So I am not optimistic, particularly in a high-profile trial like this one, that Bheki will even be able to smuggle in a gold or green tie to go with the natty black suits of the accused. On the other hand, if anybody can find a way to make this happen, it's Bheki. He has that kind of reputation.

49

It is four o'clock in the morning on Thursday 27 April 1989. I have been awake for more than an hour, not moving, eyes closed, thinking about the coming day and what it will hold. The slow dawn brings definition to Caroline as she sleeps peacefully beside me. The house is still.

I get up and wander through to Simon's room. Watching him lying there fast asleep, so tiny and beautiful in his crib, I am overwhelmed by fear. Fear for him and Caroline, fear for the country, fear of an uncertain future subject to the random acts of selfish and brutal people who play with lives and destroy countries. I have some notion of what this country holds, its capacity for hope and beauty as well as violence. I pull myself out of this maudlin contemplation. On this day of all days, I have to be positive. Looking into the garden, I see the wonder of it: a paradise of plants and flowers surrounding green lawns, and I marvel that it can exist in such an imperfect place.

Detached and quiet inside, I pick up Bheki at our office in Braamfontein and we drive through to Delmas along the highway past the airport. Bheki has brought music for the car, Beethoven's seventh symphony. The planes are coming in bringing commercial travellers from Cape Town and Durban, and excited tourists from Europe to see the game parks and the sculptured beauty of Cape Town. We pass the Benoni lake with a mist over the water and in the willow trees, then the towns are behind us, before us highway and a cold clear sky.

The first police roadblock is just off the highway on the road into Delmas. It's a serious one. As we round the corner, I spot the light machine gun with the distinctive v of the barrel support breaking the contours of the roadside bush. Slapdash, they haven't taken the trouble to camouflage it. The police are in full combat gear, ready for action. This is what they wear in the bush in Namibia and Angola. Menacing and professional. I stop the car and the sergeant who stopped us on the first day of the trial comes to the window. He recognises our faces, grunts, stands back and waves us through.

The second police roadblock is close to the court. Here the cars are searched much more thoroughly. Bheki and I climb out while two policemen walk slowly around the car, checking underneath with mirrors attached to long poles, the way a dentist inspects the back of your teeth. They go through our bags, then they move on to the next car and we're free to go.

Outside the court, the families stand in a huddle next to the minibus that brings them daily. We join the group and quietly exchange greetings. There is not much to say, we have come to the end. Bheki goes off to ensure they get seats in the front of the court.

There's a large crowd, with more people arriving by the minute. Most of them will have to remain outside, given the small public gallery. They know this but have come anyway. I hope people will be sensible and restrained because there are six or seven Reaction Unit vehicles and a number of Casspirs parked nearby. The mood is deteriorating, largely because of the dogs in the back of the police cars barking madly at passers-by. People dart fearful looks at the frenzied animals and hurry away. The policemen lounge around, smoking smugly.

Before the buses loom into view, I hear the singing. Then buses filled with activists and supporters arrive. 'Hayi! ... Hayi Hayi!' they chant and after the last 'Hayi!' feet are smashed into the metal floor of the bus, rocking it from side to side. I pick up strains of an MK song and see the Reaction Unit police reaching for weapons and climbing out of their vehicles. I have seen this before many times and I know where it's going. The singing gets louder. Strong songs which make the packed buses rock. Five, six, seven buses, and I wonder how they got through the roadblocks. Before they've stopped, the passengers spill out and form a toyi-toying circle. Another four buses arrive. I look up and pray that there will be no violence here, not today, at this court, when there is already too much to cope with.

I see the policemen bunched together, eyeing the gathering crowd. I recognise some of the UDF leaders and approach them. I explain my concern that the crowd will get out of hand. Don't worry, they reassure me, we'll calm it down once everyone is off the buses. I know they will take it to the limit and then back away, also not wanting it to go bad.

The problem is that in situations like this there is no consensus between the crowd and the police as to exactly where or what the 'limit' is. All it really needs is for someone to try to prove a point here and this could explode and go badly wrong.

I am consoled by the number of journalists present. In their battered, multi-pocketed khaki flak jackets and Vietnam vet bandannas, half of them could be mistaken for professional soldiers, which is precisely the impression they intend to convey. Mind you, some of these foreign correspondents and TV crews have seen more action than a lot of soldiers. I know many of them through Caroline and we tend to end up at their parties.

These are the biographers of wars and tragedies, moving from Nicaragua to Cambodia, Beirut, Guatemala, Bangladesh, Afghanistan. Most of them are good people. They know that the mixture of toyi-toying activists and riot police outside a high-profile treason trial is a potentially powerful cocktail, and so they wait. By default, they offer some protection. Generally, the police are more restrained when the press are around.

I take one last worried look and enter the court. In the corridor Bheki tells me that the families have been seated and that he is on his way to see the accused. What concerns me is that there'll be an incident between the accused and the police after the judge has given sentence and that people will get hurt.

I speak to Captain Prinsloo. 'Please see that your men stationed in court keep calm. We don't want them to overreact if the accused start shouting ANC slogans.'

He looks at me. 'Peter, your people must just behave.'

'Thanks, Captain, you're a big help, as always.' He gives me a baleful glance. I move away and light another cigarette. I'm tense and chain-smoking.

In court, I talk nervously to Dennis Kuny and Elna Revelas, whom Kuny has chosen as his junior counsel. There are a lot more policemen than usual, some stationed around the dock, others leaning against the walls and at the doors.

The prosecutors have dressed for the day. Louisa van der Walt has on a smart dress for the occasion, and even Harry Prinsloo looks dapper in a grey suit. Captain Prinsloo comes back into court and studies the gallery. This is the culmination of years of work for him, and if the outcome is successful, he will earn great kudos in the service. He wants nothing to go wrong at the final moment. He moves around the court, giving instructions in a low voice. Bheki comes up from the cells and nods to me. Our clients are ready.

Captain Prinsloo signals to the court orderly to bring up the accused. The gallery goes deathly quiet. I can hear the footsteps of the orderly and the accused as they mount the steps into the court. The two policemen stationed at the top of the stairs suddenly take a step back, and one of them audibly exclaims in surprise. The court orderly appears first, shaking his head, his face red. And then I see Jabu and Ting Ting and Neo and Joseph move into the dock. Jabu firmly closes the small half door behind him. They are in full MK combat uniform, including black berets with a gold star on the front. They stand legs apart, facing the court. The gallery erupts. People shout and stamp, as the accused turn to acknowledge the crowd. The court is in pandemonium. The police climb the wooden walls of the dock to get at the accused, the accused push them back. Then the police open the door and physically try to seize the accused. Bheki and I, the respectable lawyers, jump into the fray and pull the police away. It's a riot, right here in the court. Above the chaos, I hear Louisa van der Walt screaming in Afrikaans, but I can't make out the words.

Into this bedlam walks Judge Marius de Klerk. The orderly shouts out above the melee, 'Stand in court!' Miraculously, quiet descends. The accused, still beset by policemen, shrug themselves free, adjust their berets, and stand with their hands behind their backs, as if on parade. The police retreat. There is a hint of a smile on Bheki's face, a smile of pride. The men look relaxed in their camouflage gear, strong, supple and professional, like soldiers. And they are definitely not beaten.

The judge makes no comment, merely tells them they may sit. I am amazed that he is going to allow this.

Still breathing heavily after the altercation with the police, and straightening our clothing, Bheki and I sit down and the court settles. Captain Prinsloo stares at us and I know he will want someone to pay for this. Heavily. Suddenly, it is cold in this court.

The judge gazes intently at the accused. Then looks down at his papers. His eyes fall on his two assessors as he starts to speak.

50

Judge de Klerk appears calm, making frequent eye contact with the court. His assessors stare at the desk, as if they too have important papers before them.

The judge starts with an exposition of the law. He explains that the death sentence is mandatory in a matter of this kind, where three of the accused have been convicted of murder, unless the court believes there are extenuating circumstances. Standard stuff. And then, looking directly at the accused, he hurls a thunderbolt. 'Unfortunately, the three members of this court are not in agreement on the question as to whether extenuating circumstances exist.' The prosecution cranes forward, as do we, not sure that we have heard correctly. I see Captain Prinsloo shoot his namesake in the prosecution a troubled look. I am startled. The court is split. In political trials courts are never split. I try to catch the eye of the assessors, with no success. Impossible to read.

The judge moves on to define extenuating circumstances, citing case law. Eventually he says, 'The fact that the circumstances that we are concerned with may have influenced other people in a different way is not relevant; the question is, How was each particular accused's state of mind probably influenced? Circumstances connected with, or which are involved in, or which served as motivations for the conduct of the accused are relevant. Circumstances of a solely sentimental nature are not relevant.'

He sets the scene for his analysis and then moves in an interesting direction. He points out that something should not be discarded because it is 'undesirable'. Even so, he pulls no punches in his description of the killings, saying that all of the murders committed by the accused were premeditated and executed in cold blood. He pauses and says that the findings which he will now give are his own. We look at one another as he separates himself from his assessors. Where is this going? And how will it end? In my mind, there is dawning hope.

He reiterates many of the points we have been at pains to make through our witnesses, that the accused are engaged in a just war after decades of fruitless attempts by the ANC to bring the white governments to negotiations. He accepts Professor Colin Bundy's historical assessment. He goes so far as to say that anyone who disagrees with his summary 'ignored and chose not to see what was happening around us'. Strong words. Now we are sitting bolt upright. We have never heard a judge in an ANC case take this view. I mean, he is agreeing with us, the defence! Incredible. Finally, agreeing with Bundy, he says, 'The probabilities are that the accused left the country under the influence of this history. No other probability can be postulated on the facts before us.'

He moves rapidly through the evidence of Mr Potsane and Father Risi, concluding that the violence that existed in 1976 severely and traumatically affected the minds of those touched by it. Things could not be going better for us. So far, he has agreed with all our witnesses, but we also know that the real issue is whether the circumstances set out by the judge had a bearing on the minds of the accused and whether they were influenced.

Somewhat clinically, he deals with the critical areas in which the accused might have been influenced. In doing so, I have no doubt that although there is no explicit mention of them, the judge has in mind the nationalist struggles of his own people, the Afrikaners.

'It is probable,' he concludes, 'that the social, political and economic situation, as sketched by Professor Bundy, was a burden which must have weighed extremely heavily and which provoked strong emotions. It is probable that in the minds of many people, and also that of the accused, a feeling of anger and helplessness arose. It is probable that the upsurges of emotion and frustrations in the minds of people, brought about by the events and outbursts which took place and the violence which was coupled therewith, influenced the accused.

'It is probable that they, amongst other things, and as a result of the restrictions of ways in which they could participate to improve the lot of their people, thought about violence as an option and that they therefore left the country to join the ANC. Accused number one left in 1977, he was twenty-four years old. Accused number two left in 1979, he was nineteen years old. Number three left in 1977, he was seventeen years old. Number four left in 1980 and he was sixteen years old. The accused were still at school at the time.'

He mentions the military training they received and how they were probably influenced during this time. He gets a laugh from the gallery when he says, 'No direct evidence is necessary to make one realise that in an ANC camp, where a war against apartheid was prepared, no Sunday school picnic existed.' He spends time referring to the evidence of the security police, using their remarks on the ANC to substitute for the lack of evidence from the accused. He quotes Captain Prinsloo's description of the accused as being 'well-trained, devoted, committed, convinced, fanatic ANC members' and says that point of view is corroborated by the picture which emanates from their statements and their actions.

I stare at the judge as, point by point, he strikes at the prosecution's extenuation argument and addresses the key weakness in our own case. 'The accused did not become ANC "soldiers" overnight,' he says, 'they became that through long training and through intensive indoctrination. Such a finding is not speculation. To allege that the factual basis for that finding is faulty, despite all the proven facts, is a misdirection and refusal to face what is happening around us. The accused cannot be penalised just because they remain silent and did not confirm this evidence themselves.'

Bheki tugs at my elbow and in a stunned whisper says, 'He called them soldiers.'

Kuny, normally so calm, is frowning and nodding at each point the judge makes. The accused glance at me, puzzled by these unexpected findings. The gallery is silent, reporters taking notes furiously as the judge concludes that there were circumstances which probably had an intense bearing on the minds of the accused. There is an audible sigh of relief from the gallery, not to mention the defence.

The final hurdle is yet to come. I know it will be the most difficult one. Will he find that because of the effect these circumstances had on the minds of the accused, their deeds are less reprehensible? If he does, we are through. The benchmark to be used in this test is that of the 'reasonable man', a rare enough creature in our country. Be that as it may, the judge now gives his views on how morality shifts according to the changing norms in society. He refers to Kuny's point, presented in his closing argument, that the moral judgement of people who come from the same group as the accused should be applied, and that people from another group will find difficulty imagining themselves in the position of the accused.

The judge shifts in his chair and takes a breath. I sense we are close to the end. The anticipation is unbearable. My fists are clenched. The families are listening intently, all eyes on the judge. The accused show no signs of emotion, their whispered exchanges and smiles gone. They are very serious.

I concentrate again on the judge's words. 'According to my judgement, however, the circumstances which had a bearing on their state of mind were of such a nature that it markedly reduced their blameworthiness irrespective of how blameworthy their conduct may still be.

'I am therefore of the opinion that these extenuating circumstances are significant enough to render the peremptory imposition of the death sentence improper and that a sentence within the discretion of the court be requested.'

There it is. Stunned silence. We look at one another in disbelief. From the beginning of his judgment he seemed to be headed in this direction, but I never suspected that he'd have the courage to go through with it.

The silence is broken by cheering and clapping from the gallery. The accused are on their feet, surprise on their faces. Their families in the front row are hugging each other and singing starts up in the gallery. It is unbelievable; this judge has gone where none have gone before. It is remarkable!

Bheki gives me such a hard congratulatory clap on my back that I almost choke. I turn to him and we solemnly shake hands, relief in our eyes. It is over. Then I notice the judge motioning to the court orderly to call for silence. There is something wrong. The cheering stops and it takes a while for the court to settle down.

The judge continues. 'Unfortunately, as previously mentioned, the three members of this court are not in agreement on this question. The aforegoing was my point of view. What follows is the conclusion of the two assessors who assist me.'

Quickly, he tells the court that the assessors do not find that the facts shown influenced the accused and even if they did, they would not justify extenuation. There is confusion as people turn to one another, unsure of the implications of a divided bench. It is a unique situation. Bheki says to me, 'Surely the view of the judge must win over the assessors? I mean, they are only magistrates?'

The blood drains from my face as I remember the law. My mouth is too dry to respond.

The judge gives the answer. 'In respect of questions of fact the finding of a majority, that is to say, two members of this court, is binding. In respect of legal questions, the judge alone decides, but this is a factual question, and not a legal one. With a majority of two to one, the court finds that no extenuating circumstances exist and the finding is made in respect of all the charges of murder.'

Darkness crushes everything in my head. I am filled with utter dread as I hear the judge move to give his sentence. The words float past me as I look out to the gentle sea, pure and blue in the distance, slowly polishing the brass.

'I do not wish to say much about sentence, enough has been said already in this case. Violence is not the solution for the problems of our country. People who wish to seek for a solution by means of violence will only cause more violence until there only remains blood, bones and scorched earth in our country.'

There is a rising hum from the gallery. The judge raises his voice, rushing to the end as he hands out the prison sentences, ten years, twenty-five years, more years and more years, all to run concurrently. Then, the unavoidable.

'I am bound by the majority of the members of this court, and consequently I am compelled to impose the death sentence in respect of the convictions of murder. Consequently, the death sentence is imposed on accused one, two and three.'

The noise in the gallery reaches a crescendo as he finishes and hurries from the court with his assessors. Uproar. The accused jump up, face the gallery, thrust clenched fists into the air and roar, 'Long live the ANC!' The crowd shouts it back. Jabu, Ting Ting, Neo and Joseph sing 'Nkosi Sikelel' iAfrika' and the people in the gallery join in, fists raised, singing solemnly. Beautiful and clear, the lovely hymn rings through the court house. It is slow and moving, infinitely sad and full of strength. Even the security police take a step back. I do not sing, there is too much in my head. I look at prosecutor Louisa van der Walt. She returns my gaze, her eyes bright with victory. The anger in me is so intense that it is virtually uncontrollable. There is nothing that I can do.

The singing ends and Jabu, leading the others, shouts, 'Amandla!' The gallery roars back. This is a dangerous time, with the police pulling at Jabu and the others, trying to get them down into the basement and away from the crowd. The families in the front row reach out to the accused, touching the Perspex as if they will never see their sons again. I glimpse Mrs Masina. She is not shouting. She is very quiet, sitting with her eyes closed and her hands together in prayer. And suddenly I am trying my best not to cry, not here, not in front of the prosecution and the security police. The accused have gone below to the cells. The police stationed around the walls of the court have not moved; they watch us, the lawyers, as we silently pack our books and papers into our briefcases and leave the court. Unwelcome strangers.

I go down to the cells. In their uniforms, the men do not look like accused and have nothing of the pathetic vulnerability of the recently sentenced. We hug. There is nothing to say. Jabu gives me his black beret with the yellow star on it and says I must give it to my son Simon when he is old enough to understand. Meanwhile Ting Ting, Neo and Joseph are discussing the reaction of the police to their uniforms. No one talks of the sentence, there is no need to. I arrange to visit them the following day. Now I want to see their families and make sure that a situation with the police is not developing.

The families are standing next to their minibus. Bheki is with them, contained as always. A large crowd of supporters are toyi-toying, with the Reaction Unit police in a semicircle around them, R4 rifles pointing down, edging closer and herding them onto the buses. I shake hands with the families, starting with Jabu's younger sister Busi. I say I'm sorry. 'Stop, Peter,' she says, 'it is not your fault.' But I repeat it over and over, helplessly. 'I'm sorry, I'm sorry.'

I realise that I'm saying sorry because I cannot stop what is going to happen, their sons are going to die. And silently, I start to cry. Mrs Masina grabs me by the shoulders, pulls me towards her and hugs me. I wonder how someone can take so much pain. I see policemen coming towards us. 'It's time we left,' says Bheki. The families climb into their minibus. And so we all leave, the buses full of supporters, the minibus with the family and the cars with the lawyers. Away from that place.

THE BOMB

Captain Eugene de Kock's colleagues at Vlakplaas are all trained members of the Special Task Forces. Most of them have also spent time with Koevoet fighting the war in Namibia and Angola, and have extensive combat experience. Many have had cross-border operational experience and are skilled 'interrogators'.

It is these men who lead the squads of askaris. High on a blend of dagga and liquor, the askaris vie with each other in the brutality with which they execute their deadly duties in order to impress their new bosses. The cocktail of de Kock, Koevoet, Special Task Force members and crazed askaris is a lethal one. In the police circles that know of the existence of de Kock and his covert operation, he has a code name: it is 'Prime Evil'.

51

Beyond exhaustion, I cannot sleep. It's three o'clock in the morning. The words of the judge keep echoing in my mind as I analyse each sentence of the unusual judgment. Why, given the attitude of his assessors, did he jeopardise his career? He could safely and defensibly have kept Pretoria happy. It's a shame that in the end his efforts should come to nothing.

But will they come to nothing? What if there's an appeal? Knowing that he was outvoted, he still gave sufficient grounds for an appeal. Maybe it was a lifeline. Appeals take a long time to be heard.

I get up and walk around the house. If lodging an appeal keeps the accused alive, then that is the path they must take. I know they will not agree to this if it compromises their position, but I don't believe that it does. They have made their political point and have paid the price. The senseless waste of their execution has to be avoided. In delay, there is hope.

Sitting in the darkness in my living room, I realise that three and a half years after the accused were arrested, they are still alive. And they must stay that way; this country has enough martyrs. I look in on my son and then go back to bed, but cannot sleep. My mind is on the judge's words and how they can best be used in an appeal.

At the office I telephone Modder B Prison to make an appointment to see the accused, only to learn that they have already been moved to Death Row in Pretoria. Of course, I had forgotten, you can't keep prisoners who have been sentenced to death in a normal prison. They have nothing left to lose. They can contaminate the other prisoners and cause riots. The warder's dilemma: how to punish a condemned prisoner.

Death Row can only let me see the accused in four days' time. You can't just pitch up at Death Row. I am panicky. From today, we have thirteen days to lodge an appeal, assuming my clients choose to do so.

It's a long weekend and I spend the Monday enjoying the time with Caroline and Simon. He's a happy, beautiful child who never stops smiling. At home with both of them, the world outside is a faraway place.

The phone rings, and it's my colleague Norman Manoim. He tells me that a friend, the academic and anti-apartheid activist, David Webster, has been shot dead by unknown gunmen outside his house. A point-blank assassination with a shotgun by men in a red Golf. It is a massive shock as the reality of the country comes smashing home. Norman describes the incident. David was shot in his driveway while unloading plants. A cold killing.

David was a kind and gentle man you couldn't fail to like. Yet beneath his warmth and intelligence was a steely determination to fight injustice and a refusal to be intimidated from doing what he thought was right. On one occasion, after being instructed by a church organisation, he, Daphne Mashilwe and I had been taking affidavits from residents of Colesberg township, where children were being detained and tortured by police, with a view to bringing a Supreme Court application. On the way back to Johannesburg, he insisted on making an extensive detour so that we could visit Koffiefontein, the place where a number of the past and current senior Nationalist politicians including Dr Verwoerd, the 'architect' of apartheid, had been interred during the Second World War for acts of sabotage in support of Nazi Germany. There they had remained until the end of the war, when they were released and subsequently assumed political power in the general election of 1948. As we wandered through the now decrepit camp with its fading monuments, I could see he was genuinely moved by the atmosphere and history of the old detention centre, perplexed by the cold irony of history and its unlearnt lessons.

Now David is dead, another name on a lengthening list of murdered activists.

The next morning, I travel to Pretoria. Death Row is on the hill just behind Maximum Security. For those who have an eye for scenic beauty, Death Row has a view of the city and the military complex on its outskirts. The warders at the gate are quick and efficient. I imagine that this is the top of the pile for a prison warder before moving into a management position. Anyway, I'm impressed with their attitude and professionalism.

In the waiting section at the entrance I'm joined by a khaki-clad man with a dark suntan and a heavy grey beard. He greets me in Afrikaans and then waits, like me, to be admitted. The warder calls him 'Meneer Strydom' and it strikes me that this must be the father or perhaps brother of the infamous 'White Wolf', Barend Strydom. Strydom, a former policeman, went walkabout on a hot summer day in November 1988 in central Pretoria, and shot and killed, execution style, seven black men, laughing

215

as he did so. Some days earlier, he had killed a black woman in what he described as a 'trial run'. Supported by his family and other members of his ultra-right cult, he showed no remorse when he received eight death sentences. He's on Death Row, along with my clients and a number of others. Fellow prisoners, like relatives, can't be chosen.

The warder is friendly, chatting away in the bright sun, as he escorts me from the entrance to the prison. We walk past clipped green lawns with fine gardens dotted with ducks and geese and white hens picking at seeds. It's rather like being in a children's farmyard, but with a difference. The warder proudly points to the soft touches and tells me that they try to 'make it as nice as possible here'.

Going inside and up the stairs into the elevated central courtyard, I see that the visiting cubicles are arranged in a rectangle with the concrete courtyard in the middle. Nostalgically, I remember my earlier consulting areas in the doctor's surgery and the sanatorium in the other prisons. This place is serious. There is a high tower in the centre at the rear of the courtyard where, I presume, the core business takes place. I look at the tower with grim fascination, imagining the stark functionalism of its interior and the crude equipment of execution. Standing in the middle of the small courtyard, I feel the soft warmth of the early winter sun on my face, a simple pleasure.

I am directed by a warder to one of the small cubicles adjoining the courtyard. I am separated from Jabu, Ting Ting and Neo (Joseph is being held elsewhere before being incarcerated on Robben Island) by a thick, impenetrable shield of glass. We talk through an intercom system. Ting Ting tells me that they were moved here yesterday and that the conditions are better than in Modder B, particularly the food. We discuss the judge and agree that he was very brave in a situation that called for nothing less, but that his courage and honesty were not enough. They are intrigued that the judgment will make legal history. I read them some of the headlines and articles that have appeared in the papers.

The lead article in the *Star* is headed 'Judge in Delmas Death Squad Case Made Legal History'. It goes on to say, 'It is impossible to exaggerate the legal significance of Mr Justice de Klerk's judgment in the Delmas trial of an ANC assassination squad. … For the first time in South African legal history, a Supreme Court judge has taken full account of the country being involved in a civil war in weighing the subjective meaning of the actions of those he was required to sentence … Despite the practical negation of Mr Justice de Klerk's views [by his assessors], lawyers are hopeful that it may yet prove to be a legal watershed.'

The *Sunday Star* on its editorial page has the heading '"Shift" In Attitude to ANC Fighters'. The article opens: 'The ANC quest for its fighters to be acknowledged as soldiers may have gained some recognition, however indirect, in the landmark trial of four of its men before Mr Justice Marius de Klerk in Delmas.'

Jabu nods approvingly, saying he did not think when they adopted their non-participatory position that it might help others.

'For us, the circumstances led us to take that position. We were not even considering that a judge may have sympathy for us.'

Other articles and editorials pick up on this empathetic judgment and comment that it gives hope where before there was none or very little.

'It's amazing,' says Ting Ting, 'that no matter what, our case will have made a difference.' The others nod, smiling. There is satisfaction in the air, a sense of achievement, almost wellbeing. I tell them that the case has also received extensive coverage overseas in all of the leading newspapers, including the *New York Times*.

It is important for them to know that what they have done has made a mark and, to some extent, paves the way for others. They have opened the prisoner-of-war door to extenuation, and it is now up to others to push through it.

I get to the point, a little ashamed that I am not giving them more time to enjoy the exposure, but time is now of the essence. 'Guys, the simple truth is that your current stance of non-participation is going to kill you. They will hang you quickly before a campaign to save you can really get under way. If you do not appeal, you will be hanged within three months and it will all be over.'

There is no response from them as they look at me. Silence. I fill the void, trying to get to the end before they stop me. I explain to them that they have paid their dues and made legal history for the ANC. It is now time to think of themselves and their families. They must appeal, or they will die needlessly. I push home my point. 'It's time to change strategy. No soldier is ever inflexible in his strategy, he has to adapt to changing conditions. Now you must do something for yourselves. There can be no dishonour in that, especially if it does not reflect badly on the ANC.'

Again silence. Then Jabu says with a wry smile, 'We will not change our position. We plan to stick to the principle.'

'You have only fourteen days in which to appeal,' I say, feeling desperate. 'This is your last chance. We have to find a way to keep you alive.'

Still no shift. As a last resort, I ask, 'What would you do if you were ordered by your movement, as soldiers under instruction, to appeal? Would you do it or would you disobey your commander and the ANC?'

Ting Ting shrugs and looks at the others.

'This is it,' I go on. 'There are no second chances, only this one, and when it's gone, you will be hanged in three months. I can say no more. It is your choice, as always. But if you agree to let me discuss it with the ANC in Lusaka, I will go up to brief the leadership.'

'Okay,' Jabu says reluctantly. 'We need to discuss this, give us a day.'

The next morning I arrive at Death Row only to be told that I have not booked and cannot have access to my clients. Every day and every hour is important now, I cannot afford to waste time. Eventually, after much performing and begging on my part, the warder reluctantly lets me in. This is a change from Maximum Security where the warder would have made me beg, kept me waiting for an hour, and then brought his friends and family to see my face when he told me to go away and make a proper appointment.

The accused seem in good spirits as we briefly discuss family issues. Then Jabu cuts the conversation short. He says they have discussed the appeal issue in detail and they do not feel it appropriate to start participating in their trial now. My heart sinks. 'However, if we are ordered by the ANC High Command to appeal, we will do so. That is the only thing which will make us take the appeal route, direct instructions from the ANC in Lusaka. And, Peter, we know that you and Bheki are doing your best for us, but we have made our choice and are prepared to live with it.'

'The point,' I say facetiously, 'is that you won't live with it, you'll die with it. And at this stage it is not necessary, it is a waste. You have made your point and legal history. Anyway, I will go to Lusaka and we will see what the ANC says.' I am despondent in the knowledge that the ANC will, in all probability, say that the decision is up to the accused and therefore they will not interfere.

'Peter, there is something else you must know,' says Neo. 'There is a

218

man here on Death Row who has told us that he was part of a police hit squad which has been operating for the last few years inside the country and also on cross-border raids.'

Not wanting to be distracted from the task facing me and already thinking of how the approach should be made to the ANC, I reply, 'Look, Neo, virtually all of the people who are on Death Row with you are completely desperate. They'll say anything if it will buy them more time. They will do anything to avoid that rope. Besides, if he was killing for the SAP and working for them, they would not have let him end up here where he might talk. That would be sheer stupidity on their part. Who does he say he killed? Does he give any details?'

'No, he gives no details, he just told us that he was part of a government hit squad. We have only been here a few days. Maybe he will talk to us more when there is more trust,' says Ting Ting.

I suggest they try to get more information before we take it further. I am anxious to get away, to make arrangements to get to Lusaka.

52

Thankfully the flight on Zambian Airways to Lusaka is uneventful. Bheki and I spend the time drinking whisky, in case the flight should encounter any problems. We also discuss how we should approach the MK Chief of Staff Chris Hani to ask for his assistance.

We are met at the airport by Penuell Maduna. As always, he's attentive and helpful. He lists who we'll be meeting with after our discussion with Chris Hani. We know we are lucky that Hani happens to be in Lusaka and not in Angola.

It is Bheki's first time in Lusaka. It is also his first official meeting with the ANC in exile. He is clearly excited and questions Penuell about life in Zambia. I know that the politics will follow later. Penuell, a friendly and humble man, patiently answers his questions.

That night we have dinner with Penuell and brief him on the trial, spending time on the legal significance of the judgment. We point out that ANC fighters and other lawyers must now adopt a more coordinated approach to their defence and give serious consideration to the nature of their participation in their trials. The precedent that has been set should be expanded and built on. The dinner goes on into the night as we discuss current trials and are joined by other ANC people. Inevitably, we adjourn to my room for whisky and further discussions. Bheki is completely at ease, smoking in that peculiar way of his with his cigarette and his glass in the same hand. He talks about the state of organisation in Soweto, moving from serious topics to the current high price of cars.

The next morning Penuell takes us to a room on the hotel's third floor. We are let in by a man I've not seen before. Chris Hani is seated on the bed. He gets up to greet us and I introduce Bheki, who is overawed at meeting one of the great names of the resistance struggle and of the ANC. The curtains are closed, the bright morning sun a glimmer above the top of the curtain rod.

As in my previous meeting, Hani is softly spoken and courteous as he listens closely to us. He mentions that they've been following the case and that the ANC is proud of how the unit has handled their trial. The judgment will be studied to see how it can best be used to the advantage of other fighters facing trial. There's a moment's silence and then I tackle the big issue. I explain that the men are on Death Row and will be hanged if an appeal is not lodged. Surely they've made their point and served the struggle and the ANC well, but I cannot see why they should die. The appeal will take a long time, perhaps over a year, and that will also give the ANC time to mount an international and national campaign against their execution.

Bheki talks passionately of their bravery and commitment during the trial. He emphasises that nothing will persuade them from their stance of non-participation, except an order from the leadership. Hani listens. Now and then, he asks questions, but does not commit himself. We get the impression that he is sympathetic, but that he needs more time. He will try to give us a response the next day before we leave. However, as this is an important issue he will need to consult further.

Our discussion shifts to the four members of the unit and it is clear that he is interested in them. His questions about each man are almost paternal rather than military. He mentions that Justice Mbizana has disappeared and could either have been killed by the police or become an askari. I tell him we have heard nothing of Justice. He asks about the families and how they handled the trial, showing particular interest in Mr Potsane and the evidence he gave in the extenuation case. That

Mr Potsane fought in the Second World War and was a POW for more than three years fascinates him, and he wants details about the old man, even down to his bearing on the witness stand. Eventually the meeting is over and Hani tells us we'll hear from the legal department. In all this time the other man has not spoken, but as they leave he instructs us to remain in the room for another ten minutes, after which we can leave.

During the day we hold other meetings, and that night have dinner at the house of Patrick Fitzgerald, an exile I had met when he was the ANC contact in Gaborone in the early eighties. Bheki and I nervously endure the drive as Patrick sails through red traffic lights in the Lusaka manner. At his home we dine on marinated goat meat, which is good, and drink the wine we brought from South Africa. I am just a little unnerved by an AK-47 standing nonchalantly in the corner of the dining room. In case of an attack, we are told by one of the other guests. Throughout the meal, I see Bheki's eyes flitting constantly across to the weapon.

The conversation with Patrick and the two other ANC people at the table focuses mainly on the police death squads responsible for carrying out cross-border raids, as well as the frequent abductions and disappearance of activists inside the country. I explain that it's common knowledge that a squad or a number of squads are responsible for these attacks and killings, but who they are and where they are based is unknown. They may be a unit under police or army command, or a rogue group of ex-security forces carrying out the tacit wishes of the government on a 'who will rid me of this troublesome priest' basis. Is it random or organised? We have no doubt that they receive their information on targets from one or all of the numerous intelligence agencies that litter the security landscape. I remember my conversation with my clients on Death Row and mention the man claiming to be a member of a police assassination squad.

Patrick's interested. 'We know that these squads make use of captured ANC soldiers who defect under torture or for money,' he says. 'You should follow up on this guy in case there's something there.'

My feeling is that he sounds more like a desperate criminal concocting a story that might delay his hanging than a turned ANC soldier, but I agree to find out more.

The next day we leave Lusaka without having received an answer on the appeal. This is disconcerting but I steel myself for the wait and enjoy being home with Caroline and Simon.

53

Over the weekend, I meet with the families and tell them about our discussions with Chris Hani and the ANC legal department. They are relieved that the meeting went well, but concerned that there is no answer to resolve the situation. At the same time, they have an implicit faith that the ANC and particularly Chris Hani will make the right decision. I stress that even if their sons are instructed to appeal, and they do so, they may still receive the same sentence. The benefit, however, is that the appeal will take at least a year to be heard, hopefully longer, and anything may happen in that time. As we part, I am struck by their calm belief that things will work out. It's a trait that hasn't lapsed since I first met them. I envy their faith.

Bheki briefs the accused on Death Row. We meet up later in the afternoon.

'Have we received the call from Lusaka?' he asks.

'Nothing,' I reply, adding that the silence is worrying. Actually, I'm more than a little concerned. It is four days since we met in Lusaka. We have until Thursday to lodge our notice of appeal.

Bheki says he told our clients that even without word from Lusaka he didn't believe a decision to appeal would compromise the ANC. Word on the street and in the UDF is that they should lodge an appeal.

I am surprised at his forthrightness and ask how the men responded to this.

'They didn't answer me,' he says. 'So I moved on and asked them to get more information from this self-confessed hit squad guy.'

Waiting for word from Lusaka is unbearable. Bheki and I harp on it constantly, trying to understand why we've heard nothing from ANC headquarters. Hours pass. The families phone wanting to know if we've heard yet. The day ends. I go home tense and hating the limbo.

The next morning we try to persuade our clients to take the initiative. But they remain steely calm, their position unchanged, with Jabu saying that they will not appeal unless they are instructed to do so by the ANC. Every time my phone rings, I answer it expectantly, only to have my hopes dashed when it is not the call I want.

By the afternoon I can take it no longer and phone Penuell Maduna. He's not in. Where is he? When will he be back? No one knows. Then again no one's going to give any information to an unknown person phoning from South Africa. I leave an urgent message for Penuell to contact me. At nightfall I go home with a knot in my stomach. We have three days left.

In the morning, I phone again and ask for Penuell or Zola Skweyiya, the head of the ANC legal department. I'm told both men are out. Desperate, I leave a detailed message about the appeal, explaining that if we do not appeal the men on Death Row will soon be hanged. The man on the phone, more sympathetic now, says that he will get someone to phone me.

I have given Connie Rikhotso, our receptionist, strict instructions that if a call comes through for me, she must keep the caller on hold and find me wherever I am. Bheki and I have cancelled all our appointments. We stay in the office on tenterhooks. This is one call that we can't miss. Time passes; no call. What calls we get are from the press and representatives from the embassies asking if we will be lodging an appeal. They too know that the clock is ticking.

Later that morning, I take a call from Mr Potsane. With the familiar gravel of age in his voice, he asks, 'Have you heard from the ANC?'

'No, we are still waiting.' I am past offering false reassurance.

There is a moment of silence. Then, 'What will we do?'

'I don't know,' I say, hearing the hollow ring of hopelessness in my voice.

'Please keep trying, Peter. I am asking you to keep trying, one last time.'

And I feel ashamed that I cannot offer him more and that he should ask me to do what I should be doing anyway. My job.

I put down the phone and ask my colleague Suzanne O'Donnell to try Lusaka again. She tells me that the line is constantly engaged, it sounds as if there's some problem. After a while she comes into my office, distraught. 'The post office says the lines to Lusaka are down. They don't know when they'll be repaired.'

The lines to Zambia and Mozambique often malfunction. It strikes me that, after all we've been through, my clients could die because of a faulty telephone system, or because someone in Lusaka did not get their act together.

'Shit,' I curse bitterly to Bheki, 'how is it possible, after we've made them aware of the critical importance of this issue, that no one has even taken the trouble to pick up the phone and give us a response? It's almost as if no one cares.'

Is it fair on my clients that just because someone in Lusaka doesn't make a phone call, they should hang? Perhaps I should just put in the notice anyway. I can always say I did this because the phone lines were down and my clients should not be prejudiced by a technical fault. But I know the accused will see through the excuse. We have two days left to appeal.

The next morning, I sift through the post hoping for a letter or a telegram from Lusaka. Nothing. By eleven o'clock, the lines are working and I get through to the legal department, but again Penuell and Zola are not there.

'Is there a number where I can contact Chris Hani?' I ask in desperation.

'No, there is not,' says the man on the phone.

'Listen, these men will die unless they are given instructions to appeal,' I bark at him. 'I flew up with Bheki Mlangeni a week ago and met with Chris Hani and the legal department. Yet we've heard nothing. These instructions are literally the difference between life and death for these men. I refuse to believe that we cannot get a response from Lusaka.'

The man on the phone, clearly sympathetic, says, 'Penuell and Zola are travelling. They're not in town and we can't contact them.'

'But we don't have the time to wait for them to come back, it will be too late then.'

Unflustered, he says, 'We are aware of this matter. Before Penuell left he wrote an opinion on this issue for the leadership, I am sure they will respond to you.'

I realise that he has given more information over the phone than he should have. 'Look, I'm grateful for your help,' I say. 'I hope you understand my position.'

We have booked a meeting with the accused for early on the morning of the final day on which the appeal can be lodged. This way if they do have a last-minute change of heart we can do something about it. I've resolved to persuade them to appeal anyway, although I know my chances of success are limited. Our appointment is for nine tomorrow. The appeal deadline expires in the afternoon.

The calls are still coming through from the press. Bheki and I ignore them.

At two Mrs Masina calls for news. I have to disappoint her once more. I explain that we'll be seeing her son early the next morning and will try to persuade them to appeal if there is still no answer from the ANC.

She sighs. 'Let me know what they say.' She too has no illusions.

I am in my office at about three thirty when my phone rings. Suzanne tells me I have a call and that it sounds like long distance.

I answer, the apprehension clear in my voice.

A man says, 'Is that Peter Harris? This is Thabo Mbeki.' Calmly, he says that the matter has been discussed and that Jabu Masina, Ting Ting Masango and Neo Potsane are instructed, as soldiers of the ANC, to appeal. We talk briefly. This is the first time I have spoken to Mbeki. I tell him that we were starting to panic and that I am deeply grateful he has made the call. I brief him on the case, its importance, and what Jabu and the others have achieved. He listens, wishes us luck and says goodbye. It is a short conversation, perhaps two minutes, but we have what we need.

I put down the phone, breathe a sigh of relief, and shout through to Bheki, 'We're in business!'

He comes rushing through. 'Who phoned?'

'Thabo Mbeki.'

Nodding his head in approval, grinning widely, he reaches for the phone. 'Come, let's call, let's call.'

We phone the families at their homes and give them the news. They are overjoyed. I put the phone on speaker; we can hear shouting and laughter in the background as they relay the message throughout each house.

The next day our meeting with the unit on Death Row is short. I tell them that Thabo Mbeki specifically instructed them, as soldiers, to appeal.

We look at one another. I am smiling as I sense their relief, even though there is no visible reaction.

Jabu looks at the others and then at me. 'We will obey the instruction.'

I drive back to Johannesburg very fast, thinking, for the first time, that maybe this highway isn't so bad after all. The papers are lodged with the registrar of the court that afternoon, with thirty minutes to spare.

54

The application for leave to appeal is argued before Judge Marius de Klerk. Not surprisingly, he grants our application.

Afterwards I call on the judge in his temporary chambers. He stops packing his briefcase and greets me politely. I say I've come to thank him and to say goodbye, although I don't specify what I am thanking him for. The unspoken is clear enough. Sombrely we shake hands. I leave his office thinking that perhaps there is hope for this blighted place.

From now on, the appeal process will take its winding course to the judicial capital in Bloemfontein. I estimate that it will take at least a year for the appeal to be finalised, hopefully much longer if I have my way.

In the meantime Bheki and I settle into a comfortable routine with Jabu, Ting Ting and Neo. We take turns in visiting every few weeks. Less frequently we get down to Joseph on Robben Island.

At the same time, Bheki and I are involved in the defence of another three ANC soldiers, Damien de Lange, Iain Robertson and Susan Donnelly in a big trial known as the Broederstroom Trial, held in the Pretoria court. In June 1989, they are acquitted on five terrorism charges but found guilty on a number of other terrorism charges. Like the Delmas four, they too are not prepared to deny their actions, which involved attacks on the defence force and sabotage of key installations. They receive lengthy sentences.

I am involved in other political trials and time passes quickly. We also organise visits for the four from members of their support committee. Saki Macozoma sees them from time to time, although we have to ensure that their non-legal visits do not reduce the number of family visits they're allowed.

In early September, Jabu tells me that he and the others have been spending a lot of time with the 'hit squad' prisoner. He's become trusting of Jabu and the others and has told them that although he's on Death Row for the murder of a white landowner, in fact, he committed a number of other murders as part of an undercover police assassination squad. The man is reluctant to give them any details, however, claiming that he remains loyal to his commanders in the police. Jabu tells me that they have come to believe there might be some truth in his confession. He sticks to his story despite questioning from Ting Ting, insisting that while Jabu and company will be hanged, his masters in the police will never allow this to happen to him. They cannot afford it, he says, he knows too much. The only real information he releases is that he was based in the Pretoria area. Jabu says two of their warders have confirmed that this prisoner used to be a policeman.

There's been a lot of bantering between them and the man. Ting Ting has told him he shouldn't trust the police, they don't care about him. If they did, they would never have allowed him to end up in a place where he might spill the beans. Jabu's convinced there is some substance to what the man is saying, but they cannot take it further.

'Give me his name,' I say. 'I'll get him checked out, perhaps get someone to speak to his family.'

I'm told his name is Almond Nofomela.

Two days later, Anton Lubowski, a colleague and a friend, is assassinated in Windhoek in shocking circumstances. A well-known human-rights lawyer, he and I had shared a platform in 1983 at the press launch of the End Conscription Campaign. I'd been impressed by Anton, who was larger than life, handsome with his shock of curly black hair, and articulate. Almost roguish in his charm, he took up all the space at that press conference, and the media loved him.

His open support of Swapo had caused the major Namibian law firms to blacklist him and he'd found it increasingly difficult to get work. We used him as counsel in a number of cases and he'd been particularly helpful in our efforts to bring multiple interdicts against Inkatha as conflict escalated in the Pietermaritzburg area. During those long days and nights of work, Anton's unflagging energy, his legal skill and charisma had been a constant inspiration to us. In all that time he never spoke about the harassment he'd suffered in South Africa and Namibia or about the numerous attempts that had been made on his life. In a recent incident gunmen had riddled his car with bullets but he'd escaped unharmed.

And then he'd arrived home at eight in the evening and parked his car outside his house. The street was in darkness, the streetlights off. As he walked to his front door he was shot eleven times by someone wielding an AK-47. When the police arrived, a call was put through to the electricity department to have the streetlights switched back on.

Anton's assassination was the most recent in a succession of murders and disappearances of senior anti-apartheid figures, some of whom were later found murdered, while others were never seen again.

By September 1989, there had been eighteen murders of activists. To some extent we had become inured to the increasing bomb attacks on the buildings of anti-apartheid groupings, to the murders and abductions. From a legal perspective, we would carry out investigations on behalf of the victims, many of whom were our clients. But it was difficult to conduct a thorough inquiry. Only the police had access to the crime scenes and we knew, although we couldn't prove it, that the police were the most likely perpetrators. Forensic evidence was tidied up. Sham investigations would go nowhere. No one would be arrested. Every time I met with the officers in charge of those investigations, I sensed a silent mockery as they listened and gave nothing away, saying the information could not be divulged as it might prejudice the investigation. Dead end.

But we continued to search for that elusive breakthrough, that legendary 'smoking gun' which would prove that the bombings and killings were not just random acts of a lunatic right or lone vigilantes, but coordinated initiatives that were planned in Pretoria and executed by a squad under government control.

Now there was Almond Nofomela. Could he be the breakthrough we'd been searching for? And was it possible that we should have found him on Death Row of all places?

Three weeks pass as we try with little success to get information on Nofomela. In early October, Ting Ting tells Bheki that Nofomela has become increasingly anxious. He is due to be executed on the twentieth. Although he believes that Nofomela is telling the truth, Ting Ting's efforts to get details out of the man continue to be thwarted. Mockingly, they tell Nofomela, whose specific job was to hunt down and kill MK guerrillas, that even though he went to great lengths to serve the police, including committing murder, they have used him, and now he is going to die. Nofomela concedes that he is very worried, as his former commander hasn't responded to the messages he has smuggled out.

Bheki and I believe Ting Ting should persuade Nofomela to see a lawyer and give a detailed affidavit. This affidavit can then be used to launch proceedings for a stay of execution. His police friends have done nothing. If they were going to save him, they would have done so before the execution date was set.

A few days later, Bheki hears from Neo that Nofomela is desperate. He is shortly to be moved to the 'execution cell', nicknamed 'the pot'. This is where prisoners spend their last seven days 'stewing' – hence the name – before they're hanged. Nofomela's still not talking.

A few days later, I'm at home when I receive an urgent call late at night from Steve Katzew, an advocate based at the Pretoria Bar. He tells me that he has visited Death Row and must see me immediately.

'Can't it wait until tomorrow morning?' I ask.

'No,' he says.

THE BOMB

Eugene de Kock has received orders from his superior that a bomb should be despatched to this particular target. In fact, de Kock has been obsessed with the target for some time now, and talks about him frequently. He even obtains a video of the target talking to a journalist and orders key members of the Vlakplaas squad to study it carefully. There is much hatred in their discussion.

One of the Vlakplaas operatives who studies the video is a man called Sergeant Bellingan – known as 'Balletjies' to his friends. De Kock instructs him to help in deciding on the best method of killing the target. The target is well known to Balletjies as, in earlier days, they'd listened to a lot of music together – particularly Neil Diamond, one of the target's favourite singers. This gives Balletjies an idea.

55

I've known Steve Katzew for a long time and it worries me that he has called under such urgent and secretive circumstances. Steve is not actively political. While always supportive, I have never known him to be involved.

Steve was in my law class at Rhodes University. His integrity is beyond question; he is completely trustworthy. At university, he treated everyone equally. We'd both ended up on the Students Representative Council, become good friends and kept contact after we'd graduated. I know that Steve has been doing some work for Lawyers for Human Rights to supplement his growing practice.

He arrives at about eleven o'clock, shaking with tension and excitement, and blurts out that he has had the most remarkable legal consultation of his life. I pour him a whisky, top up my own and tell him to slow down. He insists on talking in the garden in case my house is bugged. Generally cynical of such melodrama and with no enthusiasm for the cold night air, I reluctantly agree. Steve, never a big drinker, although not without thirst, surprisingly knocks back his whisky and asks for another. This must be big, I think, as I pour him another drink.

He tells me that Lawyers for Human Rights in Pretoria asked him to make an urgent visit to a condemned prisoner on Death Row. A man by the name of Almond Nofomela.

I take a slug of my whisky as the familiar name jumps out of the night at me.

It turns out that Nofomela had sent a message to Lawyers for Human Rights requesting a lawyer. Steve spent the afternoon listening to Nofomela's astonishing story of how he had been part of a South African Police death squad and carried out numerous murders.

'Did he give you details?' I ask.

'Pete, he went into such detail about certain of the murders that I am convinced he would never have known these facts unless he was there. He gave me the location of the farm from which the squad operated, the names of his commanders and other critical details. He even gave me the name of the poison they put on the meat that they threw over the wall of Griffiths Mxenge's house to kill the dogs!'

'He was involved in the murder of Griffiths Mxenge in Durban?'

'Yes, that's what he's saying, and he goes into incredible detail. He also gives the names of the other policemen who were with him when they stabbed Mxenge. He says his commander on the squad was a Captain Dirk Coetzee, who did not come into the township on the operation, but remained in Durban waiting for the squad to report back. Pete, this guy, the commander, Dirk Coetzee, is chilling, a complete killer and, you know what, Nofomela loves this guy. There is a real bond there. I'm telling you, these guys come from a different place. Nofomela's the real thing. He is scary. This is not a concocted story, there are too many names and places. He gave me details about the murders of people I've never even heard of.'

Steve speaks so fast that he gulps for breath, and I'm not sure I'm hearing everything. I ask him to slow down. I also need time to think this through.

The murder of Griffiths Mxenge is well known. An active member of the ANC's underground movement, he spent some years as a political prisoner on Robben Island. After his release, he continued his work for the ANC and also ran a legal practice as a high-profile human-rights lawyer in Durban. He was murdered in 1981 in the township of Umlazi outside Durban, stabbed more than forty times by unknown assailants. His dogs were poisoned. At the time, police tried to ascribe the murder to a botched robbery, but everyone knew it was a political assassination and that the police were in some way responsible.

Steve mentions some of the other murders and gives details about Nofomela's cross-border raids and murders in Swaziland, Botswana and Lesotho. Killing sprees where ANC people were the targets, but where civilians were often killed. Steve trembles as he tells me how Nofomela calmly described the killings and the modus operandi of the squad. Frankly, I notice the ice cubes rattling in my glass, and this has less to do with the cold than the shock of what Steve is telling me. He paints a picture of a police squad that is utterly ruthless, operating outside of any accountable framework in a dark world of kidnapping and killing across the country and beyond.

Steve rushes on, his words tumbling over one another. 'This guy Ncfomela is going to be hanged in the next day or two. He managed to smuggle a message to his commander, a Eugene de Kock, at the headquarters of the squad on a farm near Pretoria called Vlakplaas.'

I interrupt him. 'Isn't his commander Dirk Coetzee?'

'Yes, Coetzee was in charge for a while and Nofomela speaks fondly of him, but the commander now is de Kock. Anyway, you can't believe this. This de Kock sends a message back via a Captain Khoza who visits Nofomela and tells him that he "must take the pain" and that nothing can be done to save him. Well, Nofomela isn't comfortable with this kind of pain.'

'I can see his point,' I say, taking a big slurp of whisky.

Steve continues. 'This was the turning point for Nofomela. After talking to some of his fellow prisoners, he finally decided to tell his story – even if it means that he's going to be found guilty and condemned to death for the other murders as well.'

'No big deal for a guy due to be hanged in a few days' time,' I say, sounding more nonchalant than I feel. 'In his position, a week is a lifetime. But what is this guy like? Are you sure he is not inventing this story to save himself from the rope?'

'I don't see how he could have invented this story,' Steve says. 'He had to have been there. Also, it wasn't like he was searching for words. He was crystal clear. The only things he was hazy on were the precise dates of some of the activities and the names of some of the victims. But he's come to the conclusion that de Kock and the rest of the police want him dead. He feels betrayed and he's angry.'

I remind Steve that Nofomela's in for straight murder and not for acting under police orders, even if those orders were to kill people. This guy shouldn't feel too hard done by.

'Did he ever mention the assassination of David Webster or Anton Lubowski?' I ask. 'Did his squad commit those murders?'

'No,' Steve says. 'Their names didn't come up. Then again, I didn't ask him about them. The murders he told me about were some years back.'

'When does he say he joined this "hit squad"?'

'In 1981,' says Steve. 'Before that he was a member of the police security branch.'

I'm stunned. 'Yussuss, Steve, this is a hell of a story.'

It's very late and Steve is wilting, the day and the whisky catching up with him. I'm not far behind. As things stand, Steve was briefed by Lawyers for Human Rights and was acting on their instructions, so this is their call. I know Brian Currin, the head of Lawyers for Human Rights, a fine attorney with a deep commitment to human rights. He's also a lawyer who knows how to move fast when it's needed. Steve's already informed

Brian of his consultation with Nofomela, and the legal proceedings are under way to get a stay of execution through the minister of justice, Kobie Coetsee. On this evidence, it shouldn't be too difficult.

56

I sit on a board called the Independent Board of Inquiry into Informal Repression which was founded by the Reverend Frank Chikane of the SACC after he'd survived an assassination attempt. I had represented him in the matter where his clothing had been poisoned and he had very nearly died.

The board includes, among others, Archbishop Desmond Tutu, Reverend Frank Chikane, Sheena Duncan (head of the Black Sash), Lawrie Ackerman (a former judge), Brian Currin, Norman Manoim and Professor John Dugard of the Centre for Applied Legal Studies at the University of the Witwatersrand.

Since its founding, the board has played an important role in compiling a database of the various attacks on activists and resistance organisations, and drawn links between them, identifying patterns and trends.

By October 1989, the worrying thing – for the police – is that we're making progress. The board employs good and brave people. Its offices are properly secured and located on the eleventh floor of a commercial office block, which we hope will deter the security police from blowing it up.

By the time the board meets to discuss the Nofomela allegations, he has been granted a last-minute stay of execution. It is agreed that a team from the board should urgently investigate to see whether evidence can be found to corroborate Nofomela's version of events. If we can get corroborating evidence, we hope to prove, once and for all, that the police have hit squads.

It's an odd time, a time of contradictions, rumour and strange hope. The dramatic resignation of President PW Botha in August 1989 had taken most people by grateful surprise. The new president, FW de Klerk, has the reputation of being more strategic than Botha and less hardline. There is talk of more pragmatism in the cabinet although some of the sinister ministers – Adriaan Vlok as minister of law and order and Magnus Malan as minister of defence – are still in office. Needless to say, the repression, killings and bombings continue. On the other hand, resistance has reached a crescendo with the UDF and Cosatu at the forefront of a massive campaign of defiance and mass action.

The pressure on President de Klerk is intense, both from within the country and externally. The ANC has set out its preconditions for negotiations, namely the release of all political prisoners, the lifting of bans on restricted organisations and individuals, the ending of the state of emergency, the withdrawal of the troops from the townships, and an end to political executions.

In addition, the new president faces pressure on the financial front. With less than a year to go before South Africa's external debt agreement in excess of US$11 billion will expire, a number of interest groups want to link the rescheduling agreement with faster political reform. Given economic sanctions and demands such as these, there is a hope that perhaps the beast is faltering. October has also seen the release of such high-profile political prisoners as Walter Sisulu, Ahmed Kathrada, and others from the famous Rivonia Trial when Nelson Mandela was sentenced to life imprisonment.

At the law firm, we discuss what this means for our clients, particularly the ones on Death Row. Surely they will not be hanged now? But at the same time, the repression continues unabated. There is talk that if this is the beginning of the end, the security forces will never allow it to happen – they will intervene, perhaps stage a coup d'état. I have encountered some of the generals and' I cannot believe that they would just hand over power. Not these people.

57

Almond Nofomela's affidavit begins, 'I am a thirty-two-year-old male presently under sentence of death. My execution is scheduled for tomorrow morning, 20 October 1989, at 07h00. I wish to reveal facts about my past which, I respectfully contend, might well have had a bearing on my conviction and sentence of death had they been known to the trial court, Appeal Court and the minister of justice.

'During the period of my service in the security branch, I served under station commander Brigadier (Willem) Schoon. In 1981, I was appointed a member of the Security Branch's assassination squad, and I served under Captain Johannes Dirk Coetzee, who was my commanding officer in the field.

'Some time during late 1981 I was briefed by Brigadier Schoon and Captain Dirk Coetzee to eliminate a certain Durban attorney, Griffiths Mxenge. I was told by my superiors that Mxenge was to be eliminated for his activities within the African National Congress … I was the leader of the group that had to assassinate Mxenge …' And so it goes on, a litany of murder and mayhem.

A few days after Nofomela's stay of execution, I visit the guys on Death Row. I ask if Constable Nofomela is a relieved man.

Jabu laughs. 'You know, this guy, his cell is in my section and now that he has broken his silence, he won't stop talking about what he has done. I have heard the same story about twenty times and it's driving me mad. Maybe we made a big mistake in saving him.'

Ting Ting and Neo burst out laughing.

'It is okay for you guys to laugh,' says Jabu mock-seriously. 'Your section is far away, but I have to put up with this policeman telling how he has been killing our people, and at the same time telling me how grateful he is to us for saving his life and persuading him to spill the beans.'

We all crack up. There's no sympathy on Death Row.

I come in. 'Look, I know that it must be helluva irritating but this is critically important information, it is the first major breakthrough that we've had into these killings and we have to get every bit of information from this guy, so please take it seriously.'

'Ja, Jabu,' says Neo, 'take it seriously, like a debriefing, pretend to be interested.' His voice is heavy with sarcasm. Jabu smiles wanly.

Back in Johannesburg, the members of the board of inquiry decide that the investigation of Almond Nofomela's allegations should focus primarily on those aspects that are capable of corroboration independently of the security forces. Of course the police have been quick to deny Nofomela's account of his time in the force. They admit that Nofomela was once a policeman, but state that he 'went bad' and ended up being a violent criminal.

Our investigation is given a boost when minister of justice Kobie Coetsee appoints a commission of enquiry to investigate Nofomela's allegations. The appointees are the attorney-general of the Free State, Tim McNally, and the head of the Criminal Investigation Division of the South African Police, General Alwyn Conradie. Like most attorney-generals appointed by the State at this time, McNally has the reputation of being conservative, but also of being a reasonable lawyer. We could do worse. As for Conradie, we could *not* do worse. But at least there is an official investigation. Cynically aware of the political adage that you never appoint a commission of inquiry unless you already know what the outcome will be, we nonetheless decide to conclude our own investigation quickly and present the results to McNally and Conradie.

Our team of investigators goes to work under the leadership of a bright young lawyer called Chris Orr, whose youthful looks belie his courage and determination. He frequently ventures alone into tough areas and asks questions that will attract the attention and ire of the security police. The more difficult our request, the broader the strange grin on Chris's face.

The first real progress is made when we investigate Nofomela's claim that he took part in a police assassination mission in Swaziland in late 1983. In the affidavit he says they entered Swaziland through the Oshoek border post and drove to the target house. First, a hand grenade was thrown into the house and then the squad came in firing. They killed three people, while a fourth person escaped. During the raid, a fellow policeman by the name of Jeff Bosigo was accidentally shot in the foot. The group returned to South Africa by driving over the border fence near Oshoek. Nofomela took Bosigo to the Ermelo Hospital where he was admitted, treated for the gunshot wound and then discharged.

In early November 1989, the board's investigators visit the Ermelo Hospital where the hospital records document the admittance of Jeffrey Bosigo on 22 November 1983 with a gunshot wound in the ankle. A news item in the Johannesburg *Star* on 23 November reports that raiders attacked a house in Manzini, killing Zakhele Nyanda and Keith McFadden who were thought to have ANC links. The article quotes Swazi police as saying the raiders were probably South Africans.

Encouraged by this small success, the investigation team moves to another allegation. Nofomela states that he and another policeman were ordered to set up a meeting with UDF members in Lamontville, Durban. On the night of the arranged meeting, some members of the squad, including Nofomela, waited under a bridge near the township while others went into the township armed with AK-47s. Nofomela heard AK-47 gunfire. Shortly afterwards, the hit team returned and the entire squad drove off.

Newspaper reports confirm that four men from the Chesterville Youth Organisation were shot dead on 20 June 1986. The inquest file on the murders reveals that the policemen who made affidavits about the killings are those named by Nofomela as having been in the waiting car or with the assassination squad.

It gets better when the team investigates Nofomela's claim that in either 1985 or 1986 his unit was told to kidnap the brother of a 'terrorist' wanted for killing a black policeman. The brother worked as a security guard in Krugersdorp. Nofomela says the man was duly captured and taken to the hit squad's headquarters, a farm called Vlakplaas outside Pretoria. The interrogation was fruitless. After severe and prolonged torture, it was clear that the man knew very little of his brother, who had joined the ANC, and had not seen him for years. The security guard was executed by one of the policemen.

The investigators make extensive enquiries in Krugersdorp and find that in May 1985 a security guard, Japie Maponya, was taken from his workplace by police for interrogation. Maponya's family, as well as his employer, confirm that after this he simply disappeared. The local police station has no record of the incident. The Maponya family confirm that Japie's brother Odirile Andries Maponya was killed in a limpet mine explosion in Pretoria in May 1988. Odirile was thought to be an ANC member.

In his Death Row cell, Nofomela tells the team that he has a box of 'souvenirs' from his days in the hit squad, and gives them permission to collect them from his home. Among Nofomela's souvenirs is a faded photograph of Odirile Andries Maponya.

In late 1984, Nofomela and other members of the Vlakplaas squad were instructed to kidnap a prominent UDF activist in Vryburg or, failing that, to steal his car. Using a duplicate key provided by the local police, they stole the car from outside the insurance company where the man worked. The squad removed the car's hubcaps and six live chickens that they found in the boot. The car was then set on fire in a remote spot. Nofomela kept the hubcaps. More souvenirs.

The board establishes that a UDF activist, Hoffman Galeng, a worker at an insurance company in Vryburg, had his car stolen in 1985. Galeng confirms that he was arrested in February 1985 and briefly interrogated by the security police. On his arrest, he was told to leave his possessions in one room before being taken into another room for questioning. He says he suspected something was amiss as the interrogation was about 'irrelevant [matters] and had no real purpose'. Galeng gives the investigators a copy of the claim he lodged with his insurance company on 29 April 1985 detailing the theft of his car four days earlier. A list of items in the car includes the six abducted chickens which Galeng, oddly, kept in his boot. Three days later his burnt-out car was found. At Nofomela's home the investigators find four hubcaps which Galeng says look like the ones that were on his car.

We are greatly excited by the corroborating evidence found by our investigation team. However, our concern is that the evidence needs more clout, more corroboration from other sources, and so we take the dangerous decision to approach the other members of the squad mentioned in Nofomela's affidavit. Perhaps they will yield more evidence which we can then present to the McNally and Conradie inquiry. Although Nofomela has named a number of men, we decide to approach only the black policemen on the squad. Our thinking is that the white policemen will be less amenable and probably prone to immediate and very damaging violence, having their own special political pathology. It is agreed that we will start with David Tshikalanga, Brian Nqalunga and Joe Mamasela. The question is: How to ask experienced police assassins with a penchant for psychotic aggression and cruelty to tell us their sad stories?

I'm pondering this question one Friday morning as I enter my office to find Bheki sitting reading the *Vrye Weekblad*. This new Afrikaans weekly already has a reputation for its anti-government stance, a rarity in the Afrikaans media. Through their coverage of political events and courageous investigative journalism, editor Max du Preez, journalists Jacques Pauw, Elsabé Wessels and others will go on to make a real impact for such a small newspaper. Bheki holds up the front page.

This time they have really done it. Captain Dirk Coetzee, commander of a police death squad, has told his story and revealed his involvement in a trail of murder, bombing, sabotage and assault. He provides corroboration on important aspects of Nofomela's claims. It is devastating and it is perfect. This is not some Death Row prisoner trying to avoid the rope. This is the genuine article, a bona fide captain in the security police admitting that he's murdered for the State. I wonder if it was Nofomela's story that made him break ranks.

Bheki says wryly, 'This Coetzee has just committed suicide.'

I agree. I can't see him living to give evidence. But for the moment this material is exactly what we need and we agree to hold off approaching Tshikalanga and the others.

Then comes some news. At the request of the National Reception Committee, Bheki and I have been asked to be on the platform at a rally to welcome the released leaders from Robben Island. On the last Sunday of the month, we meet at the Sisulu home in Orlando West early in the morning. The small house is buzzing. Bheki, who is one of the MCs and a marshal, is dressed in a tight-fitting khaki uniform with a black beret. I am dressed in a dark suit. Down the side of the house, Bheki and the other khaki-clad marshals practise their steps. This is clearly their first time.

I am taken into the house and introduced to Walter Sisulu, who sits quietly on a bed in one of the rooms. I am struck by his humility and gentility, awed by this man who has spent twenty-seven years in prison for his fight against injustice and still has the time to talk, on this day, even briefly, to a white youngster.

The convoy of cars carrying the released leaders drives into a tunnel underneath the massive FNB stadium and stops three quarters of the way up the ramp. Sisulu leads the released prisoners into the stadium and eighty thousand people roar as they see their icons for the first time. The stands are packed to capacity, the noise deafening as the elderly leaders walk slowly around the field, followed by the platoon of marshals. From the podium, behind which is draped a huge ANC banner, I see a moving mass of people, dancing to songs led by the MCs including Bheki. I am fascinated by Bheki, by his ability to control the crowd as one would an orchestra. He raises one foot, holds his knee high, with the whole crowd following, and then the stadium shakes as eighty thousand feet slam into the concrete. Watching Bheki leading the crowd in song, synchronising so many voices, I am awed. I see him with new eyes. The entire spectacle is so formidable that I wonder how, with such evident power, the majority of this country could have been dominated for so long.

Walter Sisulu is quiet as he watches the ecstatic crowd, appearing almost bemused, a small man whose presence is palpable. The other ANC veterans are also quiet, occasionally waving, perhaps amazed that they have lived to see this day. Murphy Morobe, National Reception Committee chairman, reads out a message from the president of the ANC, Oliver Tambo. Murphy, one of the UDF leaders who has spent the last decade in and out of detention, leading a life on the run, must also be questioning this reality as he stands under the blue spring sky with the Robben Islanders and other leaders behind him. When Murphy has finished, he steps back and calls on Walter Sisulu. The stadium gets to its feet. The applause goes on and on before Sisulu waves his hand, requesting silence. Looking out at the rapt stadium, the seething joy and celebration, it is hard to believe that the government will hang Jabu, Ting Ting and Neo. It is hard to believe that anyone else will die. We are so close.

58

The weekend papers are full of Coetzee and the macabre details of his killings. Friends in London and New York phone and tell me that the story has been front-page news there and is receiving extensive coverage in the press and on TV. The *Sunday Star* carries a large picture of Coetzee gazing reflectively into the future, having taken a hard drag on a cigarette. Rugged and good looking, with blonde hair and dark brown eyes, this apartheid hit squad commander could be a stand-in for the Marlboro Man. Remembering my own clients, I check myself. They too were members of a hit squad. But this is different.

The *Sunday Star* goes into elaborate detail on Coetzee's exploits, describing a police squad on the rampage, wild and unaccountable. There's the murder of anti-apartheid activist and Durban lawyer Griffiths Mxenge, and the killing of two ANC members near Komatipoort. There's the murder of a tall thin man kidnapped in Lesotho and held at the Jeffreys Bay police station. They decided to get rid of him because they were afraid of a second Biko. The murder of activist Patrick Makau and a seven-year-old child. Coetzee says they died when he and his men blew up a transit house, called the 'White House', as well as the house of another ANC member in Swaziland. A case containing forty kilograms of explosives and two Russian time-mechanisms was placed against the bedroom wall of the transit house. 'A few days later I went to have a look at the damage,'

Coetzee tells the newspaper. 'The house was razed. It was then that I heard that a child had been killed.'

The carnage continues with the murder of Ruth First. 'Shortly after I was transferred to security headquarters in Pretoria I received orders to burgle the office of the United Nations High Commissioner for Refugees in Mbabane in Swaziland. We forced the cabinets open and stole whatever we could find: files on ANC suspects and refugees, telex tapes, stickers and a variety of envelopes with the emblem of the commissioner on the cover. Two years later I learnt that the parcel with which First was blown up had been hidden in one of these envelopes.'

There's an attempt to bomb Chris Hani, but it's unsuccessful. The squad goes freelance and murders a diamond dealer. In 1982, Coetzee says, the askaris in the squad borrowed five thousand rand from him to buy diamonds in Lesotho. When they discovered that they'd been sold cheap gems, they went back and murdered the dealer. 'The murdered man's car was sold for R5 000 and I had my money back,' recounts Coetzee, noting that he'd laughed at the askaris being taken for a ride.

Two ANC women members shot in a raid on a house in Gaborone. An ANC member, Bafana Duma, blown up by a bomb placed in his letterbox. The abduction of Joe Pillay, a Durban-born teacher living in Swaziland. On this occasion, they left the four askaris behind and the men were caught after robbing a bank. Coetzee arranged for them to be released on R800 bail and then smuggled them back to South Africa. Further details include the blowing up of a state prosecutor's car in a treason trial to anger the judge and the poisoning of an ANC suspect who was being held in detention in Port Elizabeth. Coetzee has been a busy man.

The *Star* compares certain incidents in which Coetzee claims involvement with press reports of the same incidents, and then matches those against the allegations made by Nofomela. The similarities are too great to be ignored, the information too detailed to have been given by anyone who was not present. I am struck by the nature of the squad's activities. This is not political. These acts could never be justified, and they cannot even be understood as a vain attempt to keep a desperate government in power or even to protect South Africa from the ANC. This is sheer banditry, a police squad gone feral.

Not surprisingly, the *Star* article contains angry denials by the police top brass. 'It's laughable,' says General Johann Coetzee (no relation to

Dirk Coetzee), the former commissioner of police. General Coetzee, now sitting on his farm at Molteno in the Cape, states that he twice had Captain Coetzee transferred for misconduct. On one occasion this was because he found that Coetzee was involved with 'blue movies'. This I can believe. The police leadership, steeped in the staunchly conservative Calvinist doctrine of the Dutch Reformed Church, would probably view running a hit squad as a minor misdemeanour compared to the peddling of blue movies. Lieutenant-General Lothar Neethling, head of the SAP Forensic Laboratory, scoffs at the allegations that he prepared poisons for Coetzee's death squad. 'It is so laughable, I cannot comment,' he comments. Former security policeman and current member of the President's Council Craig Williamson says that he knew Coetzee as '… a hard worker and an experienced policeman. However, he suffered from diabetes for years and began acting strangely long ago.' Not exactly persuasive, Craig, I think.

And so it goes, denial after denial. We check to see if Coetzee has recently visited Nofomela, perhaps to ensure that their stories dovetail. The records show no visits to Nofomela by Coetzee. Also, this is a man who is now quietly living his life. Why turn it upside down, leave his wife and children, even leave his country, if he has done nothing wrong? But it does make sense if he has committed the acts he has confessed to and now fears being disowned by the police as a renegade who was not acting under orders. A scapegoat.

At the office, we're convinced that Coetzee, like Nofomela, is the real thing. If the government doesn't hang Nofomela and the police don't get to Coetzee and kill him, together they will prove that the security forces are out of control.

The article in the *Star* mentions that Coetzee is giving the interviews from Mauritius. A strange place to flee to, but then I suppose hit squad commanders need to relax more than most. At least he's out of the country, although in my book he's still easily within reach of his vengeful colleagues. I don't think the police will have difficulty finding recruits for this mission. He is definitely going to need protection and the only people who can provide him with that are the ANC. The obvious problem being that this is a man who has brutally killed a number of their members, and some high-profile ones at that. Given the damage he has caused, it would take some far-sighted people to ignore his actions and focus on his future worth.

The next day, Reverend Frank Chikane calls to say that the time is ripe, we must pull together what evidence has been collected on Nofomela's claims and present it to McNally's commission of inquiry as soon as possible. After frantic late-night drafting, we compile a detailed memorandum listing the areas where we've obtained corroboration. On Wednesday 22 November we fly to Bloemfontein to submit our document. Pretty conclusive stuff, we think. The delegation comprises John Dugard, former judge Lawrie Ackermann, Brian Currin and me.

McNally and Conradie receive us courteously and listen attentively to Lawrie Ackermann present the evidence. While he talks, Conradie studies us with interest, this strange collection of lawyers. I'm reminded of how a dog eyes a cat before chasing it. 'Extremely interesting,' says McNally, assuring us they will go through the memorandum in detail. 'Oh yes,' says Conradie, 'and thank you for coming.'

And that's it, no questions or discussion of the evidence. We leave wondering why we came all this way in the first place. As optimists, we quickly reassure ourselves that once they have read the memorandum they will have to take account of its contents. By the time we reach Johannesburg, after a few drinks at Bloemfontein airport and on the plane, we are completely confident that our memorandum will form the basis, if not the crucial pivot, on which McNally will rely to confirm that there is truth in Nofomela's allegations.

THE BOMB

Sergeant Steve Bosch receives a phone call from the man making the bomb, Captain Kobus Kok. He is instructed to buy two of the items that will house the bomb, each no bigger than the palm of a man's hand. One is for testing purposes and one is for the bomb that will go on to the target. Sergeant Bosch claims the money to buy the items from a secret fund available to the Vlakplaas squad and goes to a shop in central Pretoria where he buys the two items. They come in lightweight cardboard boxes on which are printed in bold coloured lettering 'Unisef SZ10'. The machines are manufactured in Japan.

59

It later emerges that after Dirk Coetzee had made contact with Jacques Pauw they went to Mauritius, and then to London where Coetzee had lengthy discussions with the ANC. This is a major propaganda and publicity coup for them. To have a high-ranking security policeman, who has also been the commander of a police assassination unit, turn to the ANC and confess on the world stage at the height of the international struggle against apartheid, is mileage that any liberation movement would welcome. In a country where political good news has been one-sided for some time, 1989 has given opposition groupings a fair amount of hope. That Coetzee's revelations come fast on the heels of the release of Sisulu and the other high-profile prisoners fuels speculation of further political developments. It also places additional pressure on Pretoria at a time when they're trying to persuade the world that they're not so bad after all. Simply regular guys fighting the good fight against the communist terrorists of the ANC.

As the press scramble to get more information about this disaffected security policeman, it turns out that Coetzee is not your basic police type. He is, in fact, a star performer, a sort of police wonder boy. He was the best student policeman in 1970 and received the trophy as the best graduate from the minister of police on the hallowed turf of Loftus Versveld rugby stadium. The following year he received first-class passes in four legal subjects. Six months after graduating he was promoted to sergeant. Three years later, he achieved a first in the warrant officer's examination. During this period, he also qualified as a dog handler and a scuba diver.

In March 1974, Coetzee fought in the bitter and savage bush war raging in what was then Rhodesia. It was well known that the government was happy to let the brightest and bravest in its security forces fight in Rhodesia. Firstly, it helped the minority government, which, like its counterpart in South Africa, was fighting to stay in power. There was much in common between the two countries. Secondly, and probably more importantly, it gave South African security forces the combat experience that would stand them in good stead in their own coming war. A feature of the Rhodesian conflict was its lack of rules. It was there in the lush green beauty of the Rhodesian bush that Coetzee learnt his future trade. There were no boundaries in the bush. The Geneva Convention did not reach into these hidden wars in secret places.

Coetzee returned to South Africa, apparently tracked by shadowy flashes of burnt corpses in mass graves, bodies torn apart by detonated mines, human remains rotting and eaten by the scavengers of the African wilds. Disturbing visions.

The young Coetzee was stationed at Sibasa in Venda in the north of the country, where he wrote his exams for lieutenant and passed first class. Soon he was given a lectureship at the police college, a position reserved for the top candidates. A 1976 promotion posted him to Volksrust as station commander, where he performed with distinction. A year later he was transferred, much to the disappointment of the town's white citizens who wrote to his superiors in protest. That year Coetzee was invited to join the prestigious security police. He accepted and took up the position of border post commander at Oshoek on the frontier with Swaziland.

Here Coetzee upgraded the police and border post premises and set up good communication channels with his Swazi counterparts. In fact, so favourably was he viewed that he received an invitation to the Swazi king's eightieth birthday party. A guest of honour, Coetzee was escorted by one of the king's four deputies. For some years afterwards, the king sent him a gift of wildebeest or impala venison every Christmas.

Coetzee was charming and he got what he wanted. But another side was developing. In that place, with that power, and with the support of security headquarters, he was untouchable. And he started to believe it.

The press are desperate to speak to Coetzee, but it looks like Jacques Pauw and Max du Preez of the *Vrye Weekblad* have got the inside story sewn up. The real speculation relates to the whereabouts of Coetzee. It is known that he is with the ANC, but where are they keeping him? Is he in London or have they taken him to Lusaka? He could even be in the Eastern bloc. We may be assured of one thing: if security find out where he is, he will die. In the meantime, the police trash their one-time favourite son as a crazed cop, a renegade who had to be expelled. General Lothar Neethling issues summons against the *Vrye Weekblad* for one million rand for defamation. Security policeman Craig Williamson breathlessly tells the press that he will also be suing *Vrye Weekblad* and 'anyone else my lawyer deems fit'.

Our objective amidst all this is to push the government into appointing a proper judicial commission of inquiry. While our expectations are not high in this regard, a commission would provide a forum where we can lead evidence and cross-examine police witnesses.

To keep up the pressure, John Dugard, Brian Currin and I hold a press conference to publicise the memorandum we presented to McNally. The press conference is packed and the major papers run our evidence as front-page stories.

On television, SAP public relations chief, General Herman Stadler, says that they regard the allegations of a police-sanctioned hit squad in a serious light and have launched their own investigation. General Stadler admits to the existence of a police farm outside Pretoria called Vlakplaas, but says that it is a rehabilitation camp for former ANC members. A few days later, the police take journalists to Vlakplaas, where they are allowed to wander around the picturesque premises and interview some of the scrubbed-up askaris living there. They deny they are part of a police hit squad.

In late November 1989, McNally hands his report to President de Klerk. We wait for it to be made public. The government remains silent under intense international pressure. Even the normally loyal Afrikaans press supports the call for a judicial commission of inquiry as more rumours of hit squads operating within the security forces are voiced. The press smells blood. Reports in some papers refer to the evidence of a witness in a treason trial in Cape Town in June 1989, in which an askari called Bongani Jonas told how he'd been 'turned' for his own survival. He described his work as an askari as going 'around the township acting on information from the security police to seek out and kill his former colleagues'. Jonas was later jailed for three years for refusing to give evidence for the State in the treason trial.

Dawn Barkhuizen of the *Star*, one of many journalists hot on the trail, writes an article referring to reprieved murderer Robert van der Merwe, who, while on trial for his life, stated that he knew of clandestine police operations and murders. In particular, he referred to an operation carried out from the Oshoek border post in which people alleged to have been close to the ANC were murdered.

Helen Grange, a courageous young journalist on the same paper, carries out her own investigation looking for evidence to corroborate Coetzee's story. Coetzee had told the *Vrye Weekblad* that an ANC suspect in detention was poisoned. He escaped death because he didn't drink all the poison, but was paralysed and his hair fell out. Doctors at Groote Schuur

Hospital in Cape Town found he'd been poisoned. He later disappeared, along with his wheelchair, according to Coetzee.

Grange confirms that Siphiwe Mtimkulu, a former student leader, emerged from five months of solitary confinement in 1981 with pains in his feet and stomach. Two days later, he was in a wheelchair and unable to walk. Grange writes that doctors at Groote Schuur Hospital diagnosed poisoning by thalium, a rare and cumulative poison used in insecticides. His brain was also affected by the poison and he began losing his hair. While in hospital, he lodged a claim for R150 000 against the minister of police for alleged poisoning, assaults and electric shock treatment during his detention. In January 1982, he returned home from hospital in a wheelchair after his treatment. On 12 April, Mtimkulu set out for Groote Schuur for a check-up, accompanied by his friend Topsy Madaka. They never arrived and were never seen again.

By now, another accomplice of Coetzee's, the policeman we'd earlier thought of approaching, David 'Spyker' Tshikalanga, has fled the country to Zimbabwe. His statements confirm some of the allegations made by Coetzee. It's becoming a flood. Each week the *Vrye Weekblad* reveals more details about Coetzee's activities, bolstering the growing clamour for a judicial commission. Still de Klerk is silent and refuses to release McNally's report.

Amidst these revelations, I visit Jabu and the others on Death Row. They are bored. It's a time of waiting. I tell them about the rally at FNB stadium to welcome back the released leaders. They listen intently, amazed that the event was allowed to take place.

'It is exciting, Peter, maybe they will not execute us now,' Jabu says, hopefully.

'Don't raise your hopes,' I counter, 'they may have released some important people but this place is still the same. On the ground with the security forces, nothing has changed.'

I tell them a story that has recently been in the press about an unemployed man by the name of Shakes Malapane, who lives in the coal-mining town of Witbank. Shakes was wearing his much prized 'struggle' T-shirt with a photograph of the recently released ANC leaders on the front and the ANC flag on the back. While on his way to the local shopping centre he was spotted by a group of riot police. Incensed by his T-shirt, they told him to take it off immediately. Shakes refused. He had nothing under the shirt and did not want to go naked. The police went berserk. Eight of them and a traffic cop jumped on him and tried to remove the shirt, assaulting him at the same time. He fought back and in the process his T-shirt got badly torn. Eventually, he was subdued, placed in handcuffs and the troublesome shirt removed. As he was being led away, a senior police officer arrived. He remonstrated with the overzealous police, ordering them to release Shakes and give him back his torn T-shirt. Malapane had the shirt repaired and continued to wear it. He decided not to lay charges as he had no faith in the system.

'So guys,' I say, 'don't hold out too much hope that all this is suddenly going to change. If they can't bear the sight of some ANC leaders on a T-shirt in Witbank, how do you think they will react to the possibility of them running the country?'

But they are not listening to me, they're doubled over with laughter, slapping one another on the back. Not empathising with the unfortunate Shakes, but imagining him fighting off eight riot policemen and a traffic cop, hell bent on stopping him from wearing his heretical T-shirt. They crack jokes about Shakes, saying that I must get his address so that they can write him a letter.

'What about Nofomela?' I ask. 'How is he feeling?'

'Well, he is very relieved that he will not be hanged in the next few weeks,' says Ting Ting in his dry understated way. 'At least not until this investigation is over, so he is feeling a lot better about that. Jabu told him to stop talking as he couldn't take it anymore, but he just carries on. Now he's worried that they will get to him here and kill him. So I suppose he is just as scared. He has asked us to protect him.'

They all burst out laughing again. Tears roll down Ting Ting's face. He is not talking into the intercom so I cannot hear what he's saying, but it sets them off again. I find myself laughing as well. I put it down to Death Row. It gives tragedy new meaning.

60

In early January 1990, the ANC legal department asks me to travel to Lusaka. I should be prepared to stay for a few days. The purpose of the visit is to take a detailed legal statement from Dirk Coetzee. I am shocked by the request, thinking that the ANC might have kept him in a safer place. Lusaka is a short two-hour flight from Johannesburg and is rumoured to be riddled with South African intelligence agents. I am also worried that the means by which I received the message may have been compromised. If the police know we are going to see Coetzee, they might track us in some way and kill him, or worse, kill me as well.

This is the picture in my mind: I am consulting with Coetzee in some seedy, run-down hotel on the outskirts of Lusaka, with warm beer and slow-moving ceiling fans, when in crash some over-muscled, brandy-breathing, deranged former colleagues of his seeking revenge. They then proceed to finish us off. A big mess. I know it's customary for the Police Task Force units to have a few shots of brandy before their missions to 'steady' their nerves. While I completely understand the need to have a shot of brandy before embarking on an endeavour that may involve killing someone, or even a number of persons, the brandy ritual becomes offensive to me when I consider that I might be one of those persons. It seems distasteful, if not disrespectful. One would think that with all this death and murder about, I should have become inured to the carnage and the prospect of a violent end. Not at all; in fact, the opposite.

I realise that I am also worried about spending time with a man who commanded what appears to have been a very successful hit squad. I mean, we have very little in common. Besides, what do you say to a man who killed and poisoned people for a living? Do you talk about the weather? No. I also wonder how prone he might be to spontaneous violence and how he would feel talking to a human-rights lawyer like myself. These kinds of guys, I tell myself, do not like human-rights lawyers and what they do. It interferes with their work. And no one likes interference, particularly an assassin. At least I'll have Max Coleman with me, but chances are he won't like Max either.

Max is in his late sixties, a slim man with thinning hair and a pencil-thin moustache. He's fit too. We went scuba diving together at Sodwana some years back and I remember how Max coped with what can be a strenuous sport. Although there's a big age gap between us, we have a good relationship and I've always admired him for the considered manner in which he approaches everything. I think it's remarkable that he decided to get involved in resistance politics after years spent in the corporate world. His life took this course when two of his sons were detained for long periods in solitary confinement during the first two states of emergency. He gave up his profitable business and devoted himself full time to helping detainees and doing other political work. I always look forward to spending time with him. Normally I wouldn't jump at the prospect of including a hit squad commander in our conversation, but I suppose this is different. It's work. Although Coetzee is also a qualified diver. Something in common, perhaps?

As it turns out, Max is every bit as anxious as I am about meeting Coetzee and spending protracted time in his company. On the flight to Lusaka, we speculate about him and how he will react to us. And then on the drive into the city, our apprehension is heightened by the normally talkative Penuell Maduna, who is strangely silent. I note that he is not driving his white Toyota Corolla and that he has progressed to a much smarter red Renault. Attempting conversation, I ask him about his new wheels and he tells me that the car belonged to 'a black guy that we caught in Zimbabwe'.

'Really,' I say, interested.

'Oh yes,' says Penuell cryptically. 'We caught him after he had sent a TV to Comrade Mhlope.'

'Was there a problem with the TV?' I ask, wondering how the dispatch of a TV can warrant the confiscation of a car.

'It had a bomb in it which exploded and killed Mhlope,' he says, eyes straight ahead on the road.

'Fuck,' I exclaim, turning around to look at Max in the back seat. He's gone very pale. I roll down the window to let in some air.

Jacob Zuma, the deputy head of ANC Intelligence, briefs us before the meeting with Coetzee.

We meet in the reception area of the Pamodzi Hotel. Zuma is dressed in khaki slacks and an open-necked white shirt, which hangs out, African style. A solid man, bald and with slightly slanted eyes, he is articulate and warmly welcoming as he tells us what he wants from Coetzee. He also gives a quick insight into Coetzee's state of mind. 'The man's gone through a lot and we need to be patient with him,' he stresses in an almost fatherly way. 'He's also missing his family and we know there are some problems there.' Max and I nod, not wanting to pry further at this stage. Coetzee is suspicious of everyone, Zuma says, and initially expressed resistance to his statement being taken by people from South Africa. 'But I told him that we all come from South Africa. It's just that some of us have been outside for longer. And one thing's for certain: we're all going back.'

We laugh – Max and me a bit too hard. But Zuma's relaxed attitude and easy appeal lessens our anxiety as we are led to the fourth floor of the hotel and the room in which Coetzee waits.

Coetzee is charming and businesslike. Well built, his blonde hair and dark brown eyes combine with his tanned face and good features to make him a handsome man. Unlike many of his colleagues in the police, in his tight-fitting blue jeans and casual shirt, he comes across as urbane and sophisticated. It has always intrigued me that policemen or soldiers seem ill at ease in civilian clothes, as if they've put aside their power and stature, along with the uniform. Coetzee has none of that. Drawing on his cigarette, he speaks to Zuma with respect, but there is something more there, warmth. I can see that this is no longer the defector anxious about his fate; Coetzee appears comfortable with his new masters. There is a hungry, raffish air about him and I understand immediately why he was branded a renegade by the police, a man who could not take discipline. He has an air of insolent confidence which must have infuriated his superiors, this troublesome golden boy who had such great promise. We sit down and Max and I take out our notebooks.

He has an amazing memory for detail. Sometimes he forgets the exact date, but his descriptions of the various incidents tie in closely with the information given by Nofomela. In good English with a slight Afrikaans accent, he hides nothing as he goes through his upbringing and early days in the police. He speaks graphically about his superiors, at times swearing violently as he describes a colleague who let him down or betrayed him. As the day progresses and he becomes more at ease, his language deteriorates badly. He swears venomously and with real passion, his face contorting, the words exploding from him. Sometimes when he swears, I see Max start and look at him with horror.

By the early evening, Coetzee is describing some of the first incidents. We order up dinner and beers, and take a break. Max and I are tired after the flight and hours of questioning and note taking. Coetzee relaxes with a beer, cigarette in hand. He jumps ahead and tells us of an instruction to 'get rid' of a detainee who has been so badly tortured that he has to disappear in order to avoid another Biko incident. He and members of his squad take the detainee hooded and handcuffed to a remote farm in the Komatipoort area where they give him a poisoned cooldrink. The poison is care of General Lothar Neethling. The severely injured detainee falls to the ground and is shot in the back of the head.

Coetzee is in full swing now. The closed curtains make the room very small, stifling with the smoke and alcohol. He describes how he and the other policemen make two fires, one larger than the other and a short distance apart. The body of the murdered detainee is thrown on the large fire. At first the corpse blisters as it burns, the flesh peeling and blackening from the intense heat.

'Bodies take time to burn,' says Coetzee, and because he and his men are hungry they braai sausages and chops on the smaller fire. They eat and drink into the night. First beer, later brandy, known as police coffee. Sodden with meat and liquor, the policemen fall asleep with the larger fire still burning, the body smouldering, turning to charcoal. The next morning, the body is ashes. The policemen disperse the coals and ashes and, hung over, they leave the farm.

The room is silent. 'Jesus,' I say.

Coetzee looks at us, slowly nodding his head. 'Can you order more drinks?'

Over the coming days and very late nights, Coetzee tells us about each of the missions he was involved in. He talks dispassionately and clinically about the details, each shooting, each murder. Never once expressing regret or even empathy for his victims, as if recounting a story in which he had no part. Just the facts. He doesn't even try to fake concern for his victims. It was a job and he was good at it. If anything, there is an element of pride in some of the operations. Occasionally he lingers on a delicate subterfuge that threw investigators off the scent.

Often he talks lovingly of his wife and family. He is proud of his young son Dirkie.

Yet when the alcohol's in him his swearing is obscene. Against our better judgement we laugh and he plays to us. I feel guilty for laughing, somehow complicit with him in these outrageous acts. There is nothing to laugh about.

Occasionally, because he's a diabetic, he takes a needle and syringe from a bag and injects himself with insulin. Without stopping his conversation, he plunges the syringe into his leg and pushes down the plunger in a way that makes me wince and go pale. Max and I turn our heads.

Late at night in the small room, with the drink, the smoke and the swearing and the death, I feel we are clustered around that fire in the veld on which the body burns, the flesh sticking to our hands, the smell all about us.

With each passing day, Max grows quieter in the interviews, not wanting to get too close to the fire. I understand this, but we need the detail, the evidence to corroborate the information we have from Nofomela and others.

Coetzee speaks of Nofomela with great affection, much more so than he does of his other fellow white policemen. He berates these colleagues angrily. Swearing viciously in a mounting rage, he blames his commanders for what has happened to him. He has lost everything: his career, his job, his faith, his family, his cause and now his country because of them. He, the hit squad commander, has become the victim. Bitterly, he wishes he could go back. He would make them pay for what they've done to him. And I believe him, completely. This man is capable of anything. He does violence to the word violence.

Coetzee is impenitent, resentful, alone in the hands of his former enemy. Should I feel some sympathy for him? Unquestionably, his personality is a seductive one, enticing. Until he speaks of murder.

Of how he, one Koos Vermeulen and a few askaris took an ANC operative by the name of Vuyani Mavuso into the bush near Komatipoort. Mavuso had been captured during a raid in Maputo in January 1981. They decided to use him as a guinea pig for a poison supplied by General Lothar Neethling.

The poison was administered in a soft drink, and although Mavuso collapsed and spent the night writhing in pain and babbling incoherently, he didn't die. The men spent the night warming themselves round a fire, braaing meat and drinking 'police coffee'. Like medical interns, they carefully noted the stricken man's reactions and dreadful symptoms as the poison attacked his body. The next morning, they obtained more poison from Neethling. This also proved ineffective. Coetzee decided to shoot Mavuso and another askari by the name of Peter Dlamini, who was proving problematic.

Before the execution was carried out, askari Joe Mamasela decided to teach Mavuso how to pray. Mavuso was forced to kneel and told to recite the Lord's Prayer. Head bowed, Mavuso recited the prayer over and over. Every time he stopped or made a mistake, Mamasela kicked him in the face. The policemen laughed uproariously. Mavuso fell repeatedly, dragged himself back to a kneeling position, again and again trying to recite the Lord's Prayer. He did this for hours, until his face was pulp. Later, Koos Vermeulen forced Mavuso and Dlamini to lie on the ground and shot them both in the back of the head. Their bodies were burnt on the fire and the ashes thrown in a nearby river.

From time to time Jacob Zuma, always courteous, joins us in the hotel room. He sits quietly, listening to Coetzee's answers to our questions. Acknowledging Zuma's presence, Coetzee is more restrained, particularly with his language.

Occasionally, when things become too much, we leave Coetzee in the room with his 'minder' and have lunch with Zuma at the hotel restaurant downstairs. Seated on the woven bamboo chairs in the warm sun with cold beers in our hands and the cool blue rectangle of the swimming pool in front of us, I wish we were here to enjoy the beauty of Zambia and its legendary game parks. I wish we were like the tourists and diplomats at the other tables, engrossed in normal worlds. For a while we indulge ourselves with small talk and then, as always, we discuss Coetzee.

Zuma speaks about Coetzee without recrimination. He's worried about Coetzee's state of mind. Coetzee misses his wife and knows she is having an affair with a young man. The affair started shortly after Coetzee fled South Africa. The young man reports to the security police. In fact, says Zuma, the whole business was set up by the security police to get information on Coetzee from his wife. The communication arrangements that Coetzee planned with her – the prearranged phone-in times at specific public phone booths – were all compromised and passed on to security by the agent. The worst thing that could happen now would be for Coetzee to return to South Africa to exact revenge on his wife's lover. That is exactly what the security police want. They will be waiting. And Coetzee is volatile enough to do it. God help the guy who sleeps with Coetzee's wife, I think, thankful that I am far from being in his fatal shoes. Such a man will be in real trouble if the aggrieved husband gets hold of him – fires in the bushveld type trouble.

Throughout the discussions, Zuma is impressive and considered, even sympathetic to Coetzee. A true professional, chewing the information from his charge like cud, extracting the nutrients.

Now and again, other ANC Intelligence officials join us in the room with Coetzee. These include Joe Nhlanhla, the head of ANC Intelligence, and people from the legal department, fascinated and horrified as we delve into Coetzee's history and the wreckage he caused.

We work until late at night, and then we drink. Too much drink, but it opens him up and he talks of his life at Vlakplaas and how they behaved on the farm and when they were on a mission. Even in his most unguarded moments, I never get the impression that Coetzee is a racist or feels an innate superiority to black people. Whenever he speaks of Nofomela it is fondly. He empathises with the man's situation on Death Row, cursing his betrayal by their masters in the police. I realise a simple fact: killing does not bother Coetzee. He feels no remorse, no guilt. The murders, the bombings, the poisonings, they are all simply activities.

And he is not alone. Vlakplaas is full of men like this. Men who operate on the other side of the moral divide where few people ever go. Those that do, lose something forever. Inevitably, the squad at Vlakplaas under Coetzee carries the seeds of its own destruction, and degenerates. Bandit time, as the squad freelances into illegal diamond dealing, murder and robbery. Out on that perimeter, there are no boundaries. Human life loses its significance. Men become meat.

61

Taking Coetzee's statement is a long and sometimes frustrating business as, bit by bit, we put the pieces in place to substantiate his story. To do this we take each incident and painstakingly gather the evidence around it. Where were the policemen concerned at that particular time? Who occupied the house? What was the weather like on the night? Which car was seen outside? What kind of damage was done? How did the person die?

After our first visit to Coetzee, Max Coleman is happy for me to continue taking the statement without him. On my second visit, Bheki accompanies me. Frankly, I would be happy to drop out too, although I am fascinated by this venture into the heart of darkness. Also, the opportunity is too good to miss. We have Nofomela's statement from Death Row, and Jabu, Ting Ting and Neo are continually feeding me new information. He now trusts them and is confiding freely. In addition, there is the independent corroboration of our own investigators in South Africa, as well as the information being fed to us by ANC Intelligence operatives during our days in Lusaka. As the unhappy recipients of attention from Coetzee's squad in the past, the latter are able to supply information from the victims' side.

The evidence from so many angles and sources is reasonably conclusive, with the versions dovetailing in most respects. Granted, there are exaggerations in Coetzee's story, but the essence is true. And it is devastating. What emerges is a tale of a police hit squad run amok, careering around the country, ruinous and unaccountable.

Over the succeeding months, Bheki and I make a regular shuttle to Lusaka to take Coetzee's statement. Often we take with us substantiating evidence for him to confirm or deny. He sifts through the damage of past operations, picking up items of interest, giving fascinating details on individual policemen, how they operate, their foibles and weaknesses, their afflictions and addictions, the ones to be afraid of, the real professionals, those susceptible to money or women, or both. All this information flows into the already detailed files of ANC Intelligence. At times the evidence opens a floodgate of memories, and then Bheki and I spend hours working through the fresh material, searching for life in the ruins.

Very late one night Bheki intervenes with a question. 'Dirk, how were the askaris at Vlakplaas paid?'

Eyes bloodshot, he replies, 'Very little money. We gave them drink and dagga as well. If you give them too much money they get independent and leave, maybe speak to people, very danger-fucken-rous.'

Coetzee is one of the few people I've met who, as a matter of course, breaks up his words to insert four-letter expletives. On occasions, to our amazement, he even inserts two shocking epithets into a simple three-syllable word.

I find that while I spend time with Coetzee we never really get close. The gap is far too great. It is purely business and no bond develops. I can tell that he senses this. Bheki, on the other hand, has a great interest in

Coetzee and is happy to spend hours in his company, listening to his stories and asking questions. Strangely, while we're in Lusaka, Bheki develops an affection for Coetzee, putting aside the atrocities he has committed as if the fact that he has simply changed sides is enough. Bheki's attitude is not that different from Zuma's. Except that Bheki has a morbid fascination with this man. He wants to get inside his head. To understand what drives him, how he felt when he murdered.

Bheki becomes obsessed with Coetzee, speaks about him constantly, questioning his motives, analysing his actions. He wants to understand how Coetzee can talk of his part in the terrible death of a man with the same absence of emotion the weatherman shows when he describes tomorrow's weather. It perplexes Bheki that the only time Coetzee shows emotion is when he talks of the treachery of his colleagues.

In between Lusaka visits, Bheki makes contact with Coetzee's brother Ben and takes a statement from him at our office. Ben is a computer boffin, a civilian without Coetzee's clipped rigour. Tall and craggy, rounder and softer in character, and devoted to his brother, he brings messages which we pass on to Coetzee. Any news of his family, Coetzee consumes hungrily.

Things are not good on the home front. On one of our visits to Lusaka we find Coetzee furious and distraught. After receiving no news for a while, he snapped and phoned home. First he spoke to his son Dirkie. When he asked to speak to his wife Karen, Dirkie told him she was in the bathroom with the 'other man' and the door was locked. 'Jesus man, in my own house!' he shouts, smashing his fist down on his leg. 'Having a bath, with this guy, in front of my kids in my house. Nee, yusssus, this guy is dead, de-fucking-ea-fucking-ead, I tell you, *dead*, he just doesn't know it yet.'

Bheki and I are silenced by the violence of this outburst. 'Have you spoken to Zuma about this?' I ask nervously.

'Ja, he is trying to help, but I can't just sit here, I tell you, in these shit hotel rooms day after day by myself. I have to do something. And all the while he's there with her. Fuck!'

Bheki and I meet with Zuma to tell him that his man is spinning. In this state he could do anything. Zuma's well aware of this and is making plans to get Karen Coetzee to Lusaka for a few days. We fly back to Johannesburg later that day, worried that all we've achieved so far is in jeopardy. Will Coetzee resist the temptation to sort out the amorous man in his bathroom? Even from afar, the security police are pressing all the right buttons.

We hear from Coetzee on our next visit that Zuma did have Karen flown in and that they have 'patched it up'. Over a period of days, they were reconciled, although it went badly at first. While she was there, Zuma generously covered all the bills. He's convinced that the affair will end. Things are back on track. Coetzee tells us that shortly after Karen arrived, Zuma had asked his permission to talk to her alone. When she came back from that meeting, she told him she was committed to the relationship. The next few days were blissful, and Coetzee is particularly grateful to Zuma, whom he credits with saving his marriage. This is a turning point for Coetzee; he is now Zuma's man.

THE BOMB

The next telephone call Sergeant Bosch receives from Captain Kobus Kok is a request for him to buy a sheep's head. This is an easy task, sheep's heads being for sale at most butcheries. Sergeant Bosch goes to his nearest butchery but as the cost of a sheep's head is fairly expensive, he opts instead for a pig's head which costs about ten rand. He lets Captain Kok know what he's done. The captain has no objections.

62

On 31 January 1990, the day before Dirk Coetzee is due to address his first international press conference in Harare, President de Klerk announces that Mr Justice Louis Harms will conduct a one-man judicial commission of inquiry into 'murders and deeds of violence allegedly committed with political motives'.

Harms, a cum laude graduate of Pretoria University, has a reputation for being 'clever' and not suffering fools gladly. He also does not share the shocking reputation of some right-wing judges who can always be relied on to do the State's bidding. The media describe him as 'incisive'. This, coupled with President de Klerk's promise that the commission will 'cut to the bone' to reach the truth about the alleged death squads, raises our hopes that, finally, here is someone who will take no nonsense and who will conduct a proper and fair inquiry. At the law firm, we receive instructions from Jay Naidoo, the general secretary of Cosatu, Brother Jude of the Southern African Catholic Bishops Conference, the Reverend Frank Chikane of the SACC, the Independent Board of Inquiry and numerous families of murdered and missing activists to represent them at the Harms Commission.

Apart from the revelations of Coetzee, Nofomela et al, police inquiries have also uncovered evidence of hit squad activity which de Klerk can no longer ignore.

During investigations into the murder of Anton Lubowski a man by the name of Donald Acheson was arrested. Acheson told the investigating officer, Jumbo Smith, that he worked for a shoplifting syndicate in South Africa and he identified Ferdi Barnard as the man who'd recruited him. Acheson had all the necessary credentials. He was an Irish national who had joined the Grey Scouts, a counter-insurgency unit fighting the black nationalists in what was then Rhodesia. When Rhodesia became Zimbabwe on independence, he left and joined 5 Reconnaissance Regiment of the SADF, based in the north of the country. In the mid-eighties, he left the SADF and went solo.

At the same time, Brigadier Floris Mostert, who is investigating the murder of David Webster in South Africa, finds that his investigation leads him to a man by the name of Ferdi Barnard. Barnard had been a narcotics bureau detective in the SAP, based on the West Rand outside

Johannesburg. In December 1984, he had been sentenced to nine years in prison for the murder of two drug addicts, the attempted murder of another addict and the theft of three cars. After serving four years he was released on parole from Pretoria Central prison in December 1988. Brigadier Mostert arrests Barnard on 31 October 1989 and detains him in terms of the notorious Section 29 of the Internal Security Act. Soon afterwards, he detains another former policeman called Calla Botha. Botha, a bull of a man who played provincial rugby, is a former security policeman. Later in his career, he joined the Brixton Murder and Robbery Squad. In 1988, Sergeant Calla Botha was one of a group of four senior policemen who all suddenly resigned from the Brixton Murder and Robbery Squad, the others being Lieutenant-Colonel 'Staal' Burger, Lieutenant 'Slang' van Zyl and Warrant Officer Chappie Maree.

While in detention, Ferdi Barnard tells Brigadier Mostert that he is 'a member of a secret organisation committed to a strategy of violently intimidating the radical left'. Mostert soon establishes that Barnard had been in contact with Donald Acheson on at least two occasions before Anton Lubowski was killed. Furthermore, he suspects that there is a link between Barnard and military intelligence. That clue acquires new significance towards the end of January 1990 when Barnard's father, a retired police colonel, launches an urgent application in the Rand Supreme Court to have his son released. In the opposing affidavit of Brigadier Mostert, he refers to 'a secret organisation' that terrorised 'left-wing radicals'. It is his belief that this group murdered both Webster and Lubowski.

We are taken by surprise by these revelations, having thought that the Vlakplaas squad, which we know is still operating, was responsible for David and Anton's death. We have not been aware of the existence of a second organisation or squad, potentially linked to the defence force and mandated to eliminate internal opponents of the government. Although we knew that the special forces of the defence force were carrying out destabilising raids and killings in Angola, Mozambique, Botswana and Lesotho, we've never considered that they might be assassinating people inside the country. We thought that grisly function fell to the police or the right wing. We were wrong.

As the revelations continue during January 1990, the press turns its attention to the secret body detailed in Mostert's affidavit. Human-rights organisations, lawyers and the opposition Democratic Party add their voices to the media's call for a judicial commission of inquiry. Interestingly, two influential pro-government newspapers join the chorus, as do the Dutch Reformed Church, the religious foundation of the National Party and government, when one of its well-known clergymen, Willem Nicol, refers to suspicions of police involvement in assassinations.

By now it is clear that de Klerk has no intention of releasing the report from McNally and Conradie.

Perhaps in an attempt to provide a sideshow, in early January 1990 Nofomela is charged with the murder of Griffiths Mxenge. 'At least the new trial will keep him alive on Death Row for a year or two,' is Jabu's comment. Typical gallows humour. 'Nowadays you have to commit murder to avoid being hanged.' The charge against Nofomela is followed by warrants of arrest for Dirk Coetzee and the askari David Tshikalanga for their involvement in the Mxenge murder. Admirable legal moves, but somehow distracting given the revelations of government culpability in political assassinations.

In early February 1990, a few days after the announcement of the Harms Commission, Brigadier Floris Mostert reveals something else in a further court affidavit. 'I established that the aforesaid secret organisation was responsible for different incidents of murder, arson, bomb explosions, assaults and intimidation. From questioning [Ferdi] Barnard and [Calla] Botha, I established that the aforementioned secret organisation was actually a unit of the South African Defence Force that was known as the Civil Cooperation Bureau (CCB).' I ponder the dark humour that led to a defence force hit squad being named the Civil Cooperation Bureau!

With information now coming thick and fast from all quarters, including the police, I'm confident that Louis Harms will come to a positive finding. On Death Row, I suggest to Jabu, Ting Ting and Neo that they protect Nofomela to the best of their ability. It would be unfortunate if he should die in a 'fight' before he testifies to the Harms Commission.

63

It is 2 February 1990, the opening of parliament. The country is awash with rumour, both good and bad, in anticipation of the president's opening speech. In the law firm, we have no doubt that de Klerk differs from his predecessors and appears to be prepared to make bold moves. Witness the release of key ANC Robben Islanders. The counter argument has it that he can afford this gesture because they're old and he wouldn't want them to die as martyrs on the Island. Undoubtedly, the release of those prisoners has bought the government more time from the international community, who have hailed it as a step in the right direction. Similarly the announcement of the Harms Commission is another good move. But will he go further?

Many are cynical of de Klerk and his government, questioning why he would voluntarily start a process of reform which must result in his losing power. Democracy is a numbers game and the National Party have done their counting.

Nonetheless, everyone in the firm is clustered in the main boardroom at the office watching the TV. De Klerk stands before parliament shuffling his papers as he speaks in heavily accented English. In one fell swoop, he announces to an incredulous nation that the ANC, SACP, PAC, Umkhonto we Sizwe and the Black Consciousness movements, as well as thirty-one other banned organisations, will all be legalised and able to operate freely. He talks of freeing political prisoners incarcerated for non-violent activities and the lifting of certain state of emergency restrictions. We listen in disbelief. Who could have dreamt he would go this far? There is complete silence in the room. What is beyond doubt is that the political landscape is forever changed.

The one thing we've all been hoping for is an indication of when Nelson Mandela will be released. We know it has to be sometime soon. In my office, Bheki and I discuss the implications of de Klerk's speech for our clients. He'd spoken of releasing political prisoners who'd committed non-violent offences, which brings us no joy as there's nothing passive about our guys. We feel it must help them, though. The climate has changed. Whatever the assessors found, it has never been disputed that Jabu and the others reported to and were accountable to the high command of MK and the ANC.

A real worry is that the generals, the right wing and the security forces will not allow de Klerk to push through his reform plans. I'm concerned that they might carry out a coup or, at least, pull de Klerk back.

Bheki is pessimistic. 'I mean,' he says, 'can you seriously see those generals allowing Chris Hani to come back into the country? Can you see them letting him walk the streets? I tell you, the people will go mad if Oliver Tambo or Hani, even Joe Slovo, are seen walking the streets. It is just too much. And if they release Nelson Mandela, some right-winger will shoot him within days and then it will really explode. Boom! And there will be no reform process. This place will burn and the security forces will have free licence. They'll go mad. The youth will come into the towns and suburbs and strip them like locusts moving through a field. They'll fight. But this time is different from 1976. Now they have guns, grenades and RPGs. I am worried about where this is going. It's too good to be true, something is going to happen.'

I am appalled by Bheki's apocalyptic vision. We can't have got to this point just to see it go up in flames. But we are so used to things being this way, the behaviour of security, the government, the right wing, that the concept of it changing is alien, requiring real adjustment.

At the same time, there is no denying that a process has begun. Once the ANC leadership is released from Robben Island and returns from exile, there will be negotiations. Talks about talks. I've heard that already there've been meetings at a leadership level, but for the moment this is speculation by the hopeful.

And always at the back of our minds is the escalating conflict between Inkatha and ANC-aligned organisations in KwaZulu-Natal where the daily death toll is excessive. There are massacres of innocent villagers and township dwellers by unknown bands of men armed with guns and pangas. We suspect that these attacks are fuelled by what the press term a 'Third Force'. To me this simply means the police or right-wing elements in the police. But, again, I cannot prove it.

In the meantime it is back to work. We have the Harms Commission to prepare for, and the appeal of Jabu, Ting Ting and Neo is set down for 15 August. A week after de Klerk's speech, I'm on a tour of the Scandinavian countries with a fundraiser from Oxfam. We meet governments to raise money to buy a building for Cosatu to replace its headquarters which were blown up in May 1987. The tour ends for me in Helsinki. And it's in the small bar of my hotel that at sixteen minutes past four on the afternoon of 11 February 1990, I watch Nelson Mandela walk out of Victor Verster prison, hand in hand with his wife Winnie. This is the man whose speech from the dock at the end of the Rivonia Trial motivated me to become a human-rights lawyer.

It's a perfect day in the Cape. In Helsinki, it is minus fifteen degrees centigrade and the snow lies leaden white beneath a grey sky. The other six patrons in the bar stare at the screen and nurse shot glasses of aquavit, fire and ice. I notice the emotion on their faces. The barman quietly refills everyone's glasses, saying in a deep voice, 'This one is for free. Let us drink to Nelson Mandela. Skol!' We drink, eyes on each other.

Turning back to the television, the burning liquid a molten ball in my chest, I feel drained and tired, missing the elation that I'd always expected I'd feel. But I am deeply relieved that Mandela, the icon, is finally free and that whatever may befall us, the process is now close to irreversible. That man cannot be put back in prison, the country would burn.

I tell the barman to give us another round. Standing, I say, 'Skol!' and we drink again. One of the businessmen at the bar says, 'I never thought he would be released.'

'Neither did I,' I respond.

The barman looks at me and says, 'You are South African, aren't you?'

'Yes, I am,' I reply, and it means something completely different now.

THE BOMB

Some bombs, it is said, have a mind of their own and are not to be trusted, which is one of the reasons that the real professionals test their devices. Such matters are never left to chance, particularly when there is an opportunity to mix business with pleasure. Kobus Kok takes his bomb to Vlakplaas for the test run. It is there that the pig's head awaits him.

64

The highway to Pretoria is still undergoing surgery, invasive and traumatic, its arteries clogged with cars negotiating the myriad temporary signs directing traffic into even smaller lanes criss-crossing the road. This dangerous mix confuses the drivers but no one slows down to the recommended sixty kilometres an hour speed limit.

Thankfully, my colleague Norman Manoim is driving and I am in the passenger seat, my right foot pressing against the floor while Norman, generally a cautious man, plays highway chicken with the oncoming traffic. Our counsel for the Harms Commission, Paul Pretorius, has wisely strapped himself securely in the back seat. 'Like strapping yourself to the mast of a sinking ship,' I quip as he belts up. It didn't raise a laugh.

Bheki, also in the back seat, is reading through the instructions and statements that we've received from our clients for the first day of the Harms Commission hearings. He's blissfully unaware of the potential chaos outside. Norman, with half an eye on the road, maintains a steady conversation with Paul. I close my eyes and do not open them until we pull into the parking lot opposite the building where the commission will be held. Like most government buildings, it is an ugly, characterless rectangular block with long corridors off which are hundreds of rooms, sized and fitted according to the seniority of their occupants.

In the large hearing room, rows of desks have been arranged to simulate a courtroom. We find our seats in the front row, dump our bags and make our way to the judge's chambers. Paul introduces us and our clients while Harms listens courteously. He's a small balding man with glasses and a businesslike approach. While he's letting us know how he will run the hearings, McNally, the attorney-general from the Free State, walks in. We had learnt with dismay that he would be leading the evidence at the commission. Since our Bloemfontein experience, McNally has featured on my list of least favourite people. It's obvious that our task will be to place incontrovertible evidence before Harms. We leave the judge's chambers impressed and encouraged by the reception we received. He has a good reputation as a lawyer, which leads us to hope that when confronted by the facts, he will arrive at the correct legal conclusion.

But perhaps we should be more realistic about what the commission can do. As Harms reminds us at the start of proceedings, his terms of reference exclude operations conducted and atrocities committed outside the country's borders. This is a problem as many of the activities of the Vlakplaas squad occurred in neighbouring countries. If the cross-border activities could be proved, and there is a lot of evidence, then that would support the general version supplied by both Nofomela and Coetzee about their activities both inside and outside South Africa. Given the terms of the commission we can only focus on about fifty per cent of the incidents. We have already explained this to the organisations we represent.

We receive another blow on that first morning when we learn that the commission's investigation team will be made up of senior police officers. One of them is Brigadier Krappies Engelbrecht, a former commander of the Brixton Murder and Robbery Squad. He will be assisted by Colonel Hermanus du Plessis. One look at Engelbrecht and du Plessis in the company of some of the police witnesses called to testify, swapping jokes, arranging to go for drinks, asking after wives and children, leaves us in no doubt that the wolf is being asked to guard the sheep.

The proceedings get off to a reasonable start when the former Brixton Murder and Robbery policeman, Slang van Zyl, tells the commission that he was recruited into the internal region Civil Cooperation Bureau by Staal Burger in 1988. He'd met the managing director of the CCB, Joe Verster, and been told that the squad would target the enemies of the republic. His cell was known as Region Six. There were ten regions, more than forty cells, with each cell consisting of between six and twenty-nine operatives. The cells operated independently and reported to Verster. All in all some three hundred members were involved in more than two hundred projects. Verster reported to a chairman who was a member of the general staff of the SADF and also the head of special forces. The chairman and the managing director made the decisions on operations.

All very corporate, spawning jokes in the commission about the role of the company secretary, and 'expense accounts'. Except that beneath the jokes was a deadly seriousness. The commission is told that the CCB assigned a priority classification to its enemies which specified the action to be taken against them – elimination, intimidation or harassment.

These revelations cause huge excitement in the commission, with the press giving extensive coverage to the discovery of this clandestine squad allied to special forces. The evidence of the two hundred projects is eagerly awaited and there is much speculation as to which murders were carried out by the CCB and which were the work of the Vlakplaas squad. Slang van Zyl gives us a taste when he admits to blowing up the Early Learning Centre, a community hall in Cape Town, with a limpet mine. This is the first admission of an illegal act carried out by the CCB and it evokes intense interest. We wait for his next admission.

Straight-faced, he tells the commission about his other 'work'. In late 1988, he received an instruction from his managing director to hang the foetus of a monkey on the official residence of Archbishop Desmond Tutu in Bishopscourt, Cape Town. He would be provided with the foetus. Without questioning this bizarre request, the compliant Slang climbed the wall of the archbishop's garden and hung the monkey foetus from a tree. He'd received the foetus in a bottle. To rising laughter, he earnestly explains that the nails of the monkey foetus had been treated by a witch-doctor. Even Harms smiles at this point, shaking his head.

Undeterred by this lack of respect for his day job, Slang van Zyl recounts a plot to assassinate Nelson Mandela's lawyer, Dullah Omar. For this he recruited an ex-convict by the name of Edward 'Peaches' Gordon. The initial plan was to shoot Dullah Omar with a Makarov pistol. Accordingly, the gun and R15 000 were given to Peaches by Slang. At the last moment, the plan was aborted and Slang told Peaches to steal some of Dullah Omar's heart pills so that they could be substituted with poison pills. According to Peaches' affidavit he took two pills from his sister-in-law, who also happened to have a heart condition, and gave these to Slang. Some days later Slang gave him a small vial of white powder and told him to poison Omar's food. On the way back from Cape Town airport where he'd met Slang, he tossed the bottle of powder out of the window.

Peaches' affidavit details the lucrative relationship that he had with Slang. He disobeyed orders recklessly and fed his handler a load of rubbish even as he was handed payment for his troubles. He supplied wrong addresses, failed to burn the kombi of some luckless activist when told to, and generally took the gullible Slang for a ride. Not mincing his words in his affidavit to the commission, he says, 'I cheated them. They were fucking dumb.'

Unable to restrain ourselves, we all laugh out loud. On the way back to Johannesburg, I even forget about the dangerous highway as we discuss the crass stupidity of Slang and the CCB. We're looking forward to the real stuff that will come when we get to the two hundred projects.

Days later, there's great excitement in the commission as the managing director Joe Verster is due to give evidence. The Peaches and Slang show was good value, but the CCB and all its projects amount to more than a limpet mine, a monkey foetus and two fake heart tablets. A large press contingent gathers outside the building and in the corridor, jostling to get a glimpse of the man responsible for the CCB and its top secret projects. The man with the power to command murder.

Research reveals that Verster was well qualified to head up the CCB. A former parachute instructor at the elite 1 Parachute Battalion in Bloemfontein, he later underwent specialised training as a reconnaissance soldier, attending a warfare school in the Republic of China and receiving further instruction from the deadly Selous Scouts in the Rhodesian bush war. He also attended military training in Beirut and Israel and subsequently became the founder commander of 5 Reconnaissance Regiment, gaining considerable battle experience in Namibia and Angola. Joe Verster is the real thing, and everyone wants to see what he looks like. I'm wondering if he will open the CCB's files and reveal the killers of David Webster and Anton Lubowski.

Harms adds to the apprehension by dramatically ruling that under no circumstances is the head of the CCB to be identified. He is not to be photographed or his address revealed, as this could endanger his life. I comment to Norman Manoim, 'The most dangerous man in the country, a superbly trained soldier, who has fought in numerous wars and who heads up a massive network of soldiers and policemen plus a dozen hit squads, feels threatened. How do you think we should feel?' He laughs. Harms looks at us, and like schoolchildren we nod submissively and quieten down as the managing director of the CCB is led into the room.

Joe Verster is a big man. At first I am taken aback by his wild and woolly hair, long and unkempt, complemented by a great grey voortrekker beard which reaches down his chest. Hey, this is a weird-looking guy. To top it all he wears dark reflective sunglasses. This mountain man grins insanely at the court, enjoying the charade. Then it strikes us that Harms has let Verster come to court in disguise.

Verster obviously likes to dress up. Not content with merely obscuring key features, he has gone to town. He looks like Rip Van Winkle. The police grin broadly, while the lawyers for the families of the victims shake their heads, murmuring loudly that this is ridiculous. This individual could be a hobo off the street. Or a professional actor. The journalists scribble frantically, some of the press artists are already drawing a caricature of this strange creature. In all seriousness, McNally stands up and proceeds to lead this character through his evidence. And Harms lets it happen, peering enquiringly at this poor man's Father Christmas before him.

Verster is brief. Once President FW de Klerk ordered an investigation of the CCB, the project files disappeared as part of an emergency plan.

There's a growing rumble from the lawyers in the court.

Harms, clearly flustered that his commission has degenerated into farce, barks, 'Do you mean to tell me that the emergency plan has been so inadequately devised that it is impossible to get your files back? Well, then it is a hopeless emergency plan.'

The other witnesses from the CCB follow Verster's lead, appearing in a variety of disguises, strange wigs, huge sunglasses, moustaches, beards, hats, scarves and bulky jackets – each one more outlandish than the next. Cocky and confident, they step onto the witness stand, sometimes giving a code name instead of their real name, and mostly refusing to answer questions on the grounds that it may incriminate them.

Trying to track what happened to the files is frustrating. Staal Burger admits that he last saw them in a Johannesburg hotel room when he handed them to someone codenamed 'Christo Brits' for safekeeping. They were never seen again, nor was Christo Brits. Like the others, Burger refuses to answer certain questions on the grounds that he might incriminate himself.

Although the commission can subpoena witnesses under Section 205 of the Criminal Procedure Act, compelling them to testify or face imprisonment, Harms chooses not to do so. Once he's let the men of the CCB come dressed like actors to an amateur production, he and his commission are doomed. They become the subject of jokes and cartoons.

The one man who is ultimately responsible for the CCB is the former chief of the defence force and now minister of defence, Magnus Malan. Although both Harms and McNally indicate that Malan will give evidence after the CCB operatives, predictably the honourable minister isn't called. In addition, we (and the other human-rights lawyers) are not allowed to cross-examine three senior generals.

Equally disappointingly, Brigadier Floris Mostert from the Brixton

Murder and Robbery Squad has a change of heart when called as a witness. Although he's investigating the murder of David Webster and although his legal affidavits revealed the existence of the CCB, he now tells the commission he is certain that the three CCB members being held by the police were not involved in the Webster killing. Not content with this about-turn, he adds that the identikits issued by the police had proved inaccurate. And if this is not enough, he mentions that his suspicion of the CCB's culpability in the Webster murder was based on whispers in the corridors of the CCB. He steps off the witness stand having given nothing away.

Each day we leave the commission in despair, no longer cracking jokes about Slang and his CCB colleagues. It is clear that they're far from stupid. Months into the commission and all we have is a bomb and a monkey foetus. We know the CCB existed to target and potentially murder opponents of the government and we have a good idea of who some of the killers are, but no proof. Corroborating evidence – like the fact that Staal Burger flew to Windhoek on the day Anton Lubowski was murdered, and flew out again the next day – is valuable, but insufficient on its own. Each time the lawyers for the Lubowski family get close, Harms stops them, saying his mandate does not extend to murders outside the country. Eberhard Bertelsman, the family's lawyer, argues that the conspiracy against Lubowski was initiated in South Africa and therefore the judge does have jurisdiction. Harms turns him down. In disgust, we get up and leave the court.

There is one hope and that is Coetzee. The problem is that he cannot come to South Africa. So it's agreed to hear his evidence in London. This doesn't surprise me. It's generally not difficult persuading judges or prosecutors to spend time in Europe, especially London, hearing evidence. Frankly, we aren't averse to it ourselves. We also know that despite McNally and Harms, this is an area on which we have worked hard gathering corroborating evidence.

When Harms announces that he is prepared to hear evidence from Coetzee 'on commission' in London at the South African Embassy on Trafalgar Square, there are mutterings from the gallery about a 'travelling circus'. But we're excited. Coetzee in London could be devastating.

65

The ferry ride to Robben Island is turbulent, the small boat dipping and wallowing in a cold and choppy sea. White horses ride the big swells until they crash into the boat, and spray whips across the deck. Table Mountain is lost in heavy grey cloud, shrouded by its famous tablecloth. Rain, driven hard by the wind, thin and stinging, lashes my face. Spiteful stuff. It is 11 April, Cape Town's notorious winter weather has started early. I go below deck and join the few prison warders and prisoners in the cabin, moodily staring at the rolling floor, at everything except one another.

The prisoners are in leg irons. I don't recognise any of them. How long, I wonder, will it be before one of us gets sick? That will set us all off. The stink of vomit in a confined space below decks is enough to turn one's stomach. I imagine the prisoners, warders and me retching our way to Robben Island, the cabin awash with our bile and half-digested breakfast. It's a safe bet I'm the only one who started the morning with lamb's kidneys, eggs, bacon and pork sausages, followed by kippers. It's a meal I really need to hang on to. I curse the weather that has turned a normally placid thirty-minute trip into a hellish ride. One of the warders, a young man with close-cropped hair, suddenly stands up and lurches to the stairs leading to the deck. In his haste he forgets to duck and cracks his head on the top of the doorway. In too much of a hurry and probably afraid of opening his mouth, he surprisingly does not swear and clatters up the stairway. The other warders laugh and smile knowingly. The prisoners look straight ahead, registering nothing. The start of your sentence is not the time to make enemies. The young warder does not return, preferring the wind and the wet deck to the cramped quarters below.

Soon, the rocking of the ferry eases, and through the window I see the breakwater that protects the Island's small harbour. Quite pretty, really, with the row of prison offices to the left of the pier where we normally dock. On a previous visit, I bought a small round flat stone of the sort you can find on the beach from the wife of a prison warder. This enterprising woman had collected stones and pieces of wood and painted them in different colours, inscribing them all, 'Robben Eiland, 1986'. She'd placed the items neatly for sale in a glass case in the office where visitors have to sign the register. I felt sorry for her, also a captive on this desolate place, trying to bring colour to the drabness with her crude paintings.

In 1986, the Island was seldom visited, and then mainly by lawyers, families of the prisoners, those academic researchers with State approval and the occasional official government delegation. Once, after my consultation was over, I'd asked a warder to take me into the village where the warders lived. My pretext was to buy a cooldrink at the shop. He agreed and, at the same time, proudly gave me a tour of the Island, pointing out things of interest.

The warders' houses had been built in a Cape fishing village style, painted white, almost quaint, surrounding a large green park below the general store. I was struck by the children's play equipment in the park – swings, a roundabout and benches for their mothers or maids to sit on. All out of sight of the main prison but close enough for the prisoners to hear the laughter of the children at play.

The rest of the Island was harsh and unforgiving, the dry scrub and rock holding birds, perhaps, but not much else. A bleak place. Every time I come here to see clients, I feel the Island's loneliness. It has been a site of incarceration of black dissidents for centuries. A site made more bleak when contrasted with the beauty of Cape Town and the mountain across the water.

During that trip round the Island, I'd asked the warder if anybody had ever escaped. He said no, the currents were too strong and the water was freezing. He told the story of one of the prisoners, 'a white criminal', as he described him, who'd tried to escape on a warder's windsurfer. He was never seen again. There had been an earlier escape in 1819 when the Xhosa prophet, Makana, and three hundred others escaped from the Island in three boats. All but four perished.

Ironically, even in 1986, I got the impression that the warders and their wives who staffed the shop and ran some of the other amenities were aware of what made this island special: its Rivonia Trial prisoners. That is why they had started making mementos of the place, and I had bought one out of pity for the tired woman with conquered eyes who sold it to me.

I see the grey walls of the prison straight ahead. A young warder escorts me along the pier to the small building on the right of the harbour that contains the offices in which the prisoners' visits and legal consultations take place. The building is flanked by a row of grim holding cells where the prisoners wait to be called for their visits.

My trips here are functional: take the ferry, avoid getting sick, get escorted to the visitors' rooms, wait for my clients to arrive, see them, give them news of home and family, discuss the case, try to be positive, walk about a bit before the ferry leaves, and arrive gratefully back in Cape Town.

Robben Island may have legendary or even mythical status because of its prisoners and the struggle they have waged, but there is nothing romantic or inspiring about it. This is just cold incarceration in a hostile and lonely place, year after gruelling year. The prison breeds depression and kills hope. That is why I find it difficult to be positive. Normally, I try to crack jokes with my clients, but how do you cheer someone facing a lengthy sentence with no end in sight? In this place, it is a real effort.

This time, at least, I can tell Joseph there's a possibility he will not serve his full twenty-five years. In fact, with the release of Mandela there's a good chance that all political prisoners may be released at some stage in the not too distant future. But, as Joseph sits in front of me in the small room with only a desk and two chairs in it, we don't talk of what may happen, because we know that *anything* is possible – the negotiations may fail, the right wing may start a war, the National Party may revolt against de Klerk. In fact, the whole country could burn if both sides can't reach agreement, and I may still be visiting my clients here when we are old men. It stretches ahead of me – a lifetime of worrying about losing my kippers and kidneys.

It is good to see Joseph again, although he seems to have aged. The high spirits of youth have been replaced by a seriousness as he describes life as a prisoner on Robben Island. He has been categorised as a 'notch two' prisoner, which entitles him to certain privileges such as newspapers and limited television viewing. He will, he says, have to wait for a long time before he graduates to 'notch three'. It feels odd to be talking to him alone and have him tell me all these things about his life inside, news about the other prisoners. This shouldn't be the case, as we have known each other for years now. And then it strikes me that when we met and consulted in the past, both before and during the trial, I always met the four of them together except for when I took his statement in the early years. Joseph, being quiet by nature and younger, let Jabu and Ting Ting do most of the talking.

While I listen to him, it occurs to me that all the time I've known him, he's been in prison. Yet I've never heard him complain. I've heard him grumble about the food or moan about a warder and his behaviour or the fact that they aren't getting their correct exercise time, but I've never heard him express anger about his situation or bitter feelings, if he has them. His equanimity is remarkable.

Eventually the warder opens the door and asks if we are finished. He's a young man with a kind face, not pushy like the ones in Maximum Security in Pretoria. I'm enjoying listening to Joseph and he clearly wants to talk further. I ask the warder for another fifteen minutes. He nods and closes the door.

Joseph settles back in the hard prison chair and asks after Jabu, Ting Ting and Neo. He wants details of each one and their life on Death Row. He wrote a letter to Jabu a week ago and hopes that it will reach him. I tell him that a week ago, Jabu and the other eight Death Row ANC prisoners were visited by Nelson Mandela. It had been a huge event for them and for the prison. An occasion filled with symbolism. Here was the most famous prisoner in the world, now free and visiting them in the very place where so many resistance figures had been hanged. Even the warders treated Mandela like a leader. He talked to each of the ANC prisoners and told them of the discussions with government. Jabu had found Mandela remarkable. Been amazed that he'd taken the time to see them when he had so many other priorities. He'd also appreciated how Mandela had engaged with him on the political issues as they received their briefing. He'd told them he would not rest until they were all free.

'We've been told that Mandela is also coming back to the Island to brief us,' Joseph says. 'We have so many questions for him.'

I tell him about the Harms Commission and that it is moving to London to hear the evidence of Dirk Coetzee. 'Bheki and I will be there,' I add.

'That is a great opportunity for Bheki,' Joseph says. 'He deserves it. He works hard. Tell him I send my best. You know that I have started to study here, Standard Ten English and history by correspondence. I'm really enjoying it. When I get out I must have something to do. I don't want to be a soldier and I must have a proper qualification, like Bheki.'

I'm impressed. Not only with the way he's handling the present but also with his forward thinking. I ask if there's much talk of release.

'A lot, and people get very excited,' he replies. 'I don't, but then I have only been inside for a little while.'

'Not so little,' I say. 'It's now over four years!'

'The talk is very distracting and we know that this could take years. For the moment, I need to concentrate on my studies, whether I am inside or outside.'

I am struck by his single-mindedness and by the shift in him, as if the war is over and now it's the time to think of jobs and qualifications. He's a different man, focusing on a future that does not include killing.

It's time to go. Joseph asks me to send him a picture of my son Simon. The warder takes him away. I still have fifteen minutes to wait before the ferry leaves so I walk along the breakwater, the wind strong, carrying spray. It does not bother me this time.

THE BOMB

The testing of Captain Kobus Kok's bomb is carried out in the early afternoon at Vlakplaas. It is sunny and pleasant. Members of the covert police assassination squad gather to watch the test.

The dry run is carried out at the shooting range adjacent to the river and next to the mountain. The test is orchestrated by Kobus Kok in the presence of his commander, Colonel Waal du Toit, and other members of the Vlakplaas squad. The pig's head is placed on a log. White skinned and ridiculous with thick folded lips and long white eyelashes, it stares benignly in the hot sun at the small group gathered for the show. The men joke and fool around. Like children at a fireworks display.

His preparations complete, Kobus Kok stands back and motions to his colleagues that it is time. They fall silent. A cable snakes its way from Kobus Kok to the pig's head. The circuits are connected, the detonator activated. There is a loud bang. The onlookers applaud and raise their drinks in a ragged cheer. The exploded head, a mash of blood and pulp, slowly topples from the log. The test is a success.

66

Paul Pretorius, Bheki and I fly to London in early May, a few days before the Harms Commission sits. It has been arranged that Coetzee will be represented by Dennis Kuny, who has been briefed by Ahmed Motala, an attorney for Lawyers for Human Rights. The two lawyers and their legal team will prepare Coetzee for his evidence. Meanwhile the ANC have ensconced Coetzee in an apartment in central London and flown in his son Dirkie.

Bheki is keen to meet up with Coetzee. However, we first have to book into our own apartment in a building close to Marble Arch. The three-bedroom apartment has a small kitchen with all the basics and a sitting room we can use for consultations. The furniture is marginally less tired than we are after our flight, but we're excited to be together in London and looking forward to Coetzee's evidence.

It is Bheki's first time in Europe and he can't stop talking about the size of London and the incredible and well-known buildings and monuments he saw as our taxi wound its way through the streets. He's in awe of it all, clicking away on the camera he bought especially for the trip. Like kids in the big city, we chatter about how we will use our free time. Paul has booked for some music concerts at the Barbican, and I'm looking forward to the theatre. Bheki wants to see everything, from classical music concerts to the Natural History Museum. He'd been told that it was always grey and raining in London, he remarks, but look, the weather is just as good as it was in Johannesburg.

Much work lies ahead, but fortunately the major load will be borne by Dennis and his team representing Coetzee. We will simply be feeding them the corroborating evidence we've gathered as well as additional details from the statement we took from Coetzee in Lusaka.

Dennis's apartment is not far from ours and there we meet up with Ahmed Motala and Coetzee. Coetzee is tired and answers questions from Dennis tersely. They've been at it all day and Coetzee is nervous and in a bad mood, clearly wanting the work to end. We sit quietly, leaving it to Dennis, only occasionally offering information.

I am surprised to see that Coetzee has no bodyguards. I'm even more surprised when we walk out of the building at the end of the session and Coetzee invites us back to his apartment which is nearby. In the street with people rushing past, I am nervous that Coetzee is an easy target. 'This is dangerous,' I say, looking around nervously. 'They can get to you so easily here.' Bheki is also rattled. We need to get Coetzee off the street quickly. We jump into a black cab and head for Coetzee's apartment while Paul goes back to our building.

Coetzee is feeling down and I suspect could do with a drink in a pub, but we cannot risk exposing our star witness. Caution prevails and we go up to his apartment where he proudly introduces us to his son. Dirkie's a good-looking boy of about fourteen, serious and unsmiling, and clearly devoted to his father.

'Where does Dirkie go to school?' Bheki asks.

'I've taken him out of school to be with me here,' Coetzee replies. 'For now, I'm teaching him myself.'

Bheki and I exchange glances. 'Is that okay for him, I mean doesn't he need real school at this age?'

Coetzee, irritated, rounds on me. 'And what's wrong with my teaching? At school he gets bullied because of me.'

I back off. I don't want to get into an argument with Coetzee about the desirability of a former hit squad commander and captain in the security police personally home schooling his child alone in an apartment in London. I also sense that something is bothering him. Anyway, I'm exhausted myself and now is not the time to start arguing on issues that don't relate to the case.

'The problem with this place,' says Coetzee, throwing at least three expletives into the five-word clause, 'is that I am left alone in the flat all day and I have no money, no nothing. I am sick of this place. I am going mad from boredom, and I am getting nothing from the ANC. Yussus fuck, this whole fucking show is a fucking fuck-up' – neatly rounding off his sentence in characteristic fashion.

I'm really worried that he's starting to lose it and that his disaffection may result in his not giving his full cooperation. 'What do you need?' I ask.

'Yussus, just some money for a drink, man, and some other things.'

I give him thirty pounds which he grudgingly accepts.

We make small talk, trying to cheer him up. Unlike Bheki, he is not at all impressed with London. 'Basically, it's a shit place,' he says.

'Well, you haven't got a bad apartment here,' I say, trying to lighten things up. 'Hell, this is a damn expensive one and must cost the ANC a lot.' It's true. His apartment is big and spacious, high ceilings with elaborate cornices and beautiful recessed windows, old wooden floors, a large rectangular mirror over the ornate antique fireplace, Parisian style. The doors to the rooms off the main sitting room are closed so it is difficult to see their size, but to judge by the reception and sitting room, they must be large. Then I realise that there aren't many personal belongings lying around. Maybe he isn't staying here at all. Maybe this is just another safe meeting place. Or maybe he doesn't leave personal stuff lying around?

Bheki chats to Dirkie and puts his arm warmly on the boy's shoulder. I can see that Bheki is bothered about Dirkie being with his father in hiding in this foreign city. The young Dirk does not take his eyes off his father. I remember Coetzee telling me in Lusaka how he would sometimes take his son with him when he set up an operation, and how, when he returned from certain missions, he would speak to his son about them. What must go through his mind when he hears us talking to his father about the killings? What does he think of the ANC?

As if reading my mind, Coetzee blurts out, 'The ANC here in London, it's like I'm in a fukken zoo. They come and visit me just to look at me in my cage. Fukken staring at me, this strange thing that they've caught. Some of them don't even talk, they just look at me like I'm a fukken animal. Diseased. And I'm alone here all day with Dirkie and no money. The okes here are not like the ones in Lusaka. Zuma really looked after me.'

I tell him I'm meeting with the ANC the next day and will see what I can do to improve his conditions. What concerns me more is if he's feeling properly prepared.

'Is there anything you want to go over with us?' asks Bheki, shifting his gaze anxiously from Coetzee to his son and back again.

Coetzee looks at Bheki, lost in thought. After a while he replies, 'No, this stuff is all in my head and it won't go away. I am just gatvol now.' He sounds truly dejected.

'And have you refreshed your memory on the dates, the ones that you were vague on?' asks Bheki.

'Look man, I may be vague on the exact dates, it was a long time ago, but what happened happened, and I know because I was there. And let them come and tell me I wasn't,' he says, raising his voice.

It is worrying. He is on edge and almost aggressive. I can see that he feels trapped. The ANC was the only place he could go when Nofomela broke ranks, and now he is here, stuck with his unlikely saviours, compelled to do their bidding, not wanting to offend them but hating the confinement. Even having his son with him is small compensation. He remains a prisoner with an uncertain future – never to be trusted fully by the ANC, and hated by the people he has turned on. He could leave and take his chances on his own in London, but he has no money and the ANC have his passport. He can't even afford his own medicine for his diabetes. Even if he does run, he knows that sooner or later the Vlakplaas squad will find him and end it. He must please his protectors or lose their protection. There are no choices here.

We have two days to go before the commission hears his evidence. If he goes in like this, bitter and depressed, he will be vulnerable and distracted. McNally and the police advocates will eat him alive. And if they leave any scraps, Harms, on his current course, will mop them up. We have to get his head right.

67

It's a beautiful spring day, the sky crystal blue, the beds of flowers outside Buckingham Palace perfect in colour and symmetry. We go down the parade and around Trafalgar Square, Bheki enthralled by it all. I point out to him the National Gallery on our left, and Nelson's column facing the admiralty arch, rising above it all. We pass the impressive South Africa House in prime position on the square. There's a small group of protestors with placards outside the massive stone building – representatives of a faction of the British Anti-Apartheid Movement that have sworn to protest outside the embassy until South Africa is free. So far they've been at it for over a decade. I'm thinking that nothing has changed since I was a student and walked past the embassy in 1984: the same building with the same protest. We turn left into the Strand and our taxi stops outside the entrance to the embassy. Both Coetzee and one of his men, David 'Spyker' Tshikalanga, are due to give evidence to the commission.

In the beginning, Tshikalanga worked for Coetzee as a gardener. Later

Coetzee recruited him as a guard in the security police, then as an informant, and finally as a police constable. Throughout, he belonged to Coetzee, who had the uncanny ability to inspire total loyalty, particularly from the black policemen and askaris with whom he'd worked in the Vlakplaas squad. Tshikalanga accompanied Coetzee on most of his missions and even went freelance when he and other Vlakplaas operatives bought uncut diamonds with money borrowed from Coetzee. As it turned out, the diamonds were fakes. Selling fake diamonds to a hit squad was unlikely to go unpunished. For his sins the diamond trader was lured across the Lesotho border and shot dead.

Soon Tshikalanga's green fingers turned red as he murdered at the behest of Coetzee and his superiors. He was in the squad that killed Griffiths Mxenge, a particularly gruesome assassination. At some point in the attack a severely wounded Mxenge wrenched free an Okapi knife that was stuck in his chest and advanced on his attackers. As he lunged at them he was bludgeoned repeatedly on the head with a sharpened tyre spanner until he collapsed. The man who'd wielded both the spanner and the Okapi knife was David Tshikalanga.

On Tuesday 14 November 1989, Tshikalanga was taken to the Northern Transvaal by Jacques Pauw. Pauw, along with Andre Zaaiman and Max du Preez, was responsible for the defection of first Coetzee and then Tshikalanga to the ANC. Tshikalanga crossed into Zimbabwe on a journey that ultimately brought him to the South African Embassy in London to give evidence before Judge Louis Harms.

It is my first time in the embassy. As a student I often walked past it, naively wondering what dark plots were hatched inside. It was a magnificent stone fortress, seemingly impregnable, cold and oblivious to the bustle of teenagers and tourists in Trafalgar Square and the stream of cheerful red buses filled with busy Londoners.

At the entrance we are directed straight ahead 'to the cinema'. Our shoes echo on the polished marble floor as we walk through the dark, wood-panelled hall.

It turns out that the embassy's cinema has been converted into a hearing room. It's a step back in time. The ornate golden carvings on the cornices and the elegant drapes of thick velvet curtain with elaborate folds wouldn't be out of place in a gilded theatre of the nineteen-twenties.

Carved golden springbok heads gaze forlornly at us from the walls. It's fantastic. Unbelievable. I love it.

The press are of the same view, whispering to one another as one does in a museum. The film crews move in slow motion up to the grand wooden stage, their cameras swivelling to take in the spectacle. They're smiling like archaeologists who have stumbled on a hidden tomb. Two thick-set men in ill-fitting grey suits, undoubtedly policemen, hurry up and tell them they cannot film in here, they must wait outside in the antechamber to the cinema. Grinning, the cameramen obey.

In the foyer, I bump into Freek Robinson, the anchor on SABC television news. Seeing Freek crawl, nod and grin when interviewing a cabinet minister, a familiar sight on TV, is enough to make you choke. He's also the only newsman taking the venue seriously, earnestly scribbling on a small notepad, while occasionally smiling ingratiatingly at the lawyers and policemen.

The government has granted amnesty to Coetzee, Tshikalanga and their ANC minders for the duration of the hearing. This is a first. Inside the hall the tables have been arranged to simulate a court, with a stand for the witness to the left of the judge's desk, which is perched on the elaborately framed stage of the theatre. The numerous counsel, senior and junior for the various arms of the State, are assembled with the rest of us on the floor below. Lawyers like commissions of inquiry: they go on and on and on and so do the fees, mounting daily. The State has a large contingent of legal representatives, but then they have a lot to protect.

The police legal team is led by no less than two senior counsel, Louis 'Goud' Visser and Sam Maritz. There are others for the army and various government sectors and then yet others along for the ride – all handsomely paid. The investigators used by the police or the commission are here too, led by General Krappies Engelbrecht, large and towering, affably swapping jokes with McNally and Les Roberts, who will continue to lead the evidence on behalf of the commission. The atmosphere is almost festive. The large space set aside for spectators and the press is quickly filled, and the photographers and film crews in the hall outside jostle around Tshikalanga and his ANC guard.

I am inside the cinema when I hear a huge commotion. Running outside I see Tshikalanga writhing on the ground, seemingly in agony. The man is on his back, his body jerking uncontrollably, his face contorting.

We are completely at a loss, thinking that he has been shot or poisoned, until someone mentions that Tshikalanga is having an epileptic fit. We restrain him on the ground, trying to make sure he does not choke as the fit gradually passes. After a while he stands up, shakes his head like a prizefighter and announces that he is now ready to give his evidence. To our surprise he wants to give it in the Venda language. 'In Venda!' everyone exclaims in horror, knowing full well that the chances of finding a Venda interpreter in London are close to zero. I go outside for a cigarette with Bheki. This whole situation is just getting too surreal, I need air. We go back inside to find that someone has spoken to Tshikalanga and that he is now prepared to give his evidence in English. We are on.

David Tshikalanga is small but powerfully built. To give his evidence, he stands stiffly, his back ramrod straight. There's an air of self-assurance about him, and he delivers his evidence in a matter-of-fact manner, almost technical, like a mechanic telling how you strip a car. His account of the killing of Griffiths Mxenge is chilling. The small details he recalls could only be known to someone who participated in the murder. Without a flicker of emotion, he describes a wet and rainy night when the visibility was poor. He tells Harms how Mxenge pleaded for his life and what he said as he lay dying.

Bheka Shezi, a colleague and friend who is present to represent the interests of the Mxenge family, stares intently at Tshikalanga. Shezi was an articled clerk in Mxenge's law offices at the time of the murder and was very close to him. He turns to me, slowly shaking his head. Anger and bitterness burn in his eyes. I can see how much it pains him that his friend and mentor was killed like an animal by these brutal men.

Tshikalanga's evidence ties in with what Nofomela has said about the same killing. On the other incidents, Tshikalanga is equally candid and calm. We can see that he is frustrating the police counsel because the specificity of his evidence takes them by surprise and they can't challenge him on the details of the killings. Instead they attack his credibility, referring to his convictions for drunken driving and his shooting of a man in a bar. They say he is a man without character and integrity. What hitman is? I ask myself. They say that he has concocted these lies merely to support his master, Coetzee. The occasion when Tshikalanga went rogue and killed a diamond dealer receives considerable attention as an example of his dishonesty and criminality. Doggedly, Tshikalanga sticks to his story, not giving an inch. Counsel for the police can see that there's not much to be gained here so they end their questions. Kuny's questions in re-examination are brief, as are Paul Pretorius's. We too want to get to the main act: Coetzee.

On the way back to our apartment at the end of the first day, our taxi passes Hamleys, the toy shop on Regent Street. I tell Bheki that it's the most famous toy shop in the world, with five floors packed with every toy you can think of. A paradise for children.

'Stop the car!' he shouts. 'I have to see this. I love toys and I need something for my boy Mandla.' Bheki once told me that he had a lot of catching up to do with his son as he had only got to know him six months after he was born. Shortly before Mandla was born he had been detained in solitary confinement and had only been released six months after his birth.

As Paul Pretorius has to get back to the apartment, Bheki, Bheka Shezi and I climb out onto the teeming pavement and enter the toy emporium. It really is an experience from the moment you walk in. There are youngsters showing off the latest toys and gadgets, planes zooming through the air, remote-controlled cars speeding across the floor and crashing into walls, the robotic sounds of a thousand toys being operated. For a moment we are transported, lost in our different childhoods.

Bheki is fascinated by the shelves stuffed with teddy bears, and especially by a bear that is larger than him and occupies its own shelf. 'That's a lot of bear,' he mutters. We ride the escalators up to the other floors, marvelling at the huge selection of gadgets and toys, suddenly kids again, not lawyers at a hearing into horrific murders. We even have a photograph taken of the three of us that gets pasted onto a metal disc like a badge: Bheki and Bheka sit in front, bemused. My head's between them and I'm grinning like one of the Hamleys bears. It's the day before Coetzee gives his evidence.

THE BOMB

Dry run and tests complete, the construction of the real bomb commences in earnest. It takes Kobus Kok about a week. Once complete, the device is placed in its package, surrounded by sponge and further protected by a small metal plate. Cardboard is wrapped around the metal plate. The carton into which the device is packed is of a type that is not manufactured or found in South Africa, thereby contributing to the subterfuge that the senders of the bomb are foreigners. This bomb is constructed of materials and in a manner that makes it virtually impossible to detect if it passes through an X-ray machine. The only real chance of finding it is through the use of a sniffer dog, but even this must be under the right circumstances.

The length of the battery life remains a cause for concern but what other options are there? Steve Bosch from Vlakplaas goes to the technical division and assists Captain Kobus Kok to wrap the bomb in brown paper. It is securely sealed with transparent sticky tape. Both men wear rubber gloves while they work.

One of the security policemen stationed at Vlakplaas is instructed to write the name and address of the target on the brown wrapping paper. He also writes the name of the sender, a person who the target would trust and from whom the target would expect to receive a parcel or communication. The target's address is in Lusaka. The 'sender's' is in South Africa. The man writes slowly and deliberately. When he is finished the pen is destroyed.

The bomb is ready to go.

68

We meet Coetzee in the hall. He's wearing a sporty checked jacket and looking pumped up, ready for the occasion. In the past few days, Dennis Kuny has spent a lot of time with him going over his evidence. Bheki and I have also spoken to him to get his motivation right. Fortunately, reviving his spirits wasn't too difficult: all it took to get his blood up were a few reminders of how his erstwhile colleagues had turned on him. With Coetzee is his brother Ben who has come to London to be with him at this critical time and is a major stabilising influence.

I have to hand it to Dirk Coetzee, he's a fighter. He shows no fear or apprehension. I've come to realise how resilient he's been in dealing with his isolation, desperately alone, estranged from family, friends and country, and at the mercy of his former sworn enemies, the comrades of people he's murdered. That he's still alive is extraordinary, and contrary to all predictions, including mine. Nevertheless, despite the fraught situation, he's prepared to testify against the police.

The man standing next to Coetzee in the foyer introduces himself to me as Billy Masetlha. Tall and slim, in a well-tailored dark suit, he speaks quietly and with authority. I've heard the name before and know that he holds a senior position in ANC Intelligence. Presumably he's the person Zuma has asked to handle Coetzee in London. In addition to Masetlha, two other men stand close to Coetzee. Dennis Kuny comes out of the old art deco cinema where the hearing is in session, approaches Coetzee and takes him aside. I chat to Masetlha, Bheki and the other two men, discussing Coetzee's state of mind and how his evidence will be regarded in London. Masetlha is friendly but non-committal.

When Coetzee walks into the hearing room, the press come rushing to ask questions and take photographs. I intervene. Coetzee cannot make any statements until after he has given his evidence. At the same time, the two large policemen who are in charge of security tell the photographers to take their pictures outside. Respectfully, they back off. It is time to start.

There is a hush as Coetzee walks to the witness stand. The police investigators stare at him. I wonder how they will provoke him. They know he's volatile and will probably try to unsettle him before he gets into the box. As Coetzee draws level with (now) General Engelbrecht, he suddenly looks at him, and says in Afrikaans, 'Ja, Krappies, how's it going?' Engelbrecht flushes, embarrassed by Coetzee's easy familiarity, and mumbles something back. Coetzee smiles. Then Harms, dressed theatrically in his black judge's robes, dramatically strides onto the stage from the dark folds of the drapes in the wings. 'Enter Harms, left of stage,' I say to Kuny, and we are off.

It takes a full day for Dennis Kuny to lead Coetzee through his evidence, incident by incident. Coetzee is good in the box. Avoiding bravado and making no cheap points, he comes across as sincere, although at times he is perhaps a little too confident. When he cannot remember a date or a detail about an issue, he admits this rather than inventing the answer or guessing. Once again I am drawn into his world of death and violence, a world without limits.

Whenever Coetzee gets to an incident in Swaziland, Harms quickly cuts in to tell him he must restrict himself to South Africa. Coetzee, clearly frustrated at being prevented from giving the full picture, does not hide his irritation. The policemen, a wall of shoulders and heads – no necks – slowly shake their heads at this errant son. They whisper like conspirators. Occasionally, Coetzee glances at them, showing no signs of discomfort or unease.

The key, however, is not how the police feel about Coetzee but how Harms feels about him. And the signs are not encouraging. Harms interjects a number of times, especially in the late afternoon when Coetzee is tired and has become a little blasé. When he clarifies an issue with Coetzee, the judge's tone is negative. It's subtle but it's there, and I can feel it. Coetzee picks it up too. Initially he's polite and courteous in his explanations, and then less so as his exasperation grows. I notice that the reporters are scribbling frantically. I can imagine Freek's angle and make a mental note to get feedback on Freek's coverage of Coetzee on the South African eight o'clock news.

At the end of the day, Coetzee steps down from the witness stand. He's exhausted but seems satisfied that he's able to tell his story. We shake his hand, pat him on the back, tell him he did well.

'The judge doesn't like me,' is the first thing he says, squaring his shoulders. 'I can sense it.'

We make light of it but we know it's true.

The next morning Coetzee is cross-examined. Sam Maritz, one of the senior counsel for the police, puts the questions. Maritz is a quiet, fastidious man who generally keeps to himself, preferring not to socialise with his clients during the breaks. He's a more than competent senior counsel. Often the State's counsel don't make the grade, but I know Maritz is a reasonable technician who is bound to conduct a sound cross-examination. I would've preferred 'Goud' Visser, but it was not to be.

Coetzee is confident, cutting a handsome figure as he turns to face his interrogator. Maritz, like a boxer in the first round, wastes no time in getting stuck in. Openly aggressive, he attacks Coetzee's credibility. He tells him he's a liar trying to save his own skin. A renegade policeman who cannot be believed, by his own admission a liar, a thief and a murderer. No scalpel here, Maritz wields an axe and Coetzee reacts accordingly.

Maritz focuses on the illegal diamond dealing and the murder of the diamond dealer from Lesotho to show that in this incident, and by implication in others, Coetzee was not acting under orders but indulging in a frolic of his own. In other words, he was motivated by his own criminal objectives and greed. Coetzee snaps back defensively that by that stage he was so far on the other side of the law that he decided to embark on a 'private enterprise' of his own. An honest answer, but it doesn't make him look good.

Harms shakes his head, unimpressed. At this display of disapproval from the judge, Maritz goes in harder. He tells Coetzee that he disgusts him with his lies and his lack of remorse for what he's done. Coetzee returns the blow, saying he's disgusted by Maritz because he defends dishonest policemen. Finding himself in a corner, Coetzee forgets all the advice we gave him about keeping his cool. Maritz, on a roll now, sensing that Harms is with him, and not even looking at Coetzee but at the judge, accuses Coetzee of implicating his former colleagues in his own illegal acts.

Actually, Coetzee is unashamed of his actions. Although he spars with Maritz, he is almost indifferent to the electric effect of his words on those at the hearing. I remember how I reacted when he first told me his story in Lusaka. Now you can feel the chill in the room as he describes violent death as blithely as a chef listing ingredients. Maritz uses this matter-of-fact recounting to accuse Coetzee sarcastically of being unrepentant. Coetzee comes back that he killed because he was in a war and was mostly acting under orders. Listening to his story, I have to remind myself of all the corroboration from other sources, from Nofomela, Tshikalanga and the evidence our investigators collated. As outrageous as his version is, I know it is the truth.

Unfortunately, Harms appears to attach little worth to the corroboration. He sees Coetzee as a renegade. After a while, he joins Maritz in attacking Coetzee, throwing in cynical comments, being clever. Amongst lawyers it is accepted that judges like you to laugh at their jokes. We do this politely even when the judge's jokes are bad. But here only one side laughs, because Harms is going too far. This commission is about the alleged activities of hit squads and there is enough evidence for it to be taken seriously, yet the judge sees it as an opportunity to show off. At other times Harms forgets himself, plunging into a cross-examination of his own for long periods and berating Coetzee for not remembering details. During these interventions, Maritz looks on smugly. Coetzee feels beleaguered, sometimes simply shaking his head at the onslaught. There is little we can do to protect him. We have to wait our turn in re-examination.

The cross-examination of Coetzee goes on for three days.

Coetzee's grilling by Maritz, the judge, McNally and Roberts is intense. At one point Les Roberts fastens on a letter Coetzee wrote to his family hoping that he'd be appointed chief investigator in our 'Nuremberg Trials'. The security police had intercepted the letter which details the thoughts of a lonely man grappling with his isolation and new reality. In Lusaka, he'd often said that if he could only get back to South Africa and have a team to help him, he would find out who was responsible for bombing various buildings and murdering resistance activists. 'I could do it in days,' he would say. 'I know how they operate, I know how they think, I know where they go to rest after the hits and I know who to go to for the evidence.' I believed him. I'd never met anyone like him before, and certainly no policeman with his record and expertise had ever been available to us. He was totally convincing.

But this is a different situation. Here he is taunted.

'You see yourself as the chief investigator in what you call South Africa's own Nuremberg Trial,' says Roberts, a quiet man who has found confidence in London.

'I said that could happen in the future if the truth doesn't come out at this stage,' retorts Coetzee.

'And at the end of this Nuremberg procedure which you think is a possibility, after you have flushed everybody out, are you going to turn yourself in so that you can be prosecuted along with the rest?' asks Roberts sarcastically.

'That's right,' says Coetzee. 'Accused number one.'

Roberts smiles. 'That makes about as much sense as if at the original Nuremberg, they'd made Rudolf Hess the chief investigator.'

Mocking laughter from the policemen and their lawyers. Harms joins in. Coetzee bows his head, humiliated and confused. It's a disaster, but Coetzee doesn't give up. At one point, I think he is going to step out of the witness box, curse Harms foully and walk out to vanish into the ANC. To his credit, he doesn't. That he sticks to his story, does not break down and keeps on repeating it, irritates Harms intensely. Eventually the judge loses control and responds loudly, 'That's a lot of crap.' There is silence and then everyone laughs. Even Coetzee smiles ruefully and shakes his head at the judge's conduct. From the studied way he looks at Harms, I wouldn't be surprised if he's imagining how he'd spend the time with the learned judge if they were alone in a remote place.

During the break at the end of the session, Victoria Brittain of the *Guardian* and a journalist from *The Times* approach me, intrigued by the judge's behaviour. 'So tell me,' says Victoria, 'is it common practice for South African judges to swear at witnesses and tell them they are talking "crap"?'

'No,' I say, 'I think this is a first for all of us.'

Her question makes me realise once more that the commission is a farce. Here we are trading insults in an art deco cinema beneath Trafalgar Square. How can you take it seriously when even the actions of the judge are beyond the pale? I am furious. I think of the sacrifices people have made and of the work that has been done to reveal the atrocities. For what? For this circus? Selfishly, I consider how much useless work I have put into this. And yet below the farce are deadly serious circumstances: a police force that is out of control. What will they do when they see Coetzee regarded as a lunatic with deranged fantasies? What will they be capable of when they feel vindicated?

I should have walked out of this commission a long time ago. In truth, I'm furious at Harms, at myself for participating and for having had hopes, again.

The re-examination by De Wet Marais – standing in for Dennis Kuny who, with Paul Pretorius, has had to return to Johannesburg – is a brave attempt to address some of the deficiencies in Coetzee's evidence. But it is not enough. Harms constantly intervenes, clearly undeterred by the events of the previous day. I want the hearing to end. I feel sorry for Coetzee, still doing his best up there against the hostility.

Roberts confronts him with the stark accusation that his actions were motivated by his hatred of the police. 'That is the fons et origo of your whole attack, of all your stories, of all the nonsense that you have been spouting over the last few months, and there is not a word of truth in it.'

'I had the opportunity,' Coetzee replies, 'or the choice to just sit put and lie, as everyone else is doing now, or to come out with the truth. So if there is an opportunity to go back one day, I can go back with a completely clear conscience and start a new life.'

Finally, he is released from the witness stand. He joins us, hesitant but hopeful, waiting for us to speak. I can see that he still wants us to tell him that Harms might believe him. But we can't, and it isn't his fault.

We say goodbye to Coetzee on the pavement outside the embassy. There is little warmth in the day. We all feel used.

After the others have left, the calm Billy Masetlha shares a taxi with Bheki and me. Once we're rolling, he tells us that Oliver Tambo would like to see us at his house. Now. We're taken aback at his announcement, excited that we should get to meet the president of the ANC. A former science and maths teacher, Tambo left teaching to become a lawyer and joined Mandela in the law firm of Mandela & Tambo, the country's first all-African law firm. In exile he built the ANC into the movement it is today.

The meeting takes place in what I assume is Tambo's home in a suburb of north London, a modest house with a small garden. Given that Tambo must be high on the Nationalists hate list, the security at his house appears minimal. We meet in the sitting room, and one can tell by the personal items and ornaments that this is a home and not a safe house. It seems to be a busy place, comfortable but not ostentatiously furnished.

Tambo is in an armchair in a corner, an old man with grey hair and a distinctive beard. He has given his entire life to the struggle and has attained almost mythical status along with Mandela, Chris Hani and Joe Slovo. He has a gentle face framed by thick black-rimmed spectacles. I've heard that he's deeply religious, and had once been accepted for training as a priest. In August 1989, he had suffered a severe stroke in Lusaka, which had left him partially impaired in movement and speech. Speaking softly and with difficulty, he welcomes us to his home. He says he has been following the proceedings of the Harms Commission but would like to hear our views, particularly whether we think the judge will make any finding in our favour. I look at Bheki and see he is too nervous to speak, and so I summarise the key events of the commission and our expectations. I let him know that we no longer have real hopes that Harms will give us anything other than what the police have already conceded, scraps.

Bheki nervously clears his throat. 'Mr President, our strategy has been to take Coetzee's and Nofomela's evidence and that of other people and then attempt to corroborate each point. We have done this on a number of occasions. But it seems that the judge just doesn't want to join the dots.'

Tambo smiles.

Although it is late, I can see the soft light of an English spring evening through the windows, as we sit there drinking tea, eating biscuits, discussing the commission. Tambo leaves most of the talking to us although he directs our conversation. After a while, Tambo looks at Masetlha, who rises. Somewhat formally, silenced by the presence of this remarkable man, we take our leave. The silence continues in the taxi all the way back to our apartment.

That night, Bheki and I go out and have dinner at a nearby restaurant. We rehash the situation, ponder what we could have done better. Finally, we come to the bitter conclusion, as one does when getting second prize and after a good meal, that there was not a lot more we could have done. Harms just can't see the truth. It is too great a leap of faith for him.

THE BOMB

Five weeks after the request to construct the bomb was received by the technical division, Constable Simon Radebe, WO John Tait and Sergeant Balletjies Bellingan drive to the post office in Joubert Park, Johannesburg. Sergeant Bellingan and Warrant Officer Tait wait in the car and Constable Radebe goes to post the parcel to Zambia.

Zambian nationals living and working in the Joubert Park area regularly send parcels and money home to their families from this post office, so Constable Radebe is hardly out of place. He is dressed in civilian clothes and there is nothing out of the ordinary about him or his package. Radebe reaches the counter and hands the parcel to the clerk who checks the address and weighs it.

The clerk, Mrs Smith, insists that the parcel must be insured. Constable Radebe pays the insurance and Mrs Smith fixes a piece of paper stating 'Insured Parcel' to the package. She fills in the insurance slip and gives it to Constable Radebe, who walks out and climbs into the waiting car. He hands the insurance slip to Sergeant Bellingan.

In the post office Mrs Smith casually drops the package into a large canvas sack on a square steel frame. Later the packages in this sack are sorted into lots per destination. The parcel is placed among those heading for Zambia.

69

Back in South Africa, we are thrust into the preparation for the unit's appeal, in addition to the ongoing work on the Harms Commission.

In the middle of May, Bheki and I visit the accused on Death Row. The horror of the place is getting to Jabu, Ting Ting and Neo and the other ANC prisoners. They tell me of a fight between them and the 'criminal' prisoners, some of whom are members of the notorious 26 prison gang. The situation is exacerbated because the prison head, a Major Cronje, ignores the problems and won't listen to complaints.

I undertake to raise their concerns about Major Cronje with Penuell Maduna, as the ANC legal department has relocated inside the country and is dealing with issues relating to prisoners and their rights. The sheer interminable boredom of life on Death Row is eating at them, worsened by their frustrations with Cronje.

Steering the talk away from life on Death Row, I focus on the approaching appeal. The appeal might yet be three months away, but three months can pass quickly. 'I suppose things can't get much worse than being on Death Row,' I say, 'although there is one thing worse, but we don't need to discuss that now.' They laugh.

Jabu says, 'Personally, I don't trust this government. I mean, how can they negotiate in good faith with people they have called terrorists and communists? They hate us. Do you think that they will just give it away? It's not going to happen. Look at what happened in Sebokeng two months ago when the police opened fire on an ANC march, killing twelve of our people. That was after Mandela and our leadership had been released. It's a joke, these talks, and people are still dying.' His voice has risen in anger.

I share his scepticism. At the same time as the ANC is being allowed to organise and exiles are returning, the security forces have become tougher and the violence intensifies. With each passing month there are massacres by masked gunmen and drive-by shootings outside factories and at bus stops. In fact, more people are dying now. On the one hand there is fear and tension, on the other elation as people catch the faint scent of freedom for the first time.

There have been talks about talks and during these an agreement, known as the 'Groote Schuur Minute', was reached to release political prisoners, remove repressive laws and lift the state of emergency. What worries me about this agreement is how they define 'political prisoner'. Will it include the types of offences that Jabu, Ting Ting, Neo and Joseph committed? The fact that my clients have not mentioned the Groote Schuur Minute or the possible release of political prisoners is an indication that they're not placing too much store by the talks. I am not going to discuss the matter either because I do not want to raise their hopes. Besides, our immediate task is to get them off Death Row so that if the talks fail, at least they will not be hanged.

I brief them on the approach that we would like to adopt for the appeal. Ting Ting feels that Judge de Klerk's opinion was laudable. 'You know, if we get through all this, which I now think we may, I would like to meet him to say that we appreciate what he did,' he adds.

'I agree,' says Jabu. 'We owe him. I'm convinced that he changed during the course of that trial. I don't know whether it was us, our behaviour or the simple facts of the case or whether he was a man at a stage of his life where he was tired of wearing blinkers, but he saw clearly and he spoke from the heart. He didn't like what we did, but he understood why we did it.' The others nod.

I go on. 'We know about an intended change to the law although it has not yet come into force.'

'What do you mean?' asks Neo. 'Is it in our favour?'

The new law is called the Criminal Law Amendment Act and it amends the current Criminal Procedure Act, but until it's promulgated it has no effect. Basically, the amendment abolishes the compulsory imposition of the death sentence and gives the trial judge the discretion to impose the death sentence in appropriate circumstances.

The new legislation abolishes the term 'extenuating circumstances' and introduces the concept of 'mitigating or aggravating circumstances'. These broaden the matters regarded as influencing the accused's state of mind and can include factors unrelated to the crime. An example may be the way an accused behaved after committing a crime or the fact that an accused has a clean record.

'That is quite complicated,' says Ting Ting, 'but perhaps it means that if this new law had been in force at the time of our trial, the assessors would have had less grounds to disagree with the judge.'

'Possibly,' I say, 'but there is another change to the law which states that if the Appellate Division is of the opinion that it would not itself have imposed the sentence of death, the Appellate Division may set aside the sentence and impose such punishment as it considers to be proper.

'Guys, this is a really big change and it means that the appeal court has the discretion to change your sentence if they find on the evidence contained in the record that there were mitigating factors. If they find this, then they can set aside the death sentence. This gives you a really good chance of getting off Death Row.

'If Judge de Klerk found extenuating circumstances in the trial, we stand a chance that the appeal court will find mitigating circumstances as those are much broader, and, frankly, the judge set you up for an appeal in his judgment. This possible amendment changes the rules of the game and, in a way, that is in your favour.'

'Sure, Peter,' says Jabu quietly, 'but this law has not come into effect yet and so your excitement should perhaps wait until then.'

I nod. 'You're right. But rumour has it that the new law will come out in the next few months.'

'Well, the appeal is only three months away so we shouldn't get our hopes too high,' says Jabu, ever the rationalist.

I drive back to Johannesburg on the dreaded highway, depressed, wondering how many more times I will have to travel to that damned prison.

THE BOMB

The bomb in the white canvas sack with other packages is transported by airplane from Jan Smuts Airport in Johannesburg to Lusaka International Airport. It is fortunate to make it through the extensive security checks and x-rays that all packages are subject to when passing through the airport.

Its target is living under armed guard in a small anonymous hotel outside Lusaka. He spends his time in the bedroom to which he is confined writing the story of his professional career.

The bomb reaches the Lusaka post office and after a few days is processed by a clerk who notes the arrival date and weight of the parcel in a book and then places the parcel in the correct pigeonhole. The clerk fills out the parcel notification slip and posts it to the address on the parcel. The address is P O Box 34077, Lusaka. The post box belongs to an ANC member by the name of 'Farouk', who shares this box with the target.

The target and those responsible for his safety are told that there is a parcel to be collected by him at the Lusaka post office. The target is waiting to be picked up at his hotel, his bag is packed as he is about to catch a plane to London where he is to give evidence in a defamation trial. It is decided that he and his 'minder' will stop at the post office to collect the package en route to the airport.

70

Most of June 1990 is taken up by the Broederstroom trial, legal work for the returning ANC leadership and preparing for the appeal. There are also sessions with Dennis Kuny and Elna Revelas, preparing heads of argument, working through the heads of argument of the State, briefing the accused and taking instructions from them and meeting with the families.

Mrs Masina is excited by the agreement regarding the release of political prisoners and believes that Jabu and the others will soon be released. Without dampening her expectations, I tell her that this will be a long process and that we can expect many hiccups. On her face is the same expectation that I saw at the beginning of the trial – the belief that justice will prevail. This time there may be a chance.

Late on the afternoon of 25 July I get a call from the ANC legal department instructing me to rush to a house in Mayfair to represent and assist Mac Maharaj who is being arrested by the security police. Mac Maharaj had spent twelve years on Robben Island and become one of Mandela's most trusted lieutenants. He'd left the country a year after his release in December 1976 and joined the exiled ANC, eventually being elected to its National Executive Committee.

By the time I reach Mayfair, Mac is being escorted to a security police car. I introduce myself to the officer in charge who lets me know they're taking Maharaj to the Morningside police station. He adds ominously, 'This thing is much bigger than Maharaj.'

Given that Mac is being arrested under the security legislation which is still in force there is not much I can do except to vouch for his condition. At the police station I'm emphatically denied access to him by the officer in charge. And that is that. I am left powerless outside the police station where I am joined by others from the ANC legal department. From them I learn that there've been widespread arrests of ANC leaders and operatives. And from colleagues I hear that urgent calls are coming in from ANC people whose houses are the subject of search and seizure raids.

I go to bed that night wondering if this was planned. Could ANC people have been lured back on the pretext of negotiations simply to be arrested? That way there'll be no negotiations and no peace. The hopes of the past few months flicker low.

The papers are full of the arrests the next day. Headlines and articles scream the indignation of the government at having discovered an underground network led by Mac Maharaj. Clearly, government officials say, it's a plot to overthrow the government under cover of negotiations.

Maharaj, Siphiwe Nyanda (whose MK name is 'Gebhuza') and seven others are to be charged with 'attempting to overthrow the government by force'. The ANC codename for the initiative is 'Operation Vula'. There are lurid details in the press of an underground network recruiting, training and arming a revolutionary army. Armed insurrection is their intention. President de Klerk trumpets the mala fides of sinister groupings in the ANC that are not to be trusted. The search for other Vula operatives who have escaped arrest intensifies.

In reality, Vula's an insurance policy for the ANC. Operation Vulindlela, a Zulu word meaning 'open the road', is a top secret initiative launched by Oliver Tambo to enable direct communication with Lusaka. Maharaj, one of the brightest minds in the ANC, along with the highly experienced Nyanda, had entered the country illegally from Swaziland in early 1988 and set up an underground network and communications system which included communications between Mandela and Tambo. When key ANC operatives returned to South Africa for the negotiation process, it was decided to keep Operation Vula alive in case negotiations failed or the government sprang a trap. This decision also reflected Tambo's old concern that the ANC should not allow its venture into negotiations to result in the movement being 'stripped of our weapons of struggle'. Sanctions, MK soldiers, and Operation Vula would all remain active until the negotiations were irreversible. The arrests of the Vula operatives show that the process is far from irreversible.

During a visit to our clients, Bheki informs them of the latest developments and that the talks are in jeopardy as the government blusters about Vula. He reports back that the three men are unequivocal in their support for Vula. Their attitude is that if the government thought everyone would just come home, lay down their arms and be dictated to, then they were wrong. They are right behind the ANC policy of not surrendering weapons or demobilising until the government's bona fides have been tested.

They're also concerned that the talks will come unstuck and that their position will become more tenuous.

'All the more reason to concentrate on the appeal and get us off Death Row,' Neo had told Bheki.

Bheki finishes briefing me and stares at the floor, lost in thought.

'Are you okay?' I ask.

He looks up. His hair's greying despite his young age, lines beginning to etch into his face. 'I don't know, Pete,' he says. 'I don't know how much longer I can take this one step forward two steps back stuff. It's depressing and things were going so well. I didn't even think we'd need the appeal. I thought they would be out by Christmas. Now, who knows?'

I know how he's feeling. 'We're a lot further than we were this time last year and the year before,' I argue. 'Hell, in 1988 there was no end in sight.'

'That's the point, Pete,' he says. 'We've been given a brief glimpse of the sun and that almost makes it worse, not knowing whether we will see it again.'

'Well, at least we have seen it.' I'm more buoyant because the previous day the Criminal Law Amendment Act had been promulgated and is now in force.

The appeal is in a little more than three weeks' time.

THE BOMB

The ANC official responsible for the safety of the target of the bomb is a man by the name of 'Stanley' who works in the intelligence department. On this assignment he reports directly to Jacob Zuma. Powerfully built, Stanley is well aware that should anything befall his charge he will be held accountable.

In view of the special status of the man he is looking after, Stanley is particularly careful that nothing should go wrong. Food is checked, access to the small hotel is curtailed and monitored, and the limited post that arrives in different forms is strictly scrutinised.

So when contact is made with Stanley and he is told that there is a parcel from South Africa at the post office addressed to the man he is responsible for, he is immediately suspicious. At the same time, he knows that the man he is guarding is desperate, if not frantic, for news from his family back home.

71

A friend of mine once caustically described a small town as being rather like Bloemfontein, but without the nightlife. His sarcasm sinks in the night before the appeal, as I gaze through the window of my room in the Bloemfontein Holiday Inn at the deserted streets. I'm nervous that the time has now arrived, and the empty town does nothing to reassure me.

The next day, I arrive at the Appellate Division buildings with Dennis Kuny and Elna Revelas at nine thirty. The appeal of Jabu, Ting Ting and Neo against their death sentences is set for ten o'clock. The buildings are of white stone blocks, impressive and august, reflecting a bygone era far removed from the small country courtroom of Delmas where the legal journey had begun. It's strange that we have reached the end of the line. If we lose here there is nowhere else to go. We could petition State President de Klerk, but Jabu and the others will never countenance that. The five appeal judges hearing our case are Joubert, the Acting Chief Justice, Smalberger, Milne, Eksteen and Friedman.

In court Louisa van der Walt sits at the front desk arranging her books and reference materials. Behind her is Captain Hendrik Prinsloo. We greet each other tersely without shaking hands.

The court is empty save for two officials and three women at the back with notepads on their laps, reporters, I assume. I'm struck by the quietness, remembering the hubbub of the crowded court in Delmas and the constant presence of security police and police Reaction Units. The difference, of course, is that the accused aren't here. They're on Death Row, as appeals are argued on the record and the law. So here we are, the lawyers, the judges and a few reporters, a solitary finale to a course of events that started with the killing of the policeman Chapi in Soweto in 1986.

I walk outside for a cigarette where I'm joined by Captain Prinsloo. He looks much the same except that his face is darker and more lined, the eyes still disconcertingly steady and inscrutable. He lights up.

'Hello, Peter,' he says in his deep voice, bringing back memories of the trial.

'How are you, Captain?' I ask.

'Not bad, Peter, they keep me busy,' he replies. The familiar use of my first name irritates me as it always has. I can't resist it. 'So what do you think of all the talks, the negotiations, it's a big thing, huh?'

'You know, Peter, I leave that to the politicians,' he says with an air of resignation. 'I just do my job. At the end of the day, the police have a job to do and we will do it. That's what it is, just work.'

I almost believe him. 'Sure,' I say, realising that this is going nowhere and regretting that I raised the issue. What did I expect him to say to me? Tell me how he really felt about the talks with the ANC? We crush out our cigarettes and go inside.

The hearing is quick. Dennis Kuny and Louisa van der Walt make their arguments, with the judges asking questions, mostly of Louisa. And then it's over. Judge Smalberger, who has taken the lead, says they'll deliver their judgment in due course, and the five of them sweep out a side door, their footsteps echoing on the old wooden floor. We pack our bags, leaving Louisa van der Walt and Captain Prinsloo in the court. There are no goodbyes.

THE BOMB

Stanley and his charge arrive at the post office en route to the airport where they are to catch a flight to London. The purpose of the trip is for Dirk Coetzee to give evidence in a defamation case brought by General Lothar Neethling against the *Vrye Weekblad*. The paper has published Coetzee's allegations that Neethling had supplied poison that he, Coetzee, had used to kill various 'targets'. Coetzee is the newspaper's star witness and his evidence will be critical in their legal defence.

Stanley parks the car and both men walk into the post office and approach the counter. Stanley gives the notification slip to the clerk. Stanley says, 'This is Dirk Coetzee, the person to whom the parcel is addressed.' Coetzee shows some identification to the clerk, who searches for the package among the rows of parcels stacked on wooden shelves.

The clerk returns with a small square parcel wrapped in brown paper and gives it to Dirk Coetzee, requesting his signature. Coetzee takes the parcel and looks carefully at the writing, checking the name and address of the sender. It is clearly addressed to him. He carefully turns the parcel, judging its weight. He doesn't shake it. Again he examines the wrapping. Stanley watches him.

Coetzee slowly shakes his head. 'I cannot accept this,' he says to Stanley. 'I think it's a bomb and I cannot take a chance. Besides, no one has told me to expect a parcel.'

Coetzee gives the parcel back to the clerk saying that he refuses to accept it. The parcel lies on the counter between Coetzee and the clerk. Stanley tells Coetzee that they have a flight to catch to London and that they must leave. They walk quickly from the post office, leaving the parcel on the counter.

The sender's name is given as Bheki Mlangeni.

72

The judgment of the five judges is delivered on 13 September 1990 by Acting Justice of Appeal Friedman with the other four judges concurring. It is clear and concise. Friedman refers to the 'very careful and well-considered judgment' of Judge de Klerk and then to the findings of the assessors. 'Both of these findings,' he states, 'amount to misdirections.'

Commenting on the sentence given in the trial court, he says, 'Having regard to both the aggravating and mitigating factors referred to above, I do not consider that the sentence of death was the proper sentence in this case.' He concludes, 'The appeal succeeds. The sentences of death in respect of all three appellants are set aside and there is substituted, in respect of each of the appellants, a sentence of twenty-five years imprisonment on each of the four counts of murder, such sentences to run concurrently with the sentences at present being served by the appellants.' These are words I never thought I'd hear when we started the case.

There is no chance of getting this news through to my clients on Death Row so it will have to wait until tomorrow. But I can phone the families. In each house the news is greeted with jubilation and sometimes by sobbing.

Mrs Masina, strong as ever, says, 'Peter, we must thank you and Bheki for what you have done. It is a miracle and may God protect you both.'

The next day I meet with Jabu, Ting Ting and Neo. They receive the news calmly although I can see their immense relief. We discuss the case and, again, Judge de Klerk's name comes up and they speak about their debt to him. We catch up on personal matters and then I leave. It's a short visit.

THE BOMB

In the international departure hall at Lusaka airport, Dirk Coetzee meets up with journalist Jacques Pauw. Coetzee is excited and immediately tells Pauw that he has been sent a bomb. Pauw asks for details and Coetzee recounts how they had stopped at the post office on the way to the airport and how he was deeply suspicious of the parcel he had been handed by the post office clerk.

Coetzee tells Pauw that he is sure that Bheki Mlangeni, the alleged sender of the parcel, would have warned him if he had sent it. Of this he is quite sure. Coetzee, convinced that the parcel contains a bomb, asks Pauw to warn Bheki about this package.

Pauw thinks that it is unlikely that the Vlakplaas operatives would use this method to kill Coetzee, and shows his scepticism. Coetzee is irritated by Pauw's reaction and frantically turns to his minder Stanley and asks him to phone Bheki the moment he gets back to his office. 'Please do it,' he pleads.

Stanley leaves them in the airport, and Pauw and Coetzee catch the flight to London. Both Stanley and Pauw forget to make the call.

73

Shortly before the end of the month the three are moved to Johannesburg Prison. We arrange for Cyril Ramaphosa and Walter Sisulu to visit them, which they do on separate occasions. Cyril, Jabu's classmate from school, is now the ANC's chief negotiator in the talks with Government. The men are honoured and grateful for the visits.

The firm has many clients in prison as political prisoners and the uncertainty that hangs over their position is tangible. The prisoners that I regularly visit on Robben Island are anxious. They know that Mandela has been out for some time and hope that their turn will come soon. They remain fearful of being forgotten in the sweep of the tumultuous events taking place. They wonder if they'll be granted indemnity. And if so under what conditions. Some are desperate to get out.

Not so with Jabu, Ting Ting and Neo. Although grateful for the visitors, they're upset that no one from the ANC legal department has come to consult them about indemnity. They write to Nelson Mandela in November to say, 'We have refused to sign the [indemnity] applications until and unless the ANC provides us with an explanation regarding the basis upon which this agreement was reached between the government and the ANC regarding these indemnities. In this regard, we requested someone from the ANC to come and see us and to explain the position. We once again make this request. We have a fundamental difficulty in agreeing to apply for indemnity and we urge you to visit us and to explain the basis of the agreement reached.' The letter concludes by saying that they admire the stand taken by Mandela in not accepting conditional release and 'we hope that you will understand our reservations about accepting such indemnity'.

'Are you sure that you want to send this letter?' I ask them. 'Now is not the time to get too precious. These negotiations can go either way and if they go bad, you want to be on the outside rather than the inside.' My normal expedient self, rising to the fore.

Jabu reponds. 'We started this with honour, Pete, and we are going to end it with honour. There is no reason for us to make compromises now that we did not make when we were in a weak position and at their mercy. So why change now when we are in a much stronger position?'

They have a point. I undertake to deliver the letter.

In mid-December, I get a call from Penuell Maduna to say that he has been mandated to see Jabu, Ting Ting and Neo. In early January 1991, I accompany him on a visit. My clients are irritated that they have not been properly consulted and they make this clear. Penuell quickly disarms them by apologising profusely and entering into a detailed explanation about the negotiations and the issue of indemnity. It's a constructive conversation and Penuell is reassuring. He also allows them to interrogate the basis of the indemnity. They ask for time to consider their response and request that he should come back in a few weeks. I feel sorry for Penuell, who is probably having similar conversations in most of the prisons around the country.

As far as the 'talks about talks' are concerned, that month Mandela's call for an 'all-party congress' to negotiate the route to a constituent assembly breaks through the deadlock. At the same time, the political violence escalates and the death toll climbs daily.

THE BOMB

The clerk at the post office in Lusaka looks at the parcel on the counter, perplexed at the conduct of the two men who have just left. Why would they not want to accept a parcel? He has a problem now. He thinks he heard one of the men mention the word 'bomb' but he's not sure. If the man doesn't want to accept his parcel that is his business, and the procedure in such cases is that the parcel must be returned to the sender. The clerk takes his black felt-tip pen, draws two lines through the name Dirk Coetzee on the parcel and writes 'Return to sender'. The parcel is then placed in a rack under the heading 'South Africa' for collection and shipment to the person and address given as the sender. The bomb is going home.

74

A month after my clients' appeal hearing, in October 1990, the findings of the Harms Commission are released. Judge Louis Harms finds ten incidents require further investigation and action. With the exception of the murders of medical doctor Fabian Ribeiro and his wife Florence, the incidents are all relatively minor. Consequently his report doesn't cause much excitement, rather the opposite. No findings are made in relation to the numerous other murders and illegal acts about which extensive evidence had been led. He does, however, criticise the CCB, mentioning that their conduct before and during the commission raised the possibility that they'd been complicit in many more violent crimes than the evidence suggested. He reserves his most scathing criticism for Dirk Coetzee, describing him as a man with strong psychopathic tendencies whose evidence could not be trusted. Similarly, the evidence of Almond Nofomela and David Tshikalanga are dismissed. He also finds that no death squad exists at Vlakplaas.

It is no surprise that Harms lets the police off the hook. In doing so he ignores critical corroborating evidence that has been laid before him by the investigation team of the Independent Board of Inquiry and others. I am disappointed, but at least the report is scathingly criticised by most of the newspapers. The *Sunday Star* devotes an entire page to the Harms report under the header, 'The toothless watchdog that stayed toothless to the end'. Centre page is a cartoon of Harms' face in triplicate, caricaturing the 'see no evil, speak no evil, hear no evil' pose.

While we hadn't expected much from Harms after his performance in London and his refusal to call key witnesses such as General Magnus Malan and Adriaan Vlok, we had not expected him to be so gullible and naive. Across the country, disappointment turns to anger as the implications of Harms' findings sink in. The police have been exonerated and now have virtual carte blanche. This is borne out when the minister of defence announces that the SADF has emerged with honour from the commission. It is a depressing time for those of us who'd gathered evidence. I console myself with the knowledge that the evidence remains even if Harms does not want to see it.

Nevertheless, three months later, in January 1991, a judge is prepared to take a different view on Dirk Coetzee. A judge by the name of Johann

Kriegler. In his original claims, Dirk Coetzee had said that he'd been supplied with poison by Lieutenant-General Lothar Neethling, head of the SAP Forensic Laboratories. In turn, Neethling had sued the *Vrye Weekblad* and the *Weekly Mail* for one and a half million rand. The defamation case had been heard by Judge Kriegler who, in his judgment, believes Coetzee's account of the death squads, and orders Neethling to pay the two newspapers' legal costs.

In a detailed two-day judgment, Kriegler states that it 'hit him like a thunderbolt' that a man of the stature of General Neethling would mislead both the Harms Commission and the Rand Supreme Court about extremely important evidence. On the other hand, Coetzee's statements to the news media, his testimony before the Harms Commission and his reactions during cross-examination were 'wholly believable in all the important aspects of his story'.

It is a tremendous victory and much celebrated. Many commentators find it an important step in restoring faith in the judiciary. At the firm we toast Jacques Pauw and his editor Max du Preez at our Friday night drinks session. We also toast Dirk Coetzee, grateful that he has been believed, finally.

THE BOMB

The bomb arrives with other parcels and mail at the Braamfontein post office in Johannesburg. The clerk fills out the notification slip and posts this to the sender's address. The parcel has travelled thousands of kilometres over a period of nine months to reach a point not far from where it was dispatched at the Joubert Park post office.

The notification slip sent from the Braamfontein post office for the parcel bomb reaches the law firm of Cheadle Thompson & Haysom. The slip lies in a tray in the mail room and some hours later an administrative employee puts it aside in a tray with the outgoing letters, which will be posted at the Braamfontein post office the following day. It is intended that the parcel will be collected at the same time as the letters are posted.

Joe Mamorare, the firm's messenger, collects the parcel from the Braamfontein post office. Joe has been with the firm since it started in March 1984. He's a messenger by day and at night he studies for his law degree. Joe clears out the firm's post box and places the parcel along with the post and other legal documents and notices in the boot of the car. He carries out some deliveries and then takes the parcel and the post back to the office.

Joe places the parcel and the post on the table in the mail room for sorting and distribution. At midday, a clerk opens each letter and the document is stamped with the date and time that it was received. The person undertaking this task looks at the parcel, considers opening it, turns it around in her hands and decides that it looks personal rather than professional. Instead of opening it she places the parcel with its tattered brown wrapping in Bheki's pigeonhole.

The parcel remains in Bheki's pigeonhole for the rest of Tuesday, Wednesday and Thursday. Bheki has taken a few days' study leave to prepare for his attorneys admission exam. He has been working at home and avoiding the office, knowing that if he visits too often he will get caught up in work and he cannot afford that.

Thursday is 14 February, Saint Valentine's Day. That night in the small house in Jabulani, the family enjoy a wonderful meal prepared by his mother Cathereine. To celebrate the day Bheki and his wife Seipati decide to cut their wedding cake, which they had not cut on their wedding day, preferring to save the occasion for another day.

Bheki, to applause from the family, stands up and solemnly cuts their wedding cake, carving slices for the family. They all enjoy the cake.

Bheki collects the parcel and the other mail in his pigeonhole in the early afternoon of Friday 15 February 1991. He briefly checks the wrapping on the parcel and sees the name of Dirk Coetzee. He assumes that Coetzee sent it from Lusaka and strips off the disintegrating brown paper wrapper which he discards in the wastepaper bin in the mailroom. In his hands is a small light cardboard box bound by transparent sticky tape. He decides to open it later as he's in a hurry. He picks up his black legal briefcase and, with the parcel in his other hand, quickly leaves the office.

He takes a taxi from Braamfontein to meet his wife in town. He has been studying hard all week and is desperately in need of a break. They decide to see a movie at the Kine Centre in Commissioner Street. Bheki places the parcel in his briefcase before entering the cinema.

The title of the film, *Reversal of Fortune*, based on the true story of the death of a young socialite heiress. Her husband, Claus von Bülow, is charged with her murder. The film upsets Seipati.

75

It's Friday 15 February and the drinks and snacks session in the firm's main boardroom is in full swing. Apart from the staff, there are a number of clients present.

The boardroom is full, it has been a busy week with a number of the partners involved in major cases and also playing key roles in the talks between the ANC and government.

The weekend stretches before us. Standing there with a whisky in my hand, listening to the chatter of colleagues and friends, I feel lucky to be a part of this excitement. A colleague, Tefo Raditapole, asks me if I saw Bheki today. I shake my head. I'd been in court all day and didn't know he'd been in. Tefo tells me he bumped into Bheki and that he'd said he was on his way to the movies. I make a mental note to phone Bheki over the weekend to see how his studies are going.

THE BOMB

After the film, Bheki and his wife Seipati have a coffee at a café in the Carlton Centre. He takes out the parcel and shows it to Seipati, saying that it is from Dirk Coetzee. He opens the box and Seipati can see a Walkman cassette player inside. Bheki says, 'Maybe there is nothing on it, but let's see,' closing the box and putting it back in his briefcase. Bheki and Seipati take a taxi home to Jabulani. At home, Bheki takes his briefcase, his post and the parcel into the house. The couple live in a room that he had had built once they were married. The room is divided by a cupboard into sleeping quarters and a small study area in which there is a desk at which Bheki and Seipati take turns to work. Bheki had paid for the building of the additional room.

It is Friday night and the sounds of music and people are everywhere. Friends drop by. Outside in the streets people are drinking and having fun. There is an air of celebration, and the main topic of conversation is that the country is going to be liberated and there will now be freedom and justice. The talk is of the future and the hope that it promises. There's also talk of Bheki's studies for his attorneys admission exam and the difference being an admitted attorney will make to their lives.

Bheki excuses himself from the house and together with Seipati goes to his bedroom and study. He decides to open the package and sits at his desk to do so. Inside is the Walkman player with the headphones wrapped in plastic around it. He lifts out the tape player and its headphones from the Unisef box and places the polystyrene and sponge packing back in the box. He throws this into a bin beside his desk. It's a normal Walkman, and through the transparent plastic of the cassette holder he can see a cassette. A second cassette contains a Neil Diamond tape.

He presses the eject button. The cover of the cassette holder slowly opens and he takes out the cassette. On it is written 'evidence of hit squads'. He slides the tape back into the slot and gently closes the lid. It clicks shut.

Bheki puts on the headphones and prepares to listen to the tape. This is evidence. He stretches out his hand towards the machine and presses the play button.

EPILOGUE

In June 1991 Jabu Masina, Ting Ting Masango, Neo Potsane and Joseph Makhura were released from jail. Jabu Masina currently lives in Mamelodi and works for the South African National Intelligence Agency. Ting Ting Masango also lives in Mamelodi and works for the SABC as a newswriter. Neo Potsane holds a senior position in the national Government in Pretoria. Joseph Makhura is based in Cape Town and is the provincial commander for Crime Intelligence operations in the Western Cape. We meet regularly.

Dirk Coetzee was granted amnesty at the Truth and Reconciliation Commission in August 1997 and now works in a private security firm in the Johannesburg area.

Captain Eugene de Kock received amnesty from the TRC for a number of murders and illegal acts, but for six murders and other, lesser, crimes he did not receive amnesty. He is currently serving four life sentences in Pretoria C-Max Prison. It later transpired that one of the assessors in the trial, Mr de Kock, was his father.

Louisa van der Walt and Harry Prinsloo resigned from the Department of Justice and became defence lawyers. Their clients include the two right-wingers convicted of the murder of Chris Hani in April 1993, as well as key accused in the 'Boeremag' treason trial of twenty-two right-wingers charged with high treason.

Captain Hendrik Prinsloo resigned from the South African Police in 1996.

Thabo Molewa was murdered on 11 December 1993 on the East Rand at the height of the political violence that engulfed the area, a massive loss.

Bheki Mlangeni was murdered at his home when the bomb intended for Dirk Coetzee exploded, killing him instantly. His mother called me soon after it happened and I went to Jabulani with a colleague, Khalik Mayet. When his body was carried to the ambulance in the early hours of the morning, the crowd that had gathered stood in the cold glare of the township arc lights, fists raised, and softly sang 'Hamba Kahle Mkhonto we Sizwe', the song that is sung at the funerals of MK soldiers.

Nelson Mandela was the main speaker at Bheki's funeral on the Saturday following his murder. He described Bheki as one of the finest young leaders of the ANC and his death as a great loss for South Africa. I miss him.